Virtually Criminal

Amidst the sensationalist claims about the dangers of the Internet *Virtually Criminal* provides an empirically grounded criminological analysis of deviance and regulation within an online community.

Virtually Criminal is one of the first studies to further our understanding of the causes of cyber deviance, crime and its control. The study takes the Internet as a site of social and cultural (re)production, and acknowledges the importance of online social/cultural formations in the genesis and regulation of cyber deviance and crime.

A blend of criminological, sociological and linguistic theory provides a unique understanding of the aetiology of cybercrime and deviance. Focus group and offence data are analysed and establish an interrelationship between online community, deviance and regulation. The book concludes that the importance of the social within online interactions precludes a purely technical or legal solution to regulation, promoting instead more adaptive multi-modal forms of governance.

This innovative book will be of interest to students and researchers across the disciplines of Sociology, Criminology, Law and Media/Communication Studies.

Matthew Williams is a lecturer at Cardiff University School of Social Sciences. He has published and conducted research in the areas of cybercrime and online research methodologies. Recent publications include 'Avatar Watching: Participant Observation in Graphical Online Environments', *Qualitative Research* and 'Policing and Cybersociety: The Maturation of Regulation in an Online Community', *Policing & Society*.

Virtually Criminal

Crime, deviance and regulation online

Matthew Williams

Routledge
Taylor & Francis Group

LONDON AND NEW YORK

First published 2006
by Routledge
2 Park Square, Milton Park, Abingdon, Oxon OX14 4RN

Simultaneously published in the USA and Canada
by Routledge
270 Madison Ave, New York, NY 10016

*Routledge is an imprint of the Taylor & Francis Group, an informa
business*

© 2006 Matthew Williams

Typeset in Sabon and Courier by
HWA Text and Data Management, Tunbridge Wells
Printed and bound in Great Britain by
MPG Books Ltd, Bodmin

British Library Cataloguing in Publication Data
A catalogue record for this book is available from the British Library

Library of Congress Cataloging-in-Publication Data
A catalog record for this book has been requested

ISBN10: 0–415–36404–3 (hbk)
ISBN10: 0–415–36405–1 (pbk)
ISBN10: 0–203–01522–3 (ebk)

ISBN13: 978–0–415–36404–1 (hbk)
ISBN13: 978–0–415–36405–8 (pbk)
ISBN13: 978–0–203–01522–3 (ebk)

In loving memory of Dilys Megan Goodwin

Contents

Figures

Acknowledgements

In writing this research monograph I have incurred many debts which I am glad to have this opportunity to acknowledge. Fellow colleagues within the Cardiff School of Social Sciences that deserve particular mention include Paul Atkinson and Lesley Noaks, whose guidance and time are greatly appreciated. Further gratitude is extended to those within the school whose support and intelligence maintains my faith in criminology as a discipline – Amanda Robinson, Trevor Jones, Adam Edwards, Rhiannon Bayliss, Mike Levi and Mike Maguire. David Wall and Nigel Fielding are also thanked for their advice and support during the writing of this project.

A special thank you is also granted to my close friends for watching over me in demanding times – Philip Satherley, Ed Green, Kris Parr, Chris Couzens, Kate Stewart, Jasmin Tregidga, and again Amanda Robinson. My loyal office partner, Steven Stanley, has also inspired and encouraged me throughout times of writing. A very special thank you is also given to Dean Doyle for his constant care, love and attention without which my personal and working life would not be the same.

My family also deserve my gratitude, especially my parents Patricia and Lyndon and my brother and sister, Gareth and Jodi. Their enduring love, support and encouragement will forever be appreciated.

Finally I would like to extend my gratefulness to those who took part in the study. Their stimulating discussions made this project realisable even in the most arduous of times.

1 Introduction

It was in the winter of 1998 when I stumbled upon an online advertisement promising the 'purely virtual experience' in a place filled with hundreds of new towns and cities, its thrill compared to the excitement of nineteenth century frontier America, with a citizenship of over 20,000, growing minute by minute. Intrigued, I followed the instructions on the advertisement and waited impatiently for the 'virtual experience' to take me by storm. Following my immigration into this virtual space I was prompted with the question 'who would you like to be today?'. Carefully choosing my name and physical representation, I was donned with my new persona. I first entered a space called the Gateway, a common meeting place for friends, relatives and even lovers who frequented this place. Dozens of animated characters could be found engaged in conversation and exploring the fertile virtual grasslands. Some would enter buildings and scale their virtual heights in elevators, while others could be seen busily rushing around a large space that was cordoned off with tape which bore the inscription 'vandalised property – under reconstruction'. Moving on to a more secluded area, near what seemed to be the entrance to a shopping mall, I overheard one couple introduce themselves. The scantily clad woman visiting from Spain was commenting how lovely the morning was in Javea, as a young man visiting in the early hours from Phoenix, Arizona, listened impatiently. At first the chat seemed polite, until the boy turned the conversation, aggressively asking personal questions of a sexual nature. Following a few expletives two others arrived in uniform, separating what had become perpetrator and victim. After a few warnings the boy vanished into thin air. Quickly one of the uniformed men exclaimed 'another one banished, can we please try and keep it civil'. Feeling as if I were intruding on a virtual crime scene I turned to look up to the snow-top covered mountains on the horizon. I noticed pathways leading off into the distance. Intrigued I followed one. At the end I found portals; gateways to other worlds like this one. Fascinated with what I had already seen I donned my explorer's hat and stepped through.

These were my first experiences of a place called Cyberworlds. It is a social space consisting of a vast array of towns, cities and worlds eclectically populated by over one million citizens and tourists. Its members holistically identify as a 'community', evidencing the qualifying characteristics of a shared history, shared language and rituals, a shared virtual geography, universal laws and regulations and a common belief system. Cyberworlds, like almost all other communities, also has a 'crime' problem. However, as the name denotes, Cyberworlds does not exist in the 'terrestrial' world. It is an elaborate computer program that is distributed over computer networks to all its citizens and tourists. As a result of its 'virtual' status the citizens and tourists of Cyberworlds never actually leave the comfort of their homes, schools or offices when visiting. Interaction is performed and relationships are sustained at-a-distance. The Cyberworlds 'community' forms the focus of this study; its social structure, 'crime' problem and regulatory mechanisms are examined by employing a 'virtual' ethnography.[1] Analysis focuses upon one 'virtual' community in order to better understand how social networks are sustained, how deviance manifests and how social control methods operate within a particular online setting. Where relevant, themes emerging from the data are also applied to the wider Internet context. Acknowledging a paucity in the empirical and theoretical understanding of online deviant activity, this research seeks to deepen and complement the current breadth of knowledge.

Cyberworlds is indicative of what might be termed late-modern forms of communication and interactivity. Increasingly experience is being mediated through networks (Castells 1996). The convenience and convergence of mobile communications and computer-mediated communication has seen terrestrial populations become increasingly dependent upon technology to mediate their everyday practices (Lash 2001). In particular, the Internet and its associated technologies are being employed to facilitate one-to-one and one-to-many communications on a daily basis within the arenas of social, political and economic life. Of particular interest are those groups of people who not only use new forms of technology to mediate their existing 'real' lives, but take a further step, using technology to create a new life. Groups of individuals are beginning to flee the physicality of their 'real' world, opting instead to take up residence in 'virtual' or online social spaces. Citizens and visitors of Cyberworlds, one of a myriad of online social spaces, often report spending over six hours a day within the 'community'. The proliferation of 'netizens' has led commentators to proclaim that the Internet, and the alternative social arena it offers, acts as a 'new community' to replace failing social relations in the 'real' world (Rheingold 1993). Others have come to perceive it as the new 'third place', a communal space, separate from the other spaces of work and home, which individuals frequent in search of solace and friendship (Oldenburg 1999). What is evident is that a new social space has opened up where, for the most part, the constraints of everyday terrestrial life are suspended. Interactivity has taken on a markedly different form and populations are engineering alternative communities with their own social practices, rules, regulations and problems.

The empirical themes covered in this study examine the claims that online community exists in some form, and that online deviance and regulation are intrinsically linked to these online social networks. First the notion of online community is discussed in detail, initially focusing upon academic debate, progressing to an analysis of data gathered from within Cyberworlds. Second, recent debate over the phenomenon of cybercrime is delineated. Data elicited via online focus groups is then analysed to theoretically explore the manifestation and aetiology of deviance within Cyberworlds, deepening our overall understanding of cybercrime more generally.[2] How cybercrime and deviance within Cyberworlds are regulated forms the focus of the final empirical theme. The maturation of regulation within Cyberworlds is mapped and is compared and contrasted with wider modes of Internet regulation. Through each empirical theme runs the theoretical underpinnings of the study, focusing on the importance of a bond to online community in preventing deviance (Hirschi 1969) and the hidden power of language to harm online (Butler 1997).

Of the most significant problems facing the Cyberworlds 'community', deviant and anti-social behaviour has proved the most arduous to overcome. This is not a unique problem. Cyber deviant phenomena plague all online social spaces. The advent of networked computer technologies has opened up countless deviant and criminal opportunities to both the classical offender and those previously ill-equipped potential offenders. The specific characteristics of the Internet have opened up a new 'virtual criminal field' (Capeller 2001). New technologies are both facilitating traditional criminal activities and creating avenues for new and unprecedented forms of deviance, yet to be rationalised in legal discourse. The devolution of computer network access to the domestic arena can be seen as a milestone in cyber criminal and cyber deviant entrepreneurship. During the Cold War, in response to the launch of Sputnik in 1957, the US established the Advanced Research Projects Agency (ARPA), the birthplace of what is now commonly known as the Internet. ARPA's remit was to develop a networked computer infrastructure for use by the military which could survive a nuclear attack. The need to expand the network beyond the military and private sector to universities was quickly realised resulting in the establishment of ARPANET. During the latter years of the 1980s the Internet slowly began to be devolved from the private and university sector to the domestic arena. Since this time the Internet has experienced exponential growth. In 1997 only 2 per cent of the UK's population had access to the Internet compared to 55 per cent in 2005. Currently 17 per cent of the world's population have Internet access (CIA 2005).

The pervasiveness of communications technology means that a user no longer needs the esoteric knowledge of a computer programmer to become a cyber criminal. In its infancy cyber criminal activity was the avocation of a small number of computer programmers and others with similar technical expertise. These were the game hackers and crackers of the 1980s

(Taylor 2001). The impetus behind cyber criminal activity was usually non-malignant and based on a utopian idealism of non-centralised computer hardware and software access. The illicit activities of these individuals were not widely detected or publicised. During this time law enforcement was far from capable of either proactively or reactively tackling the problem. More accurately, cyber criminal activity was not considered a problem until the mid-1990s. Increasingly there were reports of the misuse of the Internet and similar technologies. Community members, newsgroup members and website owners began to complain of online harassment and defamation, breaches of decency due to the online dissemination of 'obscene' materials, instances of vandalised web pages, and even cases of 'virtual rape' (MacKinnon 1997b). A clear shift occurred from the relatively benign cyber deviant activity of the 1980s to the malicious cyber criminal activity of the mid- to late 1990s. The problem has been perceived to be so acute that governments are establishing contingency plans in the event of cyber-terrorist attacks, and are creating specialised law enforcement agencies to tackle cyber criminal phenomena (Jewkes 2003). Due to the moral panic that has recently arisen around dangerous sex offenders and their use of the Internet, the domestic arena, particularly parents, have been targeted with 'cyber safety' advertisement campaigns, highlighting the 'darker side' to the Internet. What was once touted as cyber utopia has become tainted by misuse and misfortune.

However, to state that the Internet is a dangerous and unruly place is mistaken. While its features have allowed individuals to access illegal material and to defame others, a hierarchy of social control is firmly entrenched and can often redress many of the wrongs done (Wall 2001). Rules, regulations, values and beliefs are evident in almost all online 'communities', including newsgroups and Internet Relay Chat. More systematically Internet Service Providers (ISPs), who supply the Internet to domestic users, have their own codes of good practice when using the technology. Via a slow process, bodies of law have been adapted to include certain cyber activities as criminal. At the supranational level conventions have been established in an attempt to regulate what has become the global problem of cybercrime. What exists then is a highly ordered structure of governance (Wall 2001).

Formal offline regulatory mechanisms, along with the taxonomy of cyber criminal activity, have received some detailed academic attention (see Akdeniz *et al.* 2000; Grabosky and Smith 1998; Taylor 1999; and Wall 2001 for an overview). However, little research has examined the ways in which online 'communities' govern themselves or the nature and extent of the deviant acts that plague their citizens. There is much to be learnt about online 'community', social control and regulation from the netizens that were integral to its creation and maturation. Understanding these 'native' processes is essential to the development of more general regulatory practice, beyond individual online communities. Similarly, while our understanding of 'conventional' cybercrimes is quite extensive, little knowledge exists on the more indigenous forms of deviant activity that infest online communities.

While we understand how new technologies have facilitated certain crimes, such as theft, we understand less the ways in which the same technologies have created new avenues for deviant enterprise, such as 'virtual vandalism' and 'virtual rape'. This study aims to fill this knowledge gap by exploring the online indigenous forms of 'community', social control and deviant activity.

The site of inquiry

Cyberworlds is one of a handful of graphically represented three-dimensional virtual reality online social spaces that forms part of the Internet (see Figure 1.1). These online arenas can be described as second generation Multi-User Domains (MUDs); less technologically advanced methods of one-to-many text-only online communication first developed in the late 1970s[3] (see Figure 1.2). MUDs were first designed by programmers as gaming arenas, much like an online version of the classic role playing game 'Dungeons and Dragons'. In traditional MUDs, action, description and communication take place purely through text. Users have to rely on their imagination to create the environment that is being described to them. Cyberworlds takes advantage of broadband network communications, meaning much more information can be transmitted in shorter periods of time. This allows for information to be represented by more that just simple text. A graphical window allows a user to see themselves represented as an avatar, a three-dimensional persona. Via this interface users can locate each other and navigate around their three-dimensional environment. Text still functions as communication, and is essential to the maintenance of the 'community', but it has become relegated where visual components now represent action and description. Cyberworlds and other 'advanced' MUDs have grown in popularity over the last decade due to the level of social and 'physical' immersion they provide to the user. Essentially they are the closest domestic technology to more elaborate and expensive Virtual Reality (VR) platforms.

Over decades, as increasing numbers of people became connected to computer networks, gaming spaces transformed into more general social spaces, providing an escape from the terrestrial world. MUDs and the social networks they harbour have been the subject of much research in media and communications disciplines (see Jones 1995, 1997, 1998 for an overview). Many studies have focused upon the substantive issues of race, gender and sexuality within MUDs and other associated technologies (such as newsgroups and Internet Relay Chat). The effects of anonymity and disembodiment, experienced by each MUD user, have forged much of what is now understood of online social experience (see Kramarae 1998; Danet 1998; Poster 1998; Dietrich 1997; Shaw 1997). However, graphical MUDs, like Cyberworlds, have received little academic attention. Further, few studies have attempted to empirically examine the phenomena known as cybercrime or cyber deviance within these social settings.

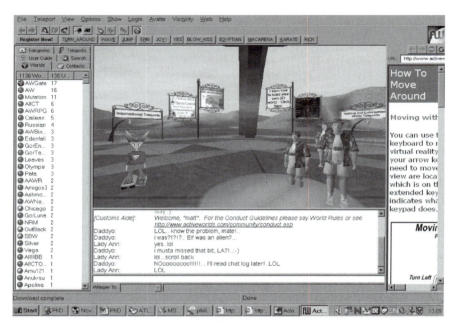

Figure 1.1 Virtual reality graphical MUD

```
Telnet - lambda.moo.mud.org                                        _ □ X
Connect  Edit  Terminal  Help
You press the button.
A trap door suddenly opens up beneath you!
You fall through, into some kind of chute.
The chute twists this way and that, until you completely lose your bearings.
You bump into a panel that seems to give, and suddenly find yourself in The Livi
ng Room!
The Living Room
It is very bright, open, and airy here, with large plate-glass windows looking s
outhward over the pool to the gardens beyond.  On the north wall, there is a rou
gh stonework fireplace.  The east and west walls are almost completely covered w
ith large, well-stocked bookcases.  An exit in the northwest corner leads to the
 kitchen and, in a more northerly direction, to the entrance hall.  The door int
o the coat closet is at the north end of the east wall, and at the south end is
a sliding glass door leading out onto a wooden deck.  There are two sets of couc
hes, one clustered around the fireplace and one with a view out the windows.
You see Welcome Poster, a fireplace, the living room couch, love seat, Cockatoo,
 Helpful Person Finder, lag meter, The Birthday Machine, and a map of LambdaHous
e here.
HFh (distracted), Abraxas (out on his feet), Ko (out on his feet), Goat (out on
his feet), Ragnarr (all set), pfc.ugly_kitty (dozing), and pupa (asleep) are her
e.
You say, "hello i am nnnew"
Abraxas has disconnected.
I don't understand that.
```

Figure 1.2 Text-based MUD

Broadly this study takes Cyberworlds as a site of analysis to ethnographically explore the emergence and maturation of online 'community', deviance[4] and regulation and to examine how each is interrelated. In its constituent parts the study focuses on three aspects of the Cyberworlds community, which translate into the four areas of inquiry. The first focuses upon the question of Cyberworlds as a 'social' space; essentially the characteristics of its social networks and the extent to which it can be said to be a 'community'. Second, focus shifts to an examination of how deviant and anti-social activity manifest within Cyberworlds, and how the existence or absence of a bond to community relates to its aetiology. Third, how deviant activities are textually performed within general Internet social spaces and Cyberworlds specifically and their capacity to harm are subject to analysis. Finally, the history and effectiveness of the mechanisms put in place to curtail deviant and anti-social activity within Cyberworlds are examined. The subsequent discussion applies these key themes to the wider Internet space more generally.

Overview

The second chapter provides a context within which the study is situated. The research straddles three main bodies of literature which includes theoretical and empirical work within the area of 'information society', recent explorations of online social networks and 'community', and literature on cybercrime, legislation and regulation. Discussions over the informationalisation of social, political, economic and working life are delineated to provide a general theoretical context for the research. The rise of information society ties in directly with the rise in online 'community'. The chapter evaluates current literature upon online 'community' and advocates its continued use in face of criticism. Finally, the abundance of literature on cybercrime is outlined, providing current typologies and discussions on prevalence, harmfulness and regulation. The chapter concludes by identifying the types of cyber criminal/deviant activity that will be focused upon in the study and highlights the important link online 'community' has with the prevalence of these activities.

The third chapter presents the first theoretical contribution. Both control (Hirschi 1969) and low self-control theory (Gottfredson and Hirschi 1990) are taken as the backbone to a theoretical explanation of the aetiology of deviant activity within Cyberworlds. Sykes and Matza's (1957) theoretical work on techniques of neutralisation is also used to rationalise the increased prevalence of deviant behaviour within the online setting more generally. Finally, the anthropological work of Turner (1967) is used in conjunction with the psychological work on disinhibition (Matheson and Zanna 1988; Reicher *et al.* 1995; Lea and Spears 1992; Spears and Lea 1992; Siegel *et al.* 1986; Kiesler *et al.* 1984) to formulate a general theory of cyber deviant activity.

An empirical and theoretical exploration of sociality and community within Cyberworlds forms the body of the fourth chapter. The chapter highlights, through several stages, that a community exists within Cyberworlds. The unique features of the environment forge an online social space that promotes friendships and relationships between members. The chapter challenges the notion that new communication technologies reduce levels of social immersion. Instead, the unique effects of disinhibition and liminality help dissolve offline hierarchies allowing for more open and rewarding exchanges. However, while individuals are allowed to engage in less inhibited exchanges, they simultaneously lose feelings of trust in fellow community members. The chapter concludes noting how members' bonds to the community of Cyberworlds vary, based upon the ways in which they both use the technology and how they perceive its function.

Chapter five builds upon the previous by examining the relationship between weak bonds to the Cyberworlds community and cyber deviant activity. The typology, prevalence and dispersion of cyber deviant activity within Cyberworlds are outlined. Offence data gathered from the community are analysed and presented showing significant relationships between patterns of offending and member status. The chapter provides evidence that shows tourists are more likely to engage in less serious but more prevalent deviant activity, whereas citizens are more likely to engage in more serious but less frequent offences. These relationships are explained in terms of a member's bond to the community. Attachment, commitment, involvement and belief (Hirschi 1969) are taken as analytical categories to further explore these relationships using data from the online focus group.

The second theoretical contribution forms the sixth chapter. The potential harms of online textual derision are focused upon. First, the belief that there is a disassociation between 'real' and 'virtual' life, a mechanism often employed by those who neutralise their online deviant activity, is challenged. Second, the mechanics of cyber deviant activity are examined through speech act theory (Austin 1975; Butler 1997). The distinction made between illocutionary and perlocutionary speech acts and their application to the online setting are discussed. A more general claim is made that the potential for individuals to be harmed in online settings is directly related to their reliance upon text as the sustaining force behind their online persona. Finally, narratives from community members describe how they perceive harm within Cyberworlds, both individually and collectively.

The final empirical chapter explores the emergence and maturation of systems of regulation, mediation and social control within Cyberworlds. The chapter outlines the tri-modal nature of regulation within Cyberworlds and traces shifts from oligarchic and vigilante mechanisms to more systematic and formal modes of policing and social control. The use of both reintegrative and disintegrative shaming within Cyberworlds and wider Internet populations is discussed in-depth. Detailed narratives from community members paint a picture of disenchantment and distrust in relation to online social control. The chapter concludes advocating the necessity for a balance to be struck between social, legal and technical controls when regulating cyber deviant phenomena.

2 The Internet, crime and society

Introduction

This chapter will 'set the scene' by contextualising the study within debates surrounding the two key areas of online community and cybercrime. First, contemporary analyses of 'late modern' society will be outlined as a background to the emergence and importance of online community. Second, definitions of community and its contentious application to online social formations will be discussed, formulating an argument that supports its continued use. Third, the phenomenon of cybercrime will be delineated, highlighting the problems of definition, measuring prevalence and regulation. Both the areas of online community and cybercrime are substantive. This chapter is not meant to be an exhaustive literature review, but more of a springboard for the main components to the study.

Information society and the growth of online community

Many social scientists, economic experts and political leaders now believe that we are living in an 'information society'. The diffusion and deepening of the information technology revolution has seen the proliferation of networks connecting economies, social and political structures, scientific communities and disorganised and diffuse populations. These processes have created what Manuel Castells (1996) calls the Network Society. Other theorists, before Castells' (1996) interpretation, also speculated that some social transformation was occurring in the latter part of the twentieth century. Daniel Bell's (1976) writings on post-industrialism, Jean Baudrillard's (1975) and Mark Poster's (1990) writings on post-modernism and Michael Piore's and Charles Sabel's (1984) writings on flexible specialisation all highlighted new features in the economy, culture, spatial boundaries, and occupations that were quite distinct from the characteristics of modernity. This section aims to outline some of these current debates surrounding the already established and/or emerging information society. It is within this framework that debates over the demise of offline communities and the rise of online equivalents are firmly entrenched. Discussions over the formation of communities in online environments will be outlined in tandem with criticisms over the application of the term to, what some critics consider, fleeting meaningless online encounters (Healy 1997; Lockard 1997). In light of these criticisms the notion of network sociality will be examined as an alternative way of interpreting online interactions (Wittel 2001). Finally, the term 'community' will be revisited and its applicability to the online environment re-evaluated in light of recent empirical evidence.

Theories of information society

Theories that postulate that the world is entering an 'information age', supported by a 'global information economy' and 'information societies', need to be understood by their constituent parts. Webster (1995) delineates what might define the 'information age'. Five definitions are provided – economic, occupational, spatial, cultural and technological – which aid in unpacking what is actually meant by a world dependent upon and shaped by information.

It is difficult to write on the topic of 'information society' without making continual reference to Manuel Castells' trilogy (1996, 1997, 1998). A thorough description and analysis of his work is beyond the scope of this study, however, a brief introduction to the main concepts is important in establishing the current thought within this area. The first area Castells (1996) subjects to analysis is the economy. He notes how the economy adopts a network structure in the process of globalisation. During this process an information-technology paradigm develops which has five features: 1) information as the new raw material; 2) the pervasiveness of information technologies used; 3) the networking logic of any system using them; 4) flexibility; and 5) convergence of technologies. When aggregated these characteristics of the new economy are called informationalism. Information processing, generation and transmission become the resources of productivity and power.

Basing an analysis on Machlup's (1962) work on the economy and information, we find five broad industry groups identified as 'information industries' – education, media, hardware, information services and research activities – that make up a significant proportion of today's modern economy. The slightly more sophisticated analysis of Porat (1977) identified that over 46 per cent of the US gross national product was accounted for by the information sector leading to the conclusion that the US was an information based economy. While quantitative indices may provide evidence in support of an information driven economy, it cannot be presumed that qualitative measures would prove likewise. For example, information may prove to be less important to the everyday social life of some citizens and groups.

Frequently combined with the economic measure is occupational definition. This measure can be twofold. First, a quantitative indication of an increasing pervasiveness of information in society is the comparative prevalence of 'information workers' to 'traditional industrial workers'. So for example, if researchers, lawyers, teachers and secretaries outnumber steel workers, builders and coal miners then we might consider the economy to be information driven. Second, the extent to which individual occupations are 'informationalised' is also an indication of an increasing dependence upon information. This can be considered a qualitative indication. There are clear methodological difficulties in qualifying and quantifying changes in occupations, too numerous to adequately cover here (for a detailed criticism see Webster 1995).

More relevant to this study are the changes that have and are occurring in the areas of technology, culture and space. To continue with Castells' (1996) view, within this networked world individuals and groups are able to communicate and exchange goods and ideas far more freely than ever before. Primarily, the Internet, and other forms of information and communications technologies (ICTs) facilitate these exchanges. The speed, efficiency and anonymity granted by new ICTs mean that the barriers that once hindered or made impossible exchanges are now crossed with ease. National boundaries, space and time have now become conquerable on a global scale. It is due to these dramatic and rapid changes that technology has become the hallmark and primary indicator of an 'information age'. Those who perceive that we are living in an 'information age' predominantly adopt this technological definition. This is not surprising considering that without the technology the dynamic networks that allow the economy, occupations and culture to be informationalised would not exist.

In relation to space, information networks have allowed previously distanced places to be connected. First, homes, schools, villages, towns and cities were connected via nascent technology networks. This reduced the time and relative distance it traditionally took to send and receive textual information. As technological networks increased in their complexity more information could be sent just as rapidly. Images and even live video can be transmitted over networks, allowing spaces to be permanently connected. Typical examples are the use of live web-cams. A resident in Cardiff can easily view and hear what is happening in real time on Times Square in New York by visiting www.earthcam.com/usa/newyork/timessquare/. While information of this kind has been available for some time, it is the speed at which individuals can receive it via information networks, and increased dissemination, that recasts the way in which space and time are experienced.

Culturally, the information society has provided the masses with an overwhelming amount of information in many guises. Satellite and cable television provide an abundance of multi-media information. Technology convergence has meant that once separate units of information provision (the Internet, newspapers, television etc.) are now combined into one easily accessible interface. This information and provision of services has a profound effect on the way in which individuals interpret and understand the world. Exposure to multiple cultures through converged technologies allows individuals to evaluate their own way of life and adapt. Established cultural anchor points can be submerged, even subverted, by the burgeoning amount of information accessible through information communication technologies.

Technology plays a pivotal role in the changes occurring in both spatial and cultural planes. In this regard questions relating to the prevalence of new technologies cannot be overlooked. While it seems appropriate to concede that technology is the defining feature of the information age, we cannot escape the need to both quantify and qualify its pervasiveness. Measuring the diffusion of information technology is complex. First, data would have to be gathered on how much technology was actually 'out there'. Second, knowledge of how this technology was being used and individual and organisational dependence would need to be attained. Following this a measure of 'information society' would have to be developed. For example, when does a society stop being industrial and become informational? Exactly how much technology does a society have to have, and be dependent upon, to qualify as an 'information society'? Currently no such reliable information exists and theorists are having to make non-empirical judgements upon the development of an 'information society'.

Some commentators are satisfied with the fact that new technology in and of itself heralds an 'information society' (Webster 1995). As a result this label has been ascribed to entire countries, including the US, UK and Singapore, 'the information island', with little empirical evidence to substantiate these claims. Paradoxically the same commentators talk of the 'digital divide', the notion that only the most advanced first world countries can take advantage of new technologies, while the second, third and fourth worlds are left in abjection. This divide is also apparent within first world countries. Predominantly it is the middle class young male who has access to new information technologies[1] (Compaine 2001).

A part of the genesis of these technologically deterministic assumptions is the practice of futurology. Ezponda (1998), for example, devotes an entire article to the mapping of the telepolis, or the global city. He identifies that with the increasing pervasiveness of ICTs individuals and organisations are increasingly playing a role in the generation and sustenance of the global city-at-a-distance. With little more than contemporary examples of changing working environments, increased use of ICTs at home, school and work, and the expanding information sector, Ezponda paints a picture of a city characterised by non-physical spaces, speeded-up social interactions and relationships at-a-distance all attributable to telecommunications and specifically computer-mediated communication. What Ezponda and others like him do is to place technology above social, economic and political realms in their tales of the information-driven future. The social, economic and political are relegated into an entirely separate division of technological innovation leaving a self-perpetuating technology to impress itself independently on all aspects of social life.

A departure from such technologically deterministic analyses might be Scott Lash's (2001) conception of 'technological forms of life'. Lash intrinsically meshes together 'life' and 'technology', arguing that forms of life are actually 'ways of life', or modes of doing things. In anthropological terms he shows how culture is a set of practices for doing things, and as such is a way of life. In a period where technology mediates an increasing amount of interaction, through email, mobile telephones, pagers and the like, technology becomes a way of life, a way of doing things. Without this technological interface individuals cannot access their life or culture which is now at-a-distance. Sociality is now only achievable via the machine interface. In this view, culture and technology are intrinsically linked. A reciprocity exists which ensures that neither technology nor culture-at-a-distance could exist independently. Without a culture of networks there would be no need for the technologies of mediation; without the technology there would be no culture-at-a-distance.

Lash (2001) goes on to describe how 'technological forms of life' are characterised in terms of being 'non-linear' and 'lifted out'. The first highlights the lack of reliance on the meaningfulness of both discourse and narratives. Instead 'technological forms of life' interpret and experience the world through units of information. These units are distinct from discourse and narrative in that they lack meaning until the sense-maker actually comes into contact with them. Inherent to this process is the speeding-up of forms of life mediated by technology. Narratives need time for reflection if they are to be understood. This is absent in technological forms of life, meaning units of information, that require little reflection, take precedence. Another consequence is that relations become ephemeral due to the speed of interactions. Individuals make and maintain more contacts, but at the sacrifice of depth. Relations are then 'stretched out' along thin networks of communication based on tenuous units of meaning. Second, 'technological life forms' are separated from origin and place. Intrinsic to these life forms are their tenuous and weak ties to culture-at-a-distance. Culture-at-a-distance occupies generic space and as such a life form's identity is absent of context. Resonance with Castells' (1998: 343) notion of 'real virtuality' can be identified here, where 'network society disembodies social relationships'. These characteristics of the 'information age' signal a departure in the ways in which individuals carry out their everyday lives. One notable change is the increasing use of computer-mediated communication and the increasing population of online communities.

The growth of online community

The cultural, spatial and technological shifts that characterise the 'information age' have also been used to explain the increasing use of computer-mediated communication for social interaction. Steve Jones (1998: 3) notes that 'Crucial to the rhetoric surrounding the Internet …

is the promise of a renewed sense of community and, in many instances, new types and formations of community'. In a time where an increasing number of individuals may be experiencing culture-at-a-distance, they may also be experiencing community-at-a-distance. Like Jones (1998), others have written on the growth and development of social formations online (Rheingold 1993; Turkle 1995; Markham 1998; Baym 1998; Reid 1999; Wellman and Gulia 1999). The core to much of the literature are debates about the existence of 'virtual community'. Rheingold (1993) was the first author to represent these increasingly complex social relations and formations as a form of community. He attributed the increasing levels of online social interaction to the demise of contemporary offline communities. The networks Castells (1996) writes of are an avenue for the revitalisation of community. In the same way that Lash (2001) talks of 'technological forms of life', Rheingold (1993) sees the proliferation of social groups sustained by non-tangible spaces. However, Rheingold's utopian perception is quite unique. Lash writes of the thinning and stretching of social relations in a time of technological dependence, while Rheingold considers online social formations to be so rich and meaningful that they warrant being called communities. This bifurcation is at the centre of the 'virtual community' debate. Essentially can social formations be maintained in a non-tangible environment, where interlocutors experience interaction at-a-distance, and if so are they meaningful enough to warrant being considered communities?

The work of Beniger (1987) and Peck (1987) on pseudo-community has been used as a comparison to 'virtual community'. The demise of gemeinschaft community, characterised by communal relationships, and the subsequent rise of gesellschaft relations, typified by impersonal indirect relations, is taken as the basis of pseudo-community. Beniger discusses the demise of personal relations in terms of increasing mass communication. The primary criticism here is the lack of authenticity in pseudo-community communication. Clear parallels can be drawn with online social relations. Simply put, non face-to-face communication, with a reduction in social cues and a lack of presence, results in fleeting encounters characterised by ephemerality and a lack of depth. Rheingold's (1993) central question was whether computer-mediated communication would allow for a community divorced from Beniger's (1987) and Peck's (1987) pseudo-relations.

Before this question can be adequately answered, the criticisms of those who oppose the use of the term community to describe online social formations have to be addressed. Fernback (1997: 39) draws attention to the central difficulty when dealing with such slippery concepts:

> Community is a term which seems readily definable to the general public but is infinitely complex and amorphous in academic discourse. It has descriptive, normative, and ideological connotations ... [and] encompasses both material and symbolic dimensions.

The most common conception of community in academic discourse is grounded in the view of Tönnies (1979). There are physical, temporal and moral dimensions to community. A common geographic territory is shared, there is a common history, a common value system and often a shared religion and language. Using this definition several conflicts begin to become apparent. First, while the Internet can be considered to be a space, it is not physical. Individuals cannot physically live in cyberspace. Second, there are questions over the extent to which groups in cyberspace can have a shared history, value system, religion or language. Lockard (1997) is reluctant to apply the term community to online social formations. He states that communication alone cannot replace community's manifold functions. Healy (1997) argues that with such a small fraction of the world's population online social formations do not oblige their participants to deal with diversity. In this sense online social formations are no more than voluntary associations of like-minded people, without the additional demands of offline community which help forge its very nature.

Further criticisms revolve around the technological deterministic nature of Rheingold's (1993) claims. Morely and Robins (1995) reject Rheingold's ideas labelling them conservative and nostalgic. The idea that technological change and innovation can turn around the social and cultural decay in contemporary American societies is naive. In line with contemporary thinking about the demise of offline community and the emergence of culture-at-a-distance, Wittel (2001) draws attention to the way in which much of the literature discusses the imaginary aspects of virtual community (Anderson 1983). This in itself is an indication that online social formations are not communities in the traditional sense. Further, the idea of the '*virtual* community' is flawed in its presumed dichotomy between the 'real' and the 'unreal'. Many writers have taken the presumed dichotomy of the 'real' and the 'virtual' for the basis of their analyses (see Baudrillard 1998; Virilio 1997). However, the empirical studies that exist in this area have repeatedly shown that experiences online are not considered as 'virtual' or apart from 'real' life, and that this presumed dichotomy is a false one (Markham 1998; Miller and Slater 2000).

In face of these criticisms Andreas Wittel's (2001) notion of network sociality may prove an appropriate alternative definition. He notes that in contrast to community, which involves strong long-lasting ties, proximity and a common history, network sociality is based on informational relations, devoid of history, and more based upon an exchange of data and on 'catching up'. Network sociality is linked with Sennett's (1998) commentary upon the decline of long-term, sustained, deep relationships. Sennett's analysis is a stark contradiction to Rheingold's utopian vision. Instead of computer-mediated communication providing a stage for a renewed sense of community, Sennett paints a dystopic picture of relations devoid of trust, commitment and loyalty. Wittel's network sociality is a less bleak interpretation of contemporary social relations. While it does not depend upon shared history and narratives, replacing them with exchange of experiences and biographies, trust and commitment can still be engineered. Instead of basing trust upon the knowledge of someone's character, knowledge of their resources or social position can be used. Giddens' (1994) notion of 'active trust' is such an example.

With the lack of meaningful encounters Lockard (1997) speaks of, and the banality of interaction Healy (1997) mentions, network sociality seems far more an accurate analysis of online social relations. However, most of the analysis in the early to mid-1990s of computer-mediated communication seems parochial. Only recently has the Internet been considered a site of empirical enquiry and a phenomenon intrinsically linked to cultural and social processes that occur offline. This empirical work has also highlighted how the Internet is a collection of very different social spaces, all with unique characteristics which shape the way in which individuals interact. To talk of the Internet or computer-mediated communication as *one* form of communication is short-sighted (Miller and Slater 2000). Further empirical work has highlighted how individuals use computer-mediated communication very differently (Markham 1998). Aggregated experiences of Internet social interaction are no longer an accurate reflection of social relations online.

Of the studies that have been conducted on virtual communities, the majority have focused upon text-based environments, limiting the ability to form a general analysis of computer-mediated communication as a whole (for examples see Baym 1998; Danet 1998; Kolko and Reid 1998; Markham 1998; Burkhalter 1999). However, the substantiated analyses from these studies have been controversial in that they challenge the majority of the criticisms of online community. The idea that networked society has 'thinned' out interaction, and that notions of history and narrative are no longer integral to sociality are being questioned. More importantly the same cannot simply be said about interactions within online environments. Analyses presented later in this text support both Markham's (1998) and Miller and Slater's (2000) analyses. These analyses argue that history and meaning are an integral part to some online social formations, and that while exchanges are ephemeral, they are not mere informational exchanges. Based on this analysis online social formations will be referred to as online communities from this point.[2]

The darker side of the Internet

While ICTs allow legitimate global economies and knowledge networks to exist, they also allow for a darker side that sees the illegitimate use of information networks. Castells (1998) identified what he called the Global Criminal Economy as a defining feature of Network Society. Organised criminal groups, that were once national in scope, can now employ global networks to further their illicit dealings. Information technology has enabled criminal groups to interact with other criminals on a global scale, to traffic illegal goods more effectively and anonymously and to identify potential victims at a click of a button.

While Castells (1998) was more concerned with organised 'mafia' criminal structures, his study allows us to understand how and why criminals have incorporated information technologies into their deviant behaviours. From large scale money laundering to petty instances of computer hacking, the criminal has turned to IT to further facilitate 'traditional' criminal activity, and to create new ways of committing crimes. Essentially with new opportunity follows crime. The digital networked age provides not only established criminals with new ways of committing crime, but also empowers previously non deviant individuals, drawing them into new criminal behaviours. At one end of the spectrum we see organised criminals taking advantage of new technologies and networks to facilitate their illegalities, while at the other extreme the 'empowered small agent' is able to commit crimes that were previously beyond their means (Pease 2001).

Untangling the web: defining cybercrime

Before categorising types of cybercrime it is important to distinguish what is criminal behaviour and what is not in relation to computer use/misuse. As advances in technology escalate at a rate unparalleled by everyday institutional mechanisms, it is no surprise that the law is slow to respond to high-tech criminal activity. The McConnell report (2000) identifies 42 countries which are yet to update their legal systems to cope with the threats of cybercrime. Such lack of foresight was further emphasised by Attorney General Reno at a meeting with senior law enforcement officials from the G8 countries:

> [U]ntil recently, computer crime has not received the emphasis that other international crimes have engendered. Even now, not all affected nations recognise the threat it poses to public safety or the need for international cooperation to effectively respond to the problem. Consequently, many countries have weak laws, or no laws, against computer hacking – a major obstacle to solving and to prosecuting computer crimes.
>
> (US Attorney General Janet Reno 1997)

Where advances have been made, it is questionable whether the scope of new and adapted bodies of jurisprudence can remain ahead of deviant enterprise. While certain forms of hacking, obscene electronic materials and online stalking have been met with legal regulation, many other forms of computer related activities escape regulation due to their esoteric nature. For example, certain activities, such as bomb talk (discussions surrounding the manufacturing of explosives), some forms of online textual violence (see MacKinnon 1997b), and until recently racist and xenophobic online behaviour[3] (see Mann *et al.* 2003), escape regulation but are still arguably harmful. As a result it has become acceptable, and more analytically fruitful, to consider harms instead of crimes in relation to computer use/misuse.[4] Examining how one's behaviour on a computer network can negatively affect an individual, be it financially or psychologically, allows for a greater scope in understanding both criminal and non-criminal computer related activities.

In attempting to define crimes and harms that take place on computer networks, it is important to consider the spatial and temporal dimensions of crime and deviance. Traditional or terrestrial crimes exhibit certain general characteristics. Often they are static in terms of time and space. Perpetrators very often have to be present at a certain time and in a certain place to carry out a crime. The same might be said for the target of crime; targets of crime (victims, property etc.) must share the same temporal-spatial dimensions as their perpetrator.[5] For a crime to be committed it must also be recognised as a crime within these temporal-spatial constraints. Therefore the law and conventional social understanding at the time and place must recognise behaviour as illicit for it to be labelled as criminal. Finally, unlike the 'typical' characteristics of the terrestrial offender, the virtual criminal is more likely to exhibit traits attributable to those from an affluent and well-educated background. Partial evidence to corroborate this can be found in the findings of the 2002/3 British Crime Survey and 2003 Offending, Crime and Justice Survey. Both surveys show that peak Internet usage was among middle income households, and that there was a significant correlation between increased Internet use and increased household income. Correspondingly Internet use was low amongst those living in council estate and other low-income areas. The level of physical disorder in the immediate area also impacted on levels of Internet use, where those living in areas categorised as having relatively high physical disorder were less likely to use the Internet. Those in full-time education, compared to those in full-time employment, were also significantly more likely to admit to sending viruses, engaging in hacking activities and sending threatening emails (Allen *et al.* 2005).[6]

The characteristics of cybercrimes and harms can vary from those of terrestrial crimes. There is little adherence to the spatial-temporal restrictions characteristic of conventional crimes. This is primarily due to the burgeoning growth of new electronic information and communications technologies (ICTs) (Woolgar 2002). Networked societies allow for time and space to be distanciated, meaning that an action in one spatial-temporal boundary may have an effect outside of that restriction (Giddens 1990). In relation to criminal activity this means that individuals are able to attack their victims at-a-distance. The temporal dimension of crime is also affected; new ICTs allow criminals to make deals or harass a victim in compressed periods of time, given the distance covered. A fraudulent transaction can take place over thousands of miles in milliseconds while a harasser can subject their victim to derisory discourse at great distance in real time.

Given these inconsistencies, there is contentious debate over what constitutes a cybercrime (Wall 1999). This uncertainty is further reflected in legal discourse, where issues over jurisdiction inflate the debate. As cybercrimes can span national boundaries and legal jurisdictions, questions over what body of law should apply complicate issues of retribution. In contention, Wall (2001) identifies that the trans-jurisdictionality of some cybercrimes can prove beneficial in attaining a conviction. The notion of 'forum-shopping' has allowed prosecutors to identify in which region an investigation and conviction would be most successful. The two case examples Wall (1999) gives come from both sides of the Atlantic. In the case of *R v. Arnold* and *R v. Fellows* (1996) jurisdiction was handed over from US to UK law enforcement as it was thought a conviction would be more likely. Similarly in *United States of America v. Robert A. Thomas and Carleen Thomas* (1996) the prosecution was moved from California to Tennessee given that the differing body of law in the latter state would be more effective at securing a conviction.

The contention surrounding legal discourse in relation to cybercrime is mirrored in other political and social arenas. Three multilateral organisations are currently involved in shaping high-tech crime policy: the European Union (EU), the Council of Europe (COE) and the G8. Other organisations, such as the Organisation for Economic Co-operation and Development (OECD), the United Nations, Interpol and Europol, have been involved to a lesser extent. None of the organisations has offered a definitive definition of cybercrime. The United Nations highlighted the problem of definition in its *Manual on the Prevention and Control of Computer-Related Crime* (United Nations 1995), stating that while there is consensus amongst experts, these definitions have been functional and hence too specific. A similar position was held by the Council of Europe. The European Committee on Crime Problems decided to leave out any definition of high-tech crime in its *Convention on Cybercrime* (2001), allowing individual jurisdictions to apply their own definitions based on their specific body of law. The Council of Europe does, however, provide a working definition for Europol, the European law enforcement organisation responsible for fostering effective cooperation of member states in order to tackle organised crime. However, this definition is narrow, in that it only relates to 'attacks on automated data-processing systems' (2000). This is in part due to Europol's existing mandate which already covers certain crimes that can be committed over computer networks (drug and arms trafficking, counterfeiting, trafficking in human beings, child pornography, illegal immigration networks etc.), nullifying the necessity for a more comprehensive definition of cybercrime.

Recognising the complex nature of cybercrimes, others have had more success with defining them. Wall (1998) categorises cybercrimes in three distinct ways. First, technology has provided a vehicle for the further facilitation of existing harmful activities. Wall identifies that computer networks have become a communications vehicle which facilitates the commission of 'traditional' criminal activities. Everyday crimes have then migrated, or have been re-engineered to function online. A typical example might be the use of the Internet by paedophiles who have utilised the anonymity that is granted to every Internet user to 'groom' children in unregulated chat rooms, and to maintain and build networks where illegal images and even victims are exchanged. Further, Mann and Sutton (1998) show how a group of burglars posed as trainee locksmiths on a locksmiths' newsgroup in order to obtain new methods of lock picking.

The second category of computer related crime identified by Wall involves the creation of new opportunities for harmful activity that are currently recognised by existing criminal or civil law. Examples would be the creation of new kinds of obscenity though computer-generated images (pseudo-photographs), and computer fraud. Third, entirely new forms of harmful activities, that are of dubious legal status, have emerged with the increased use of the Internet. Essentially the Internet has allowed for the creation of a new environment within which novel forms of misbehaviour are engineered. At one level these include the unlawful appropriation of intellectual property such as images, software, music and video products. At the extreme, cases of virtual violence have been reported on many occasions, where online community members have been verbally attacked and harassed by another net user. Cases of virtual rape have even been reported (MacKinnon 1997b). It is these kinds of computer related deviant activities that are posing the greatest challenge to legal systems and are undergoing constant evaluation in terms of understanding and interpreting the kinds of potential harms they can cause.

Wall (2001) further formulates a fourfold typology that proves useful in trying to understand these types of deviant cyber activity: *cyber* trespass, *cyber* obscenity, *cyber* theft and *cyber* violence.

Cyber trespass

Cyber trespass is the invasion of private space on the Internet by a hacker. Young (1995) identifies several types of hacker including utopians that believe they are helping society by demonstrating its vulnerabilities, and militant activists, who are aggressively anti-establishment and use their technical knowledge to cause harm to their targets, be they individuals or institutions. Wall (2001) identifies four categories of illicit activity conducted by these individuals. First is the deliberate planting of viruses. These could be designed to disable a particular function or they could be sleeping viruses designed to be neutralised only after a ransom has been paid. On a less organised level viruses are sometimes distributed via the Internet and email to cause general chaos – the so-called *Love-Bug* realised in 2000 being an example.

The second type of activity is the deliberate manipulation of data, such as web pages, so that they misrepresent the organisation or person they are supposed to represent. Several political party websites have been targeted by hackers in the run up to general elections in the UK. Manifestos have been re-written in sarcastic and satiric fashion (Reuters 16 June 2003). In more serious circumstances, following the introduction of Megan's law (Sex Offender Registration Act 1996), the misrepresentation of paedophiles' names and addresses on the Internet in some American states could prove detrimental, both physically and mentally, to innocent individuals. The anonymity granted to every Internet user often means the process of identifying the perpetrator of such acts is very difficult if not futile.

The remaining two kinds of activity are associated with Wall's further categorisation of hackers: the *cyber* spy and the *cyber* terrorist. *Cyber* spies break access codes and passwords to enter classified areas on computer networks. The primary aim of the *cyber* spy is to appropriate classified knowledge. In comparison *cyber* terrorism can take many forms including denial of service (DoS) attacks where entire servers are brought to a standstill, halting business and sometimes even whole economies. Richard Clarke, the once White House 'terrorism czar' highlighted, if not a little too fervently, the risks associated with new networked technologies:

> [CEOs of big corporations] think I'm talking about a 14-year-old hacking into their websites. I'm talking about people shutting down a city's electricity, shutting down 911 systems, shutting down telephone networks and transportation systems. You black out a city, people die. Black out lots of cities, lots of people die. It's as bad as being attacked by bombs…Imagine a few years from now: A president goes forth and orders troops to move. The lights go out, the phones don't ring, the trains don't move. That's what we mean by an electronic Pearl Harbour.
>
> (quoted in Sussmann 1999: 452–3)

While a little emphatic, Clarke's concerns were partially justified. It is no secret that military strategists are preparing to counter 'information warfare', so defined when intruders enter major computer systems and cause damage to their contents thus causing considerable damage to the target. It is known that such intruders can infiltrate and tamper with national insurance numbers and tax codes, bringing economies to a standstill (Wall 2001). Such evidence suggests a gap seems to be opening between society's increasing dependence upon ICTs and its ability to maintain and control them (Taylor 2001).

Taylor (2001), having conducted extensive research into hackers, provides alternative characterisations based on function. First, he outlines Levy's (1984) hacker 'generations', detailing the 'true' hackers of the 1950s and 1960s who were seen as the pioneers in their field, hardware hackers who were responsible for opening access to hardware during the 1970s and game hackers of the 1980s, who generated games for the hardware. Taylor adds three more types of hacker, bringing the typology up to date. He describes the hacker/cracker as an individual who illicitly breaks into other computer systems, much the same as Wall's *cyber* spy. Microserfs are those individuals who once belonged to, or are still associated with, hacker groups but work within corporate structures, such as Microsoft. Finally Taylor talks of hacktivists, those hackers who are motivated by political drive.

Cyber obscenity/pornography

It is important to distinguish what is meant by pornography and how it manifests on the Internet. A distinction can be drawn between child pornography, which is illegal, and mainstream pornography, which is legal. Child pornography is a special case and is generally considered illegal in many countries. For this reason it provides a challenge for regulation on the Internet (Grace 1996). It is also recognised that there is no settled definition of 'conventional' pornography in a multi-national space such as the Internet. Further, cultural, moral and legal variations make it difficult to define 'pornographic content' in a global society (Akdeniz 1997). The debate over obscene material on the Internet is contentious because the laws that govern this material differ so drastically between countries. In Britain, for example, individuals regularly consume images that might be classed as obscene in many Middle-Eastern countries. In seeking to clarify this issue the European Commission's *Green Paper on the Protection of Minors and Human Dignity in Audiovisual and Information Services* (1998), highlighted the need to distinguish between illegal acts, such as child pornography, which are subject to penal sanctions, and children gaining access to sites with pornographic content, which is not illegal but may be deemed harmful to children's development. Nonetheless, differences in classification between countries create problems when information of a seemingly pornographic content is internationally transmitted via the Internet.

Several studies have been conducted focusing on the availability of pornographic material on the Internet. While the Carnegie Mellon Study was methodologically flawed its finding that at least half of Internet content was related to pornography drew mass attention from the media which saw the genesis of the first Internet moral panic (Rimm 1995). Another project, employing content analysis, examined Internet pornographic graphic images (Mehta and Plaza 1994). Other studies have conducted similar content analysis of written pornography found on newsgroups (Harmon and Boeringer 1997). Each study voiced how simple it was to access various incarnations of pornography via the Internet. Content analysis of written pornography also showed a tendency to use violence within the narrative, more so than magazine pornography (Harmon and Boeringer 1997).

Pornography on the Internet is available in many different formats, ranging from pictures and short animated movies to sound files and textual stories (Akdeniz 1997). These sites and newsgroups are accessible through the Internet by any online user. While some discussion groups are free to access, most of the websites with pornographic content require proof of age and payment by credit card to access their materials (Akdeniz 1997). The legal requirement of proof of age verification and the cost that customers are obliged to pay meant that the online pornographic industry was one of the first to venture into e-commerce. The online sex industry is one of the more successful e-commerce ventures, and paved the way for other online businesses. The desire to legitimise the industry resulted in the establishment of Adult Sites Against Child Pornography (ASACP). This organisation, and others like it, go to form part of a wider network of Internet governance (Wall 2001).

Prosecutions for the production of online pornography are rare. In the majority of situations the producers of this material go to great lengths to secure their websites from under-age access. Age verification systems are in operation on many sites, while others require the use of a major credit card. However, regulation is complex given trans-jurisdictionality. When addressing the issue of pornography the limited police resources are directed towards more serious infringements of the law – such as online paedophile networks. However, current legislation does stipulate that it is an offence to send 'by means of a public telecommunications system, a message or other matter that is grossly offensive or of an indecent, obscene or menacing character' (Akdeniz 1997). While arrests have been made in the US for sending similar obscene messages (see *United States of America v. Jake Baker and Arthur Gonda* 1995), similar trends have not been mirrored to such an extent in the UK.[7]

Policing of the Internet and newsgroups is beginning to emerge as part of the Home Office's drive towards further proactive policing methods. Operation Starburst in the summer of 1995 was one of the first international investigations into paedophile rings and the Internet. Resulting from the investigation nine British men were arrested (Akdeniz *et al.* 2000). Operation Starburst was the first investigation to uncover a direct link between child abuse and the use of the Internet (Akdeniz 1997). The recognition that the Internet is an avenue for the trafficking of illegal pornographic images was also embodied in criminal law. The Criminal Justice and Public Order Act of 1994 widened the definition of a publication to include a computer transmission, which led to the prosecution of Fellows and Arnold in *R v. Fellows* and *R v. Arnold* (1996). Governance of Internet content is, at present, a contentious debate. The reasons for regulation may seem obvious at first, however, currently it might be thought inappropriate to regulate mainstream pornography on the Internet while it is readily available on the high street.

Cyber theft

Wall (2001) identifies two types of *cyber* theft. The first is the appropriation of intellectual property where, for example, music or video has been recorded and digitally reproduced and distributed over computer networks. The most notorious successful prosecution for this type of *cyber* theft was in the case of *AandM Records, Inc. v. Napster, Inc.* (2000) where the defendant was accused of distributing and selling copyright musical material. The Digital Millennium Copyright Act 1998 (DMCA) was introduced to update US law for the digital age. Certain aspects of the Act made Internet Service Providers (ISPs) liable for copyright violations. While the DMCA was comprehensive enough to satisfy the World Intellectual Property Organization's (WIPO) treaties, there were still concerns over its inadequate protections for copyright owners. The proposed Berman Bill (2002) in the US allows copyright owners to effectively violate the law in protection of their products. The Bill allows for the hacking of any computer that is downloading copyright material from a peer-to-peer network. It becomes clear that the Bill, if ever implemented, would allow for action tantamount to vigilante justice with copyright owners acting as prosecutor, judge and jury. Due to such opposition from digital civil libertarians it is questionable whether the Bill will actually be implemented.

The second type of *cyber* theft is the appropriation of virtual money, or more accurately the appropriation of credit card numbers. The important issue here is that the offender does not actually need to have the physical credit card. All of the relevant details are available from discarded credit card receipts, or can be obtained through unsecured (unencrypted) online credit card transactions.

Cyber violence

Cyber violence is the term used to describe online activities which have the potential to harm others via text and other 'digital performances'. These activities manifest in textual, visual and audio form, meaning the violence is not actually physically experienced. *Cyber* violence can be delineated by its perceived seriousness. Least serious are heated debates on message boards and email, often referred to as flaming (Joinson 2003). At worst, a defamatory remark may be made about someone's inferior intellect or flawed argument. These exchanges are considered minor in terms of violence due to the fact that their consequences never mount to anything more than a bruised ego.

More serious are 'digital performances' that are hate motivated. To take two examples, racial and homophobic hate-related online violence are in abundance in the form of extremist web pages (Mann *et al.* 2003). Protected under freedom of speech laws in the US, these sites employ shocking tactics to drum up support for their extremist viewpoints. In particular, some sites go as far as to display images of hate-related homicide victims in distasteful ways to heighten their very often misguided outlook on society's minorities (Schafer 2002). The use of derogatory homophobic and racist text in these sites, combined with the use of inappropriate imagery and sound, results in a digital performance which is violent and potentially psychologically harmful, not only to the victim's families but also to the wider community.

Of potentially more harm are the violent activities of online stalkers. Cyber stalking involves the use of electronic mediums, such as the Internet, to pursue, harass or contact another in an unsolicited fashion (Petherick 2000). Most often, given the vast distances that the Internet spans, this behaviour may never manifest itself in the physical sense, but this does not mean that the pursuit is any less distressing. Petherick (2000: 1) states that

> there are a wide variety of means by which individuals may seek out and harass individuals even though they may not share the same geographic borders, and this may present a range of physical, emotional, and psychological consequences to the victim.

Yet there still remains some concern that cyber stalking might be a prelude to its physical manifestation (Reno 1999).

The Internet allows communication with another person unconstrained by social reality, thus creating a certain psychodynamic appeal for the perpetrator who chooses to become a cyber stalker (Meloy 1998). Only written words are used, and other avenues of sensory perception are eliminated; one cannot see, hear, touch, smell, or emotionally sense the other person. There is also, if one wants, a suspension of real time. Messages can be sent and electronically stored, and their reception is no longer primarily dictated by the transport time of the medium, but instead, by the behaviour of the receiver. Meloy (1998: 11) explains, 'some individuals may always return their phone calls the day they receive them, while reviewing their e-mail at leisure'.

Meloy contends that this asynchronicity provides opportunities for the stalker and presents a series of suppositions concerned with the medium itself. First, Meloy notes how the lack of social constraints inherent in online communication means that potential stalkers become disinhibited. Therefore certain emotions and desires endemic to stalkers can be directly expressed toward the target more readily online than offline. Second, while online the absence of sensory-perceptual stimuli from a potential victim means that fantasy can play an even more expansive role as the genesis of behaviour in the stalker.

A more contentious debate in the *cyber* violence literature exists around the phenomenon that has become known as 'virtual rape' (MacKinnon 1997b). These cases of virtual violence have completely escaped any legal rationalisation. In the most famous case a hacker was able to enter an online community and take control over community members' actions (Dibbell 1993). Because movement and action within virtual communities is expressed through text, the 'virtual rapist' was able to manipulate people's actions against their will. What essentially followed was a salacious depiction of violent rape upon several individuals in real time. While no one was physically harmed, community members reported being traumatised by the event. This case was taken so seriously that the whole community (over 1,000 members) voted on what action should be taken against the perpetrator. The imperative point to be made here is that the physical self of the perpetrator, the individual that exists in the offline world could not be physically harmed, only his online persona could be punished. The effectiveness of such punishment is then questionable (see Chapter 7).

All forms of *cyber* violence can take advantage of the many media used to make up computer-mediated communication. The majority of this communication is purely textual, both real time (Internet Relay Chat) and delayed (email). Any form of *cyber* violence has to operate within these parameters. Therefore the violence of words, as debated by Butler (1997) and Matsuda *et al.* (1993), becomes the focus of attention later in the study in an attempt to understand the mechanics and potential harms of online violence (see Chapter 6).

Levels of computer-related crime

Attempts to quantify computer-related offences are difficult due to a lack of reporting and recording. In most cases individuals or businesses may not realise an offence has occurred, and indeed it may not have, given the dubious legal status of some cyber acts. Others may feel the acts are not serious enough, that the police would not be interested, or that an alternative method of mediation is required. However, these complexities have not prevented attempts at quantification. Since the turn of the century there has been a burgeoning of surveys attempting to measure the extent of the cybercrime problem. Governments, voluntary and public organisations are now systematically collecting data on the incidence of business and personal cybercrimes. In particular in the US the Federal Bureau of Investigation in arrangement with the Computer Security Institute conducts an annual computer crime and security survey, targeting over 700 public and private businesses. Similarly in the UK the National High-Tech Crime Unit (NHTCU) in conjunction with National Opinion Poll (NOP) conducts a similar survey. Since 1997 the Department of Trade and Industry have published their Information Security Breaches Survey. Most recently the British Crime Survey (BCS) and the Offending Crime and Justice Survey (OCJS) have for the first time shed light upon cyber victimisation and offending amongst the general population. Combined these efforts help lift the veil on the true extent of cyber-criminal activity.

Business cybercrime

The Computer Security Institute (CSI) and the FBI in the US conduct an annual computer crime and security survey, gathering information from over 700 corporations, government agencies, financial institutions, medical facilities and universities. Each year the survey provides data on the prevalence of high-tech illegal activities covering hacking, fraud and denial of service attacks, amongst many others. In 2005 the survey uncovered that 56 per cent of respondents suffered computer security breaches within the last twelve months. The most prevalent incidents were virus attacks followed by access to unauthorised information and denial of service attacks. The 91 per cent of respondents that were willing and/or able to quantify their financial losses reported losing just over $130 million in the financial year through various forms of high-tech crime.[8] Of this total amount virus attacks accounted for 33 per cent of losses, unauthorised access 24 per cent, theft of proprietary information 24 per cent and denial of service attacks 7 per cent. Interestingly website defacement was responsible for the least of the losses at 0.08 per cent (Gordon *et al.* 2005). Since 2000 there has been a steady decrease in the incidence of computer crime reported by US companies (from a high of 70 per cent in 2000 to a low of 54 per cent in 2004). Figures from 2005, however, indicate a departure from this seemingly steady decrease, providing some evidence that the high-tech crime problem is far from under control.

The NHTCU 2005 survey, which included 200 companies (30 per cent from the critical national infrastructure), indicated that the prevalence of business cybercrime in the UK differs from that reported in the US. Overall 89 per cent of those interviewed said their company had experienced some kind of computer related crime, a rise from previous years. Viruses and worms affected 83 per cent of companies, 15 per cent reported the use of their systems for illegitimate purposes, denial of service attacks impacted upon 14 per cent of companies, 11 per cent suffered unauthorised access to systems, 10 per cent reported theft of data and 9 per cent were victims of financial fraud via computer systems. A closer analysis found that the financial and telecoms sectors were more likely to have suffered from financial fraud – phishing (illegitimately obtaining and utilising consumers' personal identity data and financial account credentials), fraudulent use of stolen data and keylogging (the use of spyware to record PC user activity). Both sectors were also more likely than others to have suffered theft of information or data. Total estimated minimum financial impact on businesses with over 1,000 employees was £2.4 billion, compared to £177 million for companies with between 100 and 1,000 employees.

The UK Department of Trade and Industry have published an annual survey on information security breaches since 1991. The latest report at the time of writing highlighted that the business environment in the UK is becoming increasingly dependent upon technology. This dependency has also increased the exposure to security threats. This is evidenced by a year on year increase in security breaches with an all time high of 74 per cent of businesses experiencing a security breach in 2004. The majority of breaches were a result of virus infection (50 per cent), misuse of information systems (22 per cent), hacking attempts (17 per cent) and fraud involving computers (11 per cent). The total average costs of the worst incident ranged between £7,000 and £14,000 for small businesses and between £65,000 and £190,000 for large organisations (ISBS 2004). Aggregated this amounts to a similar overall figure as reported in the NHTCU (2005) survey.

The Australian Computer Crime and Security Survey (2005) paints a less severe picture than both the US and UK. It to focuses upon public and private companies and its current incarnation included over 181 respondents. Over all sectors only 35 per cent had experienced a computer-related attack (down from highs of 67 per cent in 2002 and 49 per cent in 2004). Virus, worm and trojan infection affected 64 per cent of companies, 24 per cent were victim to denial of service attacks, 15 per cent reported unauthorised access to information, 14 per cent had confidential information stolen, 2 per cent were subject to telecommunications fraud and 8 per cent had their websites defaced. In 2005 companies reported financial losses in excess of 16 million dollars (the highest Australian figure recorded).

The findings from all three surveys are illuminating and paint quite distinct pictures of the cybercrime problem in three nations that are far from disparate.[9] It is likely that dramatic changes in trends within countries are more attributable to police recourse allocation, increased detection capabilities and practices of recording and reporting than actual decreases or increases in the prevalence of cybercrime. Methodological differences between surveys (for example, how certain cybercrimes are categorised and what companies are excluded or included in analysis and on what criteria) are likely to account for the stark differences between countries. What is certain is that as businesses become increasingly dependent upon computer systems they open themselves up to greater risks of disruption and financial losses.[10]

Personal cybercrime

Assessing for the impact of cybercrimes on businesses and national critical infrastructures has become commonplace. However, quantifying the prevalence and impact of similar acts on domestic Internet users began as late as 2003 in the UK. The British Crime Survey (2003) was the first to include a technology crimes module. Credit card fraud, mobile phone theft, mobile text harassment, online harassment and access to obscene electronic materials were some of the areas covered by the new module. This was the first systematic attempt in the UK to understand the extent of Internet-related victimisation. In relation to credit card fraud 75 per cent of the sample admitted to being anxious about using their credit card online. This is not surprising given persistent media attention on Internet-related fraud and alarming figures indicating a continued increase in credit card losses (APACS 2005). Virus victimisation affected just over 18 per cent of households in the 12 months preceding the survey. While this is much lower than reported in business surveys, it is more likely that domestic users fail to recognise infection and neglect to report their surreptitious victimisation. Hacking affected just over 2 per cent of Internet using households, 12 per cent were victim to email harassment and 21 per cent had accessed or been sent offensive or upsetting unsolicited material via the Internet.

The UK based OCJS (2003) gathered data on cyber offenders rather than victims. While self-report studies have their methodological flaws, the data reported on is still marginally reliable and worthy of note. Only 1 per cent of 18–65-year-olds admitted to taking part in Internet-related fraud. Similar low offending figures were evident for virus sending (0.9 per cent), hacking (0.9 per cent), email harassment (0.7 per cent), visiting racist websites (0.7 per cent) and visiting websites to obtain information on how to commit a crime (1.5 per cent). The only significant rate of online offending was copyright theft – over 20 per cent of males and over 9 per cent of females admitted to illegally downloading copyright material. Overall almost 11 per cent of respondents who said they used the Internet admitted to committing a technology crime.

Aside from government surveys voluntary organisations whose aim it is to support sufferers of cybercrime also routinely collect data on their victims. While the reliability and validity of such data are contested, they do help in further mapping particular esoteric forms of cyber deviance. In particular, attempting to accurately quantify the prevalence of cyber violence is complex. The infrastructures required to identify and record such instances are yet to be fully instituted and definitional issues still complicate the matter. However, the statistics that are made available by some organisations may shed partial light on the patterns of cyber violent victimisation. In 2004 the organisation Working to Halt Online Abuse (WHOA) dealt with 196 cases of online harassment, a 40 per cent decrease from the year 2000.[11] The majority of cases were resolved by the Internet Service Provider, leaving a small percentage of cases which called upon the police and legal system. The majority of victims were white females aged between 18 and 25, and in most cases the harassment occurred either through email or instant messaging. Many organisations like WHOA collect similar data. Unfortunately collection is far from systematic, and little collaboration exists between organisations. The victimisation patterns that have been identified from these data are not an accurate picture of online crime, and a substantial dark figure still exists.

Explanations for offending

Given that the scope of computer-related offences is so wide it seems futile to provide a general theory of cybercrime. Explanations for the kinds of crimes that use the computer as a tool are similar if not the same as those theories that attempt to explain analogous crimes that occur offline. The motivations behind the activities of paedophiles, drug dealers and hate-groups online remain the same; the Internet just makes committing these crimes less problematic. The specific theorising that has been done has tended to examine acts of cyber violence, given its unique qualities and the fact that, in many respects, it is a new kind of deviance. Much of the work on 'flaming' or abusive speech online has taken a social psychological approach to behaviour. Kiesler *et al.* (1984) identified that people partaking in computer-mediated communication were far more likely to be over-personal and free than those communicating face-to-face. Individuals are more likely to give personal information about themselves, and are more likely to be social. However, a darker side was also identified. With this increased sociability comes increased levels of aggressiveness. It is identified that individuals become disinhibited when communicating online. Disinhibition essentially means a lack of self-consciousness, anxiety about social situations and worries about public evaluations. These theorists pointed to the anonymity inherent in Internet interactions, the perceived distance between people in conversation, a reduction in social cues and a breakdown of social hierarchies as explanations for disinhibition and increased levels of aggressiveness.

Attempting to expand this theoretical framework this study takes the established theory of control (Hirschi 1969) and examines the relationship of online community to cyber deviance. In particular the analysis focuses upon Cyberworlds members' bond (attachment, commitment, involvement and belief) to online community in relation to recorded instances of online deviance (see Chapter 3).

Regulating computer-related crime

Governments' desires to take advantage of networked information technologies has resulted in calls for regulation and control of certain forms of electronic information. The Internet in particular has proved a challenge to regulators in terms of intellectual property rights, access to obscene or harmful content and the protection of minors. This can be seen in the drafting of the Artists' Rights and Theft Prevention Act (2005), the Berman Bill (2002), the Author, Consumer, and Computer Owner Protection and Security Act (ACCOPS) (2003) and the Communications Decency Act (CDA) (1996) in the US and the various attempts by the EU to control Internet content and behaviours (such as the EU *Action Plan on Promoting the Safe Use of the Internet* 1997, and the *Convention on Cybercrime* 2001). These attempts to regulate and govern Internet content and behaviours have often been met with staunch opposition from cyber civil liberties campaigners. Such opposition saw the successful challenge to the CDA (1996), the Berman Bill (2002) and the ACCOPS (2003). Technically the Internet is difficult to regulate. Its capacity to span the globe, ignorant of national boundaries, means that no one body of law has precedence over what can and cannot be distributed. Barlow (1996) eloquently describes how this proves problematic for policy makers:

> … the Internet is too widespread to be easily dominated by any single government. By creating a seamless global-economic zone, borderless and unregulatable, the Internet calls into question the very idea of a nation-state.

However, it is misleading to state that the Internet and other forms of computer-mediated communication are not subject to any form of regulation. In fact, it may be more appropriate to talk of the governance of the Internet instead of regulation, as the discourse of governance lends itself to the very nature of the Internet. Governance refers to the 'regulation of relationships in complex systems' (Rhodes 1994: 151) which 'can be performed by a wide variety of public and private, state and non-state, national and international, institutions and practices' (Hirst and Thompson 1995: 422). The Internet is a complex system of interconnections between technologies, organisations and individuals. Any attempt to govern such a complex system of interconnectivities requires a diverse and dynamic approach. Walker and Akdeniz (1998: 8) provide an overview of a governing framework that is both diverse in its constituent components, and dynamic in its approach:

- Global international regulatory solutions by the likes of OECD and the United Nations.
- Regional supranational legislation such as by the European Union.
- Regulations by individual governments at a national or local level, such as through police squads and customs control units.
- Self-imposed regulation by the ISPs with industry-wide codes of conduct, which would transcend national boundaries.
- Trans-national and national pressure groups made up of end-users.
- Rating systems such as Platform for Internet Content Selection (PICS).
- Self-imposed regulation, such as through software filters, to be used by end-users.
- Hotlines and pressure organisations to report illegal content such as child pornography. The Internet Watch Foundation (IWF) is one such incarnation in the UK. The EU *Action Plan* set up in January 1999 is also an initiative which incorporates the use of hotlines.

Evidence already exists in support of this hierarchy of governance. The blurring of private and public regulation is recognisable in the increased sales of security software for end users and the continued establishment of local and regional policy development. The European Commission's *Action Plan on Promoting the Safe Use of the Internet* (1997) was one of the earliest pieces of legislation to recognise the necessity for a multi-layered and multi-juridical approach to the regulation of Internet content. The *Action Plan*, therefore, aimed to set up a European network of hotlines to report illegal content such as child pornography. It also sought to establish a clear set of criteria for the identification and filtration of what it termed 'harmful' or 'illegal' content. However, little discussion was given to what was actually meant by either of these terms in relation to child pornography. Nonetheless, the plan sought to increase the awareness amongst children and parents of the dangers of using the Internet, and to encourage vigilant self-regulation where possible.

More recently the *Convention on Cybercrime* (European Committee on Crime Problems 2001) might be considered one of the most systematic and international attempts at regulating 'harmful' and criminal activities that employ the use of computers. The aim of the European Commission was to approximate substantive law in the area of high-tech crime. It was considered that with common definitions, incriminations and sanctions, high-tech crime could be successfully regulated. Four areas were focused upon: offences against the confidentiality and integrity of computer data and systems; computer-related offences; content-related offences; and offences related to infringements of copyright and related rights. Further protocols to the convention concerning content that is xenophobic and racist have also been added. Forty-two member and non-member states of the Council of Europe signed up to the convention when it was introduced in 2001. The convention was ratified in 2004 and has been introduced into 11 member states' legal code. However, neither the UK nor the US has ratified the convention. There are still major concerns that the convention jeopardises certain civil liberties and places an unreasonable burden on Internet Service Providers. Further, it is doubtful whether the content constraints espoused by the additional protocol of the convention would be adopted in the US given first amendment rights.

Summary

The emergence of online community has occurred in tandem with the increasing prevalence of cybercrime. Many cyber criminals rely on the existence and permanence of online communities. Some require the illicit knowledge and materials that are so easily disseminated though discussion and newsgroups, while others use forms of online community to identify and attack their victims. This research is focused far more on the latter. The research aims to complicate the notion that 'virtual criminality' is synonymous with terrestrial crime (Grabosky and Smith 2001). If cybercrime is to be fully understood all levels of online deviant activity have to be considered, including the sub-criminal. When potential harms are included in the analysis various unprecedented forms of online deviance come to light that begin to share less in common with terrestrial crimes and deviance. The prevalence, manifestation and control of these less familiar acts of deviance within the online community form the focus of the study. Three empirical chapters take the debates covered here further. The notion of online community is discussed in relation to the field of study. How deviance manifests and is sustained within this online community is explored. Finally, the ways in which the control and regulation of crime are achieved, and what part community plays in this governance are outlined. The following chapter outlines the theoretical framework of the argument.

3 Control in cyberspace

Introduction

Online deviant acts which simply employ computer technologies to facilitate traditional crimes, such as the spread of online paedophile networks or the theft of cash, are still adequately addressed by the theories used to explain their occurrence offline. This study departs from these lines of theorising by attempting to explain the occurrence of deviant acts that manifest solely within the online environment. The aim is to understand forms of online deviant acts that might not otherwise occur if it were not for the existence of computer networks. In particular, acts of virtual property destruction and online violence are examined and theorised, due to their prevalence and severity within Cyberworlds. However, the theoretical framework outlined in this chapter is also helpful in explaining a range of online deviant behaviours beyond the borders of Cyberworlds. Given the threat and risk these kinds of online deviant acts may pose to individuals and groups it is pertinent to understand the aetiology of such acts in order to develop prophylactic measures. As a precursor to the empirical evidence detailed later, this chapter will outline a theoretical position, delivering possible explanations as to why and how individuals who spend time socialising within online communities come to deviate from group norms sometime during their experience as group members. The focus is the established criminological position of control as a theoretical and analytical tool in explaining deviance (Hirschi 1969). The central role placed upon community and interdependency within the theory lends itself to the Cyberworlds environment. The existence of community, and the degree to which individuals feel bonded to the community and each other become central to explaining online deviance within Cyberworlds.

Deviance and control

Hirschi's (1969) control theory was originally developed to analyse delinquency which lends itself to the analysis of sub-criminal acts that manifest online. More specifically the emphasis placed on social bonds, attachment to community members and belief and involvement in community as analytical categories within control theory allows for an application that proves fruitful in explaining antisocial behaviour online (Hirschi 1969). Introducing the notion of cyber-risks in relation to evaluations of 'risk-taking' within the online environment shows how certain techniques of neutralisation, unique to this environment, further increase the likelihood of online deviance (Sykes and Matza 1957). Using complementary sociological (Turner 1967; Bakhtin 1965) and psychological approaches (Matheson and Zanna 1988; Reicher *et al.* 1995; Lea and Spears 1992; Spears and Lea 1992; Siegal *et al.* 1986; Kiesler *et al.* 1984) to build upon and adapt control theory proves beneficial in widening its explanatory power when addressing online antisocial activity.

The central tenet in control theory is the assumption that deviant acts occur when an individual's bond to society is subject to atrophy (Hirschi 1969). The central question is 'why do individuals obey the rules of society', a reversal of the fashion in strain theories where the question posed asks 'why do individuals not obey rules' (Merton 1938). The bond an individual has to a group, as an analytical category in explaining non-conformity, has its roots in classical forms of thought and has been the subject of debate over decades (Durkheim 1951; Hobbes 1957). The usefulness of the category in relation to the online social setting becomes evident when assessing the bond an individual has to the online group or community. In any such assessment the elements of the bond need to be delineated.

Hirschi (1969) outlines four main elements that serve as controlling forces over individuals. Attachment refers to the capacity of individuals – in Hirschi's case adolescents – to form effective relationships with other people and institutions – parents, peers and the school. When attachments are strong, individuals are more likely to be concerned with the opinions and expectations of others and thus more likely to behave in accordance with them. Strong attachment meant the internalisation of group norms, much like Reiss' (1951) concept of personal control, where individuals take on board the norms of society as their own. For Hirschi attachment did not lie in some internal psychological state – although recent work in social psychology is useful in further exploring control in relation to disinhibition – but in ongoing social relations which could vary over time. The attraction here was that changes in degrees of attachment could be readily explained by relations to others and not by some innate pathology. While Hirschi (1969) was referring to adolescents in his study, a similar reasoning can be applied to online community members in this study. A lack of attachment to other community members, community founders, and institutions, such as the Peacekeeper Core,[1] may be an important factor in explaining antinormative behaviour (see Chapters 5 and 6).

Hirschi identifies commitment as the second element in the bond an individual has to society. Simply put, commitment is the 'rational component in conformity' (Hirschi 1969: 20). The premise is that individuals who invest time and energy into conventional lines of activity, such as attaining an education, developing a career or simply building a reputation, risk losing these if they deviate from group norms. This approach relies on there being a rational actor who calculates the risks and costs of committing a crime. Commitment also functions on more subtle levels as it is woven into the fabric of existence within society. Most people, simply by living in a society, acquire possessions, prospects and the like that are at risk if a decision to deviate from group norms is taken. Hirschi takes Stinchcombe's (1964) example of high school rebellion to illustrate how commitment functions on several levels. Antinormative behaviour occurs within schools when the future status of individuals is not clearly related to present performance, which suggests that conformity is not only realised by what one has but also by what one hopes to achieve. The application of conformity to the online setting is relatively non-problematic given the similarities in social structure. At the simplest level individuals who become citizens of the community have more at stake (their citizenship) than tourists if they deviate from community rules. Aspirations to join the Peacekeeper Core, the time invested in building property on land and so on are all elements of commitment that can be associated with social experience within Cyberworlds.

Involvement in conventional acts and avocations is one of the more mundane elements of a social bond to society. The assumption is that a person may simply be too busy to even consider committing a deviant act if they are involved in conventional lines of activity. Hirschi identified several elements of conventional activity such as commitment to deadlines, appointments and working hours that would restrict the opportunity for deviant activity. Unsurprisingly this rationalisation has featured in many youth crime initiatives, where recreational facilities and clubs have been supported by governments in order to involve juveniles in more conventional activities. In relation to the online setting, it is likely that community members who are involved in building property (a time intensive activity), organising social events or volunteering for community organisations are less likely to veer into antisocial activity than those who have no static vocation or avocation.

The final component of a bond to society, one's belief in the values, norms and laws of society, is central in explaining an apparent lacuna in Hirschi's work and control theory in general. Control theory assumes that there exists an accepted universal belief system at work in society. In contradiction to strain and subcultural theories control theory does not subscribe to the notion that deviance is a product of the adoption of inverted norms. On the contrary, deviants at the same time as committing an illicit act also believe that it is deviant and wrong. This rationalisation is tackled in two ways within control theory. Some control theorists have regarded beliefs with little semantic value. Beliefs are merely words and do not differentiate between deviants and non-deviants. The second approach is dependent upon the deviant rationalising their behaviour so they can simultaneously still believe in its wrongful nature while committing the act. Most notably Sykes and Matza (1957) term this process 'techniques of neutralisation'. The individual drifts in and out of states of delinquency depending upon the circumstances and requirements of the moment. This state of drift is made possible by 'techniques of neutralisation', through which the moral bind of the law can be temporarily ignored. It is at this point where a bifurcation occurs in the general argument over motivations to deviate. Hirschi (1969) argues that the motivation to deviate is innate, meaning an internal or external force is not needed for a deviant act to occur. Quite simply there is a variation in the extent to which people believe they should follow the rules of society. The foundation to this argument is that there is a variation in the belief of the moral validity of social rules. The notion that individuals have an innate motivation to deviate must be accepted if Hirschi's conception of control theory is to be adopted.

It is with this premise that Hirschi makes a strange departure from stressing the importance of the social – regarding social attachments, commitments, involvements and beliefs as more relevant than their psychological counter-parts – to relying on some universal 'inner' desire to deviate. This paradigmatic shift encapsulates the central problem of control theory. If we are not to accept the notion that humans have an 'animal impulse' to deviate, then how is delinquency explained? In defence Becker (1963: 26) explains:

> There is no reason to assume that only those who finally commit a deviant act usually have the impulse to do so. It is much more likely that most people experience deviant impulses frequently. At least in fantasy, people are much more deviant than they appear.

While Hirschi finds such arguments convincing he resigns himself to the fact that control theory was never meant to answer the question 'Why do they do it?'. The theory treats deviation as non-problematic, and was designed to answer the question 'Why don't we do it?'.

In later work with Gottfredson, Hirschi presents a General Theory of Crime building upon his original concept of control theory (Gottfredson and Hirschi 1990). In this work the classical notion of crime or the criminal act and the positivist notion of the criminal or actor are united. In line with the hedonistic calculus of classical theory, crime is defined as acts of force or fraud undertaken in the pursuit of self-interest. From this perspective criminal events can be understood using principles that explain all other human conduct. The keystone in this theory is low self-control, resulting in large from 'ineffective child rearing' (Gottfredson and Hirschi 1990: 97). The general approach taken seems to have warranted the removal of the key variables Hirschi (1969) outlined in *Causes of Delinquency*. For this reason there are limits to its explanatory power when applied to the deviant acts discussed in this study.

Self-control theory has its fair share of critics (see Geis 2000 for an overview). Areas of debate cover its definition of crime, the matter of tautology, the role played by opportunity and its views about specialised criminal behaviour to name but a few. However, there are certain components of self-control which build upon Hirschi's (1969) control theory that are helpful in explaining online deviant behaviour. First, its more holistic reasoning draws attention to the notion that low self-control is not confined to criminal acts, but also causally implicated in many analogous acts, such as, in Gottfredson and Hirschi's (1990) terms, promiscuity, alcohol use and smoking. In this respect the theory may hold some explanatory power in accounting for online deviant acts such as profanity, antisocial behaviour and online harassment, all of which have uncertain criminal status. Yet, without too many mental contortions, one can see how Hirschi's (1969) initial conception of control theory can also be used to explain 'analogous acts'. Second, Gottfredson and Hirschi's (1990: 88) discussion of opportunity, noting that 'criminal [or deviant acts] require no special capabilities, needs or motivation; they are in a sense open to everyone', resonates with Pease's (2001) notion of the 'empowered small agent', whose genesis is explained in terms of the ubiquitous opportunities to deviate that are granted by increasingly pervasive information technologies. While it is within this area where self-control theory has been criticised heavily for rejecting social learning as key in providing opportunity, the proliferation of new information technologies may indeed aid the theory in expanding general opportunity, foregoing, of course, arguments over the 'digital divide' (Compaine 2001). Third, self-control theory allows for a generic understanding of the perpetrators of crime and deviance, regardless of socioeconomic status, sex, age and race. This general approach to offenders, rarely found in criminological theory, allows Gottfredson and Hirschi (1990) to explain forms of white collar crime, as well as more predatory crimes. Similarly, this approach lends itself to the analysis of online deviant acts, predominantly perpetrated by young, middle-class white males (Compaine 2001). Lastly, the policy implications of self-control theory point towards a reduction in the role of the state, and a return of the responsibility of crime control to the community. The relevance of this policy recommendation to the online environment is realised in Chapter 7 which shows how formal tertiary methods of social control were less effective in relation to community crime control.

Due to the overarching similarities between control and self-control theories, and certain omissions and advances embodied in each, a combined theoretical approach is taken in this study. One of the key benefits of both theories is their capacity to address not only criminal events but also more mundane, yet significant antinormative acts or harms, such as those that plague Cyberworlds. In the empirical chapters that follow the components of a bond an individual has to the online community are taken as analytical categories (attachment, commitment, involvement and belief). An analysis of how this bond can be weakened by forces unique to the online environment allows for a meaningful understanding of why individuals are more likely to be deviant online rather than offline.

It is at this point where a disclaimer is required in relation to the application of alternative theories of criminal behaviour to the online environment. The decision was reached to concentrate on the application of control theory to the online environment following the evaluation and the application of a host of alternative criminological theories such as rational choice theory, routine activities theory (Clarke and Felson 1993) and sub-cultural theories (Cloward and Ohlin 1960; Matza 1964; Short and Strodtbeck 1965). While these theories are applicable to a variety of online contexts (for example see Newman and Clarke 2003; Williams 2004), control theory was considered most applicable to the Cyberworlds environment because of its use of community as a central analytical theme. The majority of deviant acts examined in this study are, in a variety of ways, attached to and dependent upon the existence of the Cyberworlds community.

Control, deviance and the online environment

In attempting to tie control theories to behaviour within online settings it is useful to look briefly at current research that focuses its attention on levels of inhibition – arguably relational to self-control. Some of the most recent psychological literature on online behaviour points to the centrality of disinhibition in many of the practices carried out by community members (Lea and Spears 1992). Disinhibition explains behaviour that is not constrained by self-consciousness, anxiety over social situations or worries about public evaluation. In other terms, individuals online experience a lessening in self-control. While this phenomenon can have both positive (increased levels of socialising) and negative effects (increased use of defamatory and harmful statements) it is the latter that is of concern. However, there is debate over the exact cause of this disinhibition. Psychological studies that explore the phenomenon of disinhibited behaviour online, elucidate that a reduction in social cues (Kiesler *et al.* 1984; Siegel *et al.* 1986), the possibility to remain anonymous (Reicher *et al.* 1995), a reduction in self-control (Spears and Lea 1992) and the ignorance of community evaluation (Matheson and Zanna 1988), are precursors to such behaviour. While these theories have their merits, they were not specifically designed to explore the aetiology of deviant behaviour *per se*. A more productive approach to explaining the phenomenon of disinhibition can be found in control theories. An examination of social attachments, commitments, involvements and beliefs that function to bond an individual to the community or group is likely to carry more explanatory power when dealing with online deviance. While control theories have a degree of applicability to online deviant behaviour, additional sociological theorising can increase their explanatory power.

Bond and online community

In examining the attachment, commitment, involvement and belief an individual has to the online group or community it is important to establish that a group or community exists online. As noted in Chapter 2, notions of community and the application of such a term to groups online form an ongoing and contentious debate. For the purposes of this chapter it is taken for granted that there exists a definitive 'collective' of individuals within Cyberworlds; more finite and substantive empirical evidence and discussion on this topic are explored in the following chapter. At a rudimentary level, the notion of citizenship within Cyberworlds seems an influential shaping force behind its social structure and is indicative of a degree of group solidarity and presence. Group norms, rules and beliefs are in operation, as well as long and short term relationships between members and institutions. Strong bonds to other members, institutions, rules and conventional lines of action, according to control theory, would mean the internalisation of group norms and a heightened consciousness of other members' opinions and expectations. Weak bonds would effectively be the reversal of the above, mirroring the effects of disinhibition theory – essentially an ignorance of community evaluation and a weak attachment to group norms.

The contention is that weak bonds online can lead to an increased prevalence of deviance, and that certain aspects of the online environment create a social space where the integrity of bonds is in constant flux. In an attempt to explain this phenomenon Turner's (1967) concept of liminality can be used as an analytical device. Turner, drawing from anthropology, details how spaces and individuals can be affected by liminality, showing how an individual in a liminal situation is 'betwixt and between' any stable or recurrent condition that is culturally recognised (1967: 94). As people are removed from their actual or real life positions, as is the case when entering an online environment, they are freed not only from the associated values and norms of behaviour but also they are 'divested of their previous habits of thought, feeling and action' (Turner 1967: 105). Liminality can thus be seen as a period of freedom: freedom from the constraints imposed by previous fixed roles and the associated actions, responsibilities and expectations of the person's 'actual' life. This loss of constraints typically allows individuals in such a transitional period more freedom to interact with others in similar circumstances, in this case the online environment. The ability to mix with others is further facilitated by the loss of hierarchies existing outside the liminal state. However, it would be incorrect to state that online community members have no distinguishing marks of social status – technological knowledge, length of community membership and placement within the hierarchical structure of the online community reflect some of the social restraints that structure 'real' life in the actual or non-liminal environment. However, it takes a degree of time for a new community member to inculcate these online hierarchies, leaving them in a period where neither themselves or others have a recognisable fixed status. Further, stratification within the online environment is far more fluid and turbulent than within terrestrial community, often resulting in less importance being placed on status. This may allow for individuals to mix more freely than they would offline.

Bakhtin's (1965) notion of the medieval carnival, explored in his work *Rabelais and His World*, can be used to further understand this transcendence of status. In this seminal work on 'folk humour and carnival laughter' Bakhtin attempts to explain how the carnival atmosphere functions as an oppositional force against social hierarchies:

> While carnival lasts, there is no other life outside it. During carnival time life is subject only to its laws, that is, the laws of its own freedom. All are considered equal during carnival ... a free and familiar contact reigns among people who were usually divided by the barriers of caste, property, profession and age. People were, so to speak, reborn for new, purely human relations. These truly human relations were not only a fruit of imagination or abstract thought; they were experienced.
>
> (Cited in Morris 1994: 198)

Presdee (2000) also uses the notion of the carnival in his analysis of culture and crime. Carnival is said to function as a playful and pleasurable resistance to authority where those normally excluded from the discourse of power celebrate their anger at their exclusion (Presdee 2000). The online environment is a carnivalistic space within which once disempowered individuals can operate outside of terrestrial hierarchies. Some individuals embark on 'edgework' – intense and often ritualised moments of pleasure and excitement which accompany the risk, danger and skill of transgression (Lyng 1990) – making the online environment unpredictable and sometimes dangerous. The notion of carnivalesque spaces also has much in common with Turner's (1967) period of liminality. Indeed both point to the stripping away of identity – akin to anonymity experienced within online environments – as a precursor to an increased prevalence of socialising, a heightened sense of freedom and weak attachments, commitments, involvements and beliefs in the community.

The process of logging on to an online community can be viewed as a transitional phase of liminality. As the individual enters the first stage of 'immigration' they choose an avatar, an alternative persona partly created by the visual representation of the entity on the computer screen, and partly by the user's imagination. The carnivalesque nature of the online environment is taken a step further with the ability to change an avatar's physical appearance at any time, possibly creating a new persona to fit the new image. This freedom to develop multiple personae, while still being accepted as a valid member of the online community, is a clear extension of both Turner's (1967) and Bakhtin's (1965) work. The ability to take on fluid identities has certain consequences for the strength of bond an

individual can forge with the online community. Following the logic of
control theory such weak bonds would result in higher levels of deviance.
Yet are weak bonds enough to plummet every community member into
deviant activity? As noted earlier, not all those with low self-control or
those who are disinhibited as a result of the liminal and carnivalesque
nature of the online environment become antisocial. There is some degree
of rationality in deviance; once the controls have been lifted an individual
must decide that deviant activity is the appropriate course of action given
the risks involved. It is hypothesised that risk and its suspension within
the online environment helps explain why some individuals decide to
take deviant courses of action and others do not. The following section
is a theoretical prelude to a deeper empirical examination of online risk
suspension which follows in Chapter 5.

Cyber-risks and techniques of neutralisation

The idea of virtual or cyber-risks is not a completely new concept. In
his seminal work *Risk Society* Beck (1992) writes of the increasing risk
associated with nuclear, reproductive and genetic technologies, in doing so
identifying certain consequences of new technologies in modern society. In a
similar vein the risk-society thesis can be applied to the online environment.
Encapsulated within the notion of the online environment are technologies
of information and communication, and those who employ such tools are
running a myriad of risks. Common examples include the invasion of the
computer virus, computer fraud, Internet addiction, cyber-cults or other
deviant groups such as paedophile rings, and the rapid spread of moral panics
and irrational fear facilitated by scare stories such as the risks associated with
genetically modified foods. These risks, however, work on a reciprocal plane
– consequences of online actions often manifesting themselves offline and
vice versa. The computer virus aims to destroy data and disrupt actual life
and time; other risks involve the computer being used as an instrument of
gain; while the spread of moral panics manifest themselves in 'actual' political
consequences. It is this reciprocity that distinguishes between the two kinds of
cyber-risk, the other being that which is evident within online communities.
This kind of cyber-risk holds a more tenuous relationship with the terrestrial
world. In other terms, these kinds of cyber-risks are engineered out of the
virtual environment within which they seek to rage their consequences. An
example would be the risk of having one's avatar's appearance or name
attacked in a derisory manner. This is not to say that the real person who
created the avatar would be immune to these consequences, it is more the
argument that these risks are truly virtual in that they are engineered from
within the online environment and are evaluated in relation to this social
space and not terrestrial external space. Without the existence of the virtual
environment these cyber-risks would have no breeding ground.

Techniques of neutralisation

Anonymity, a sense of physical detachment, time and space distanciation and transience all form part of the liminal and carnivalesque online environment, and as such assessments of 'risk taking' have to be altered in light of these characteristics. These may have a neutralising effect on risk and risk taking within the online arena. For example, those wishing to take the risk of hurling abuse at a fellow community member are more likely to do so in an online environment than one that makes the offender 'directly' liable for their actions. This is due to the knowledge that most online environments are unregulated, and those that are have little deterrent effect due to their ineffective and non-threatening prophylactic and retributive measures. Those individuals who decide to take the risk of harassing others within virtual communities can remind themselves of the distance between themselves and their partners in conversation, and in doing so disassociate themselves from accountability and self-control. Indeed, the possibility for reprisals, apart from a severe virtual tongue-lashing, is minimal given the degree of anonymity granted to the offender.

Taking Sykes and Matza's (1957) techniques of neutralisation it is possible to identify how the characteristics of the online environment allow individuals to drift into deviant behaviour while still maintaining a positive self-image. Those committing antisocial acts within online social spaces would find it non-problematic to deny injury to the victim of their assaults. Rationalisations such as 'it's only words' are verbalised techniques of neutralisation that are arguably a by-product of the ephemeral nature of the Internet and its text-based dependency for communication. In a similar vein, the perpetrator may neutralise feelings of guilt, that might otherwise prevent deviance, by denying the existence of a victim with rationalisations such as 'they aren't really there', and 'this isn't real'. Distain or condemnation of the condemners is yet another technique to neutralise the wrongfulness of antisocial behaviour online. This can be seen in the specific context of Cyberworlds, where there is an active condemnation of the regulatory body (Peacekeepers) and the corporate arm of the community (see Chapter 7). Any acts of vandalism or attacks on officials could easily be neutralised by the recognition that 'his condemners … are hypocrites, deviants in disguise' (Sykes and Matza 1957: 669).

It becomes clear that risk is suspended for those seeking to disrupt online community life. This period of suspension is evidently a temporary phenomenon; at some point community members must re-enter the offline world. Here a comparison can be drawn between the nature of the online deviant and the everyday tourist. Online community members may feel as if they are a tourist, and that this temporary status provides them with the mental mechanisms to take a 'moral holiday', akin to a reduction of belief in online community norms, values and regulations. The concerns that bond an individual in the real world from committing deviant behaviour are suspended. Baron and Straus's (1989: 110) social disorganisation index, usually employed to measure features of disorganisation in American society, can be used in an attempt to further theorise online deviant behaviour:

> [A]ny weakening of stability and integration has an emancipating effect on character and allows in varying degrees the development of irresponsibility, unconventionality, and disorganisation. Those whose lives involve a considerable amount of mobility and who thus are forced to spend a large proportion of their time among strangers are subject to this effect. They are not controlled by an organised society to the extent that settled peoples are and are thus free to express individuality to a greater extent.

The mobile aspect of online community members' experiences holds much in common with the travel of the tourist. Online community members first become mobile when entering the *pre-liminal* stage where the individual is separated from their original position – their terrestrial life. In the following *liminal* stage, where they enter the virtual environment, the individual is divested of the rules and norms that governed them in their original position. It is in this liminal stage where the individual is susceptible to low self-control, irresponsibility and unconventionality. Logging off and re-entering the offline world is considered the *post-liminal* stage, where rules and regulations of the 'real' world re-shackle the individual.

Liminality, the carnival of online environments, a reduction in societal controls and techniques of neutralisation can all help account for deviant activity within Cyberworlds. However, none of these analytical devices helps to explain the original motivation of the offender. For convenience it is acceptable to take on board Katz's (1988) or Presdee's (2000) position arguing that Internet users are seduced by the carnival online environment and become involved in cybercrime because of the excitement it can induce. Alternatively Hirschi's (1969) defence could be adopted stating instead that conformity is of interest, not deviance. Instead of asking why people commit cybercrimes or harms the study examines why members of Cyberworlds conform. However, no matter what defence is taken, it is unlikely that all readers would be fully convinced by these arguments. In incorporating a multitude of online deviant acts in the study a general theory of criminal and analogous behaviour had to be adopted. As a result the specificities of the aetiology of certain online deviant acts are beyond the scope of this analysis, and it is acknowledged that more theoretical work is required if the specifics of some cybercrimes and cyber harms are to be fully understood.

Summary

The existence of an online community within Cyberworlds allows for a relatively unproblematic application of control theory. Individuals' varying degrees of attachment, commitment, belief and involvement in the community and its rules and institutions, influenced by techniques of neutralisation and liminality, show how levels of self-control are in a constant state of flux. If this approach is taken, the problem with the over-prediction of deviance, often a common criticism of many theories of crime, has to be considered. It has been detailed previously that simply a reduction in self-control cannot account for deviance, and would surely over-predict the prevalence of antisocial activity. In response, the rationality of the deviant actor and the ability to neutralise the risks and 'wrongfulness' of committing deviant acts online has been advocated as an extension of the theory. While this may not directly allay criticisms of over-prediction, it is contended that the day-to-day infraction of community rules and etiquette, while not serious enough to be deemed criminal, still provides evidence of low levels of self-control. As Gottfredson and Hirschi (1990) note, their theory not only explains more serious crimes, but also analogous less serious behaviour that is conducted on a daily basis, that may be overlooked by authorities, but is still evidential of low self-control. The following empirical chapters establish the existence of an online community within Cyberworlds providing a framework for the application of the theories outlined in this chapter.

4   Establishing online community

Fieldnotes: I entered the world called gateway, the arrival point
in the CyberWorlds environment. Once I 'floated' down onto the
clearing beneath me (apparently this is the way everybody enters
these worlds) I could see at least twenty-five people all exchanging
conversation. Looking around I noticed masses of greenery leading
up to the mountains on the horizon. Avoiding conversation in order
to peruse my new environment I noticed how most avatars seemed
to engage in conversation, sometimes overly personal in content.
Discussion centred around a recent 'virtual' funeral where mourners
congregated to lament over the loss of a friend. I assumed that
this friend actually died, and this was not some simulacrum.
Enabled via the VR environment some avatars would make an effort to
locate their partner in conversation as if to recreate or simulate
'face-to-face' conversation. Some avatars would bundle together
in groups, while others would wander alone, as if exploring the
vast virtual landscape, while maintaining 'remote' communication.
I couldn't help but think that these avatars shared some history,
even if it was one only a few years or months old, and born of
purely 'distanced' or 'virtual' relations.

Rusty: I had never visited 'chat rooms' (and still don't), but in
early '96, I found the URL for a place called Cyberworlds. I admit
that I saw it as a kind of game. I didn't see a lot of social
interaction, although at the time, I wasn't really looking for
it. Thinking back, I'm sure it was there, I just wasn't involved
in it. I built a house, met a few people, and made a few friends,
but after a while, I got bored with it. Early in '99 I returned
to Cyberworlds, and was amazed to find a 'virtual' community of
people from all over the world. They appeared to 'know' each other.
Slowly, I became 'known' by some of the 'regulars', and soon I felt
like I had become a part of the community.[1]

Debate over the feasibility of building and maintaining a 'community' in
a computer-mediated environment has dominated cyber-studies discourse
for the past decade. Many commentators trace the debate back to Howard
Rheingold's (1993) seminal work on 'virtual community', in which he
contends that online communities form when social aggregations emerge
from the Internet where enough people carry on public discussions long

enough, with sufficient human feeling, to form webs of relationships in cyberspace. Yet many of the contemporary debates surrounding the existence of virtual communities fall back on the need to define what community really is in the offline world. The previous extracts begin to tease out features that have been used by scholars in defining community. A shared history, social interaction, a common habitat and common ties between individuals, evident in the data, are familiar traits found in many traditional and contemporary conceptions of community (see Hillery 1955; Poplin 1979). While discussions about definitions are important when dealing with the phenomenon of virtual community, it is not the purpose of this chapter to delineate such debate in any great detail (see Chapter 2 for an overview). Instead its purpose is to draw on the empirical data gathered from observations and focus groups in order to piece together a narrative of the users' experiences of Cyberworlds in light of current debates (see Appendix 2 for an overview of the methodology). Thinking around how community and crime are interrelated will also form a focus of the chapter, taking into account Hirschi's (1969) conception of community bond. Taking the idea of a bond as a framework allows not only for an analysis of 'community' within Cyberworlds, but also an examination of social interaction within the context of deviant behaviour. Taking Hirschi's attachment, commitment, involvement and belief, in their loosest sense, as analytical categories and mining the data for evidence of their prevalence in the experiences of users of Cyberworlds shows how some form of 'community' exists, whether imagined or actual, and how deviant events relate to the 'bond' individuals have to 'community'.

Several key research questions address the bond an individual has to 'community' and how it relates to deviance. First, can and how does 'community' sustain itself within a computer-mediated environment, and second, how might an individual's bond to an online community influence the way they behave. This chapter will deal with the first question by primarily addressing three main themes. First, how interaction is altered in light of increased visual stimuli within a Virtual Reality environment compared to text-only online spaces will be explored. Investigating how textual communication is influenced by increased levels of pseudo-presence via the use of avatars queries the supposition that levels of social immersion are significantly depleted within online interactions. Following on from this line of reasoning it can be assumed that increased levels of social immersion in online interactions further develop a bond to a social group.

Second, the chapter will move on to detail the use and meaning of building within Cyberworlds to show how a permanent presence is forged within an environment characterised by ephemeral encounters. The cultural significance of artefacts and buildings, and the process of building itself, are examined in relation to maintenance of history and memory within Cyberworlds. The significance of these permanent online artefacts to the strength of community members' bonds is also discussed.

Lastly, the formation of relations and friendships is studied within an online environment that is subject to states of liminality and anonymity. While many users of Cyberworlds talk of an attachment to a 'community' in terms of friendships, trust, and isolation from the offline world, others give a narrative of a dystopia, highlighting a lack of bond as a result of liminality, disinhibition, a lack of trust and anonymity (Turner 1967). These contrary accounts will form the final focus of this chapter, highlighting the factors that strengthen or weaken one's bond to an online social group. Taken in conjunction, these three themes show how Cyberworlds is considered by its members to be a viable social space, where meaningful interactions take place that have real consequences. This chapter then sets the scene, establishing that a form of community exists within Cyberworlds. The subsequent chapter builds upon this foundation, locating the aetiology of deviance in varying levels of attachment, commitment, involvement and belief in the online community.

Pseudo-presence and community

Traditional concepts of community result from an accumulation of observations regarding events, artefacts and social relations which are constrained within distinct geographical boundaries[2] (Jones 1995). The preoccupation with physical geography has been a stumbling block for many when attempting to conceptualise a community mediated by computer networks (Lajoie 1996; Mnookin 1996; Nguyen and Alexander 1996). With an absence of physicality, a lack of face-to-face communication and presence, it is no wonder many critics reject the notion that community can be sustained online (Kolko and Reid 1998). The social immersion, realism and 'shared space' that presence creates are arguably lost in a digital medium (Lombard and Ditton 1997). Herring (1999) has argued that the incoherence in interaction experienced by many users of text-only CMC, resulting from disrupted adjacency, overlapping exchanges, and topic delay, must have a negative effect on community cohesion. In response researchers have taken on board the task of understanding how social formations are sustained within spaces devoid of physicality.

Markham (1998: 86) identified a group of Internet users who considered cyberspace as a *place* where 'they can go and meet and talk with others'. Markham continues to recall the experiences of her research participants, claiming that 'although such online worlds may not have a physical substance, they are thought of as meaningful places where things happen that have genuine consequences. Some users talk about these online spaces as virtual communities. Others call cyberspace "home"' (Markham 1998: 86). Markham's study featured text-only online environments, such as chat rooms and MUDs, where any simulacrum of presence had to be imagined by the user. The technology becomes a mode of being, where individuals become the text they write. This can be seen in individualised styles of writing and the use of emoticons. Regulars to the online community begin to recognise others by expressive style and content; personality is imbued within the text written on-screen, creating a pseudo-presence. Herring (1999: 20) concludes in her paper that the 'messy texts' experienced within social interaction online can intensify interactivity, often extending 'the limits of what is possible in spoken conversation'.

The lack of face-to-face and oral interaction in text based CMC means that presence is imagined. The descriptions of spaces in MUDs and MOOs evoke vivid imagery in the user's imagination:

```
Welcome to Diversity University! Ambient lighting conveys a calm
and friendly atmosphere, and there is always plenty of space on
the red couches here. This centre is located in the Student Union,
so when you feel ready to explore, just leave for the foyer by
typing OUT.

Type HELP NEWBIE for a quick summary of commands

Exits include: [west] to the Quiet Cubicles, [out] to the Student
Union Foyer, [tutorial] to Tutorial Center, [north] to Help Desk
(not just for newbies), [southeast] to Tour Centre

You are standing here.

You see Mr. Besenstiel, a large banner, an application folder and
a map here.

You listen up to make out the words of an announcement, 'Attention
Guests! To find out how you can apply for a regular character at
Diversity University MOO, Type HELP @REQUEST.'
```
(Extract from Markham 1998: 38)

The use of vivid description and positioning ('You are standing here') creates a sense of presence. Similar methods are used in fantasy gaming and role playing (Fine 1983), and arguably some readers place themselves within novels, imagining they are part of the scene (McLaughlin 2000). The preoccupation with presence in many social practices indicates its importance to social interactivity. Presence has been captured within VR communities, such as Cyberworlds, where spaces do not have to be imagined by the user; buildings, parks, malleable objects and other community members are represented by computer graphics. Within VR communities memories can be imbued within objects, creating a sense of visual history. Interactivity is given an added social richness where users are given the opportunity to recreate social spaces in their vision employing the unique features of VR to accomplish things unachievable in the physical world.

Presence and social immersion

Presence provides for a more immersed interaction in two main ways. First, the level of intimacy is said to increase when interlocutors are physically present. Intimacy is said to be increased by close proximity, and the use of body language and non-verbal cues. Second, immediacy in conversation also increases the level of social immersion (Argyle and Dean 1965). Wiener and Mehrabian (1968) discuss how the choice of language can increase a sense of psychological closeness or immediacy. Therefore idiomatic forms of language may provide higher levels of immediacy and hence a greater degree of social immersion. If this model is to be followed, that high levels of intimacy and immediacy increase social immersion in communication, then it would be logical to assume that face-to-face communication is an ideal form.

Non face-to-face communication is not necessarily absent of presence. In the online text-only context an approximation of presence can be engineered through 'placement' techniques in written text, and the use of individual writing styles. Levels of intimacy vary by the use of emoticons replacing body language and facial cues. Native forms of language online, such as the use of acronyms (IMHO – In my humble opinion, OMG – Oh my God, LOL – Laugh out loud, and the like), combined with synchronous forms of communication, such as a chat room interface, create a high degree of immediacy in exchanges. Yet the desire to introduce physical elements into online communications has been irresistible, and is testament to how important physicality is to interpersonal communications. From 'smiley faces' created with standard ASCII characters, to conventions of describing physical movements in parentheses ('action words'), to more sophisticated avatars, the inclusion of physical elements in online encounters has increased as the technology has advanced. However, text-based group interactions should not be viewed as the poor cousin to newer, flashier, prettier media that allow sound or graphical images (moving or still, cartoon-like or photographic) to be exchanged by participants. As McLaughlin (2000) argues, text-based interactions can be as experientially real as graphical VR interactions, if not more so, in just the same way that a reader can be as emotionally and experientially involved in a novel as in its big screen adaptation. In many ways, he argues, our capacity to immerse ourselves in the text, particularly where we are active participants with limitless capacity to interpret it, is much greater than our capacity to involve ourselves in graphically presented images of the same activity, where our role is as the observer, and the interpretations of form and movement are given to us. As Markham (1998: 210) states, 'Just as the text cannot capture the nuance of the voice, the voice cannot capture the nuance of the text'. However, regardless of these arguments, the desire and the dream of many programmers and ICT users alike to emulate real life in a digital medium has forged new technologies that promise a Virtual Reality. For many, it seems, the levels of social immersion experienced in text-only environments are far from an 'ideal' mode of communication (Herring 1999).

Graphically rich online environments have been developed in an attempt to increase levels of social immersion in CMC. While some argue that the established form of face-to-face communication may not be the ideal mode (see Jones 1995), others see an approximation of face-to-face communication online, in terms of visual presence, as the next step in increasing social immersion in interaction. Cyberworlds is one such innovation that takes advantage of Virtual Reality Modelling Language (VRML), allowing for graphical representations of individuals and spaces. As noted in previous chapters, community members are embodied as avatars – graphical representations of their terrestrial selves. Presence no longer needs to be imagined, the environment creates a visual space for individuals to physically relate to one another (see Figure 4.1). Below respondents give narratives of how avatars enrich the communicative process, detailing how positioning, appearance and performance are all important parts of one's identity within Cyberworlds:

Kid606: it can be helpful to actually be standing next to them and talking with them but this is the next best thing. with avatar representation you can just chat away still standing next to them.

Laika: Yeah I agree, and further Cyberworlds is not just 'online chat.' The people on Cyberworlds tend to be more creative and intellectual types than on the standard online chat or game, and they tend also to take the time to help others out using their own areas of expertise, whether through building, object/avatar development, or bot programming.

Fieldnotes: Just entered the gateway and I've noticed the way avatars are using space and relating to each other 'physically'. It seems as if most of those talking are aware of their physical presence in the VR environment and make efforts to face each other while conversing. Spatially all the avatars are in close proximity and most of them seem to be facing inwards into the discussion circle.

Avatars allow for actual positioning within a 3D graphical environment, providing for an increased social immersion, with avatar emote commands providing more 'realistic' expression in textual/visual exchanges.[3] In response to a question on the usefulness of emote commands, several users said that communication became more meaningful and interactive than in text-only chat environments:

IDM: Tremendous advantages. You have more access to other communication and expression. You can become an avatar, you can use music, build, all in all a fuller experience than text based communication.

> Croft: I think there is more of a presence in the 3D environment.
> Pure text based feels very distant to me.

Feelings of closeness in VR environments replace a sense of distance sometimes experienced in text-only online communication. Community cohesion is fostered by task orientated practices, such as building and maintaining the 'physical' elements of the community. Experiences of increased social immersion within VR environments, due to an increased sense of presence, indicates that some users form a bond to these visually rich online communities that is in some ways different from bonds to text-only online environments. Some users become more attached, committed and involved with the online VR community when social interactions approximate real life encounters, deepening their meaning and importance. Choosing an avatar's appearance to represent the self is an example of the importance placed upon perception and interaction within the online community.

> Jonny_G: My chosen avatar represents myself and I have found that
> if I visit a world where my personal avatar is not available, I
> feel uncomfortable. I very often use the emote animations.

Note how the majority of avatars congregate under the centre of the main structure forming a discussion circle.

Figure 4.1   Aerial view of discussion circle in Cyberworlds

Pappa_m: The one's who choose large avs to look tough are generally weak feeling about themselves. The women who pick the sexiest avs are usually one's who feel they are fat or ugly. The one's who pick nice or conservative avs usually ARE nice or conservative in their behavior. I see their choices as either a 'front face' or a 'real face'...depending on which they choose to present.

Bella: Yes, indeed. I always look at the avatar and the 'actions'. As Pappa_m mentioned before, you can tell a great deal about a person by the avatar he/she chooses. You can also tell a lot by what and how a person builds in Cyberworlds. This may be wrong, but I think I can tell more by the chosen avatar and the 'actions' than by their actual conversation. Not their physical appearance or condition, but their 'real' being. :-)

The use of emote commands in VR seems to be an important extension of textual communication, in terms of meaning and interaction. The way users control their avatars, whether they express themselves regularly with a jump in the air, or even a dance, influences the ways in which they are perceived by other community members. This broadening of the stimuli bandwidth deepens interactivity and arguably feelings of attachment to one another.

Immersion within VR environments can also have negative consequences to community cohesion and maintenance. As many users signalled, the more stimuli a community member is presented with the less time can be devoted to textual interaction. The presence of objects, games, and buildings encourages community members to explore and become distracted from conventional text-based interaction.

Brainiac: My take on this comes from exposure to a number of online communities: Cyberworlds, Everquest, Ultima Online, UseNet, and IRC. What I find most remarkable is the incredible plasticity a community shows in adapting to its environment. We might be the same people when posting in UseNet or building in Cyberworlds, but our behaviors are shaped by the environment. UseNet and message boards encourage a 'letter' style of communication which is quite distinct from the conversational styles of Cyberworlds or IRC. Among a group of strangers conversational content seems to be higher in a textual environment but degrades when there are more interactive 'toys' to play with: instead of reacting to other people's words and ideas many choose to play with music playing bots or colored text effects or games. 'Ground Zero' has more conversation and activity going on than Cyberworlds 5002N 1772W[4] or people within each of about 40 or 50 'zones' talk and sell to each other in 'out of character' discussions. In Ultima Online, people who wouldn't dare to stop and talk to each other in a wilderness area frequented by Player Killers can have long talks at a bank or mage shop[5] within a guard zone. What I'm getting at here is a community cannot be separated from its environment. Change the environment, and the community changes. It is unlikely an online community will ever be the same as an offline community.

The 'physical' dynamics of a community ultimately alter the ways in which individuals interact with one another and their surroundings. In the case of VR, increasing amounts of visual stimuli prove to distract users from conversation in some circumstances, while in others bond individuals to structures and practices. While it might be the case that, unlike in text-only environments, the lack of emphasis placed on intense textual exchanges may subject a community bond to atrophy, it is important to acknowledge other forms of interactivity, other than textual communication, that help forge community. Game playing, building, exploring and volunteering for community projects are all activities that might foster connections and commitments to a social group.

Online artefacts as presence and meaning

The ability to build within Cyberworlds has had a profound influence upon the ways in which community members interact with their surroundings. Thoughts, messages and histories are imbued within artefacts manufactured by community members that are significant and meaningful to individuals and the community at large. Events and situations that affect community members in the physical world seem to penetrate into the virtual arena, creating a reciprocal link between online and offline experience.

> Remy: In one world Cricetia, a member's father was ill. There was a prayer garden built and beautiful prayers and flowers put there. He recovered. :)

Calls for support from the online community clearly indicate a bond between individuals and institutions. Significant life events are also mediated through the VR medium. Online weddings and birthdays are commonplace within Cyberworlds, where community members congregate in virtual churches and spaces to celebrate the occasion. During the course of the fieldwork a member of one of the focus groups celebrated her wedding to another online community member, while another celebrated a significant birthday.

> BennyG: Recently I had a notable birthday one of those BIG one's [at the ages you thought you would never reach - lol]. Not only did my online friends build a huge birthday site for me in Cyberworlds but many also sent cards and gifts to me at my offline address. It made my birthday something to remember. Like life in offline area - 'you reap what you sow' I guess and if you are willing to be generously spirited with others it is returned regardless of the context.

The notion that behaviour and events online have actual effects upon people's lives is an indication of the social validity community members place upon interaction within Cyberworlds. A further indication of the validity placed upon action and interaction within the online arena is found in reciprocity between community members. People come to Cyberworlds to talk with other people and initiate friendships, even intimate relationships. BennyG's comment 'you reap what you sow' is a clear indication that reputation is important in online interaction. Reputation is something that is built over time via a myriad of social interactions. Community members with reputations also have histories, and are part of the wider history of Cyberworlds as a whole. Slowly we begin to see the emergence of the characteristics used to define offline community appearing in the narratives of online community members. However, along with the positive, negative life events also seem to find their way to the virtual arena. Most notably a virtual funeral was held in Cyberworlds which challenged the way community members perceived the validity of their experience online.

> RM: I once witnessed a funeral in Alpha World. A woman who was active down there died of heart attack at the age of 40 or something. I didn't know her myself. Showed up out of sheer (somewhat morbid) curiosity. 'Virtual funerals' don't happen too often. There was a crowd of people down there. They brought flowers, crosses, candles (the COF[6] staff arranged for that people attending could build there), donated some (mostly awful) MIDI files that played, there were some speeches etc. The poor mother of that dead woman attended as well. Old woman seemingly didn't know much about the technology, couldn't figure what was actually going on, why these tons of text scroll down so fast, who's saying what etc. Consider such situation. Say you now somebody from correspondence only (I know a lot of people this way) and some day learn this person died. Certainly you drop a letter or a telegram to the family, other people you'd both know. So why not do it here in Cyberworlds? In all of Cyberworlds's aesthetics, regardless of what you think about it. Still this was something horrible and it disturbed me. It was as if they were playing childish games about some real person death. Well - this was clearly visible - people were basically all excited by the fact their virtual community is so mature, they can even have funerals down there.

RM's contradictory account of the virtual funeral seems to embody several underlying perceptions of Cyberworlds which are mirrored by other community members. While the virtual funeral is considered legitimate, comparing it to forms of asynchronous communication, RM simultaneously found it 'horrible' and 'disturbing'. Such disgust emerged from the idea that what might have actually been occurring was game-like, engineered and used as an instrumental device to somehow legitimise the community. The idea that the event was game-like may have its roots in the fantasy-gaming genre from which Cyberworlds draws its technology. More likely, however, is the possibility that RM's experience of VR life is affected by the liminality and ephemerality embedded within online interaction, often relegating online experience to play-like encounters. However, contrary to RM's experience, others recognised the limitations of the VR medium and genuinely believed that the sentiment was authentic and meaningful.

```
Zypraxia: Hmmmm, the funeral – yes it can sometimes seem weird but
I suspect ppls feelings were genuine and expressing emotionality
in text is limited consequently chat at such times can seem off
hand, distracted etc.
```

```
Justin: Death on the net is not a joke or game. I have attended
several Internet memorial services. One especially touching one
where family members lived all over the world and could not
attend.
```

```
Morlan: I have never been to an online funeral, however, I have
visited (and contributed to) many online memorials. One in
particular, I think, speaks volumes for the usefulness of the
virtual medium, enabling people from all over the world to show
their support/sympathy for others.
```

```
Amber: Would you like to know that not only have I planned my
RL funeral in RL, but in VR and a close Cyberworlds friend has
promised to build me a memorial in the America cemetery?
```

The limitations of the text-based element of Cyberworlds technology is often blamed for apparent insincerity sometimes experienced at sensitive events. During these events visitors may seem distracted or even inanimate. Exact simulated corporal immediacy is not possible within Cyberworlds, and it is the tendency of many members to blame the technology of interaction for the social failings of the community. While there may be degrees of truth in this reasoning, it is reasonable to assume that online social structures also play their part in the failings of online community (see Chapter 7). Regardless of the technological shortfalls, Cyberworlds is granted by some the same regard as offline social space. In fact, it is reported as having an advantage over offline spaces in that its lack of physicality means individuals can pay their respects from all over the globe simultaneously. Amber's wish to have a memorial built in Cyberworlds after her death indicates the importance of history and memory for the online community. Narratives from community members detail how buildings encapsulate individual identities, a constant reminder to others that there was someone here before their time.

```
Brainiac: If I turn my computer off tomorrow, two weeks from now,
people will stop thinking about where I am. When my citizenship
expires, my name will mean nothing to no one. But when someone I
know discovers my building all over again, they'll remember me. An
image of ourselves is forever engulfed in what we can see. Like
tiny trinkets collected over years of road trips, a time capsule,
or even just a childhood diary, our buildings are a stone-engraving
of our lives at that time.
```

The ephemeral nature of life within Cyberworlds, and virtual communities in general, results in turbulent and shifting populations. Individuals build so that they can be remembered by others while they are not online. Unlike life in the physical world, once the computer is turned off simulated corporal immediacy is discontinued within the virtual arena. Similarly, when users walk away from the computer, avatars seem to stand in complete silence, as if asleep or in some kind of virtual coma. Connection to virtual social spaces is purely optional. However, this tenuous link to online life, which for some is as meaningful as life offline, leads individuals to engrave themselves and their personalities into the landscape. Similarly, buildings provide a kind of virtual immortality, recognised to its fullest extent when individuals leave the community. The feeling that one's presence is not permanent within the online environment urges individuals to leave behind reminders of themselves.

```
Buxton: In the physical world friendship may also be short lived
due to relocation or moving on in some other way, but this seems
accelerated in virtual space. Maybe the lesson of the virtual world
is in coming to terms with moving on. Yet we build structures to
leave behind our virtual 'Kilroy was here' statement. It seems
in some way the very speed of the virtual world demands that we,
like fairy tale children, leave our trail of breadcrumbs behind.
Perhaps we are not yet quite accustomed to the speed.
```

The realisation that online encounters are often fleeting and non-linear (Lash 2001) results in a perceived necessity to build permanent structures that help embed meaning into interactions and identity online. The speed at which interactions take place within Cyberworlds (often foregoing the convention of an introduction, and the immediate posting of 'ASL' information – Age, Sex and Location) means members are increasingly distancing themselves from the exchange of in-depth narrative. Instead members exchange units of information as there is little time to sit back and reflect upon detailed life histories. While many members may boast a long contacts list, they sacrifice depth in interaction for quantity. Using Lash's (2001) expression, many Cyberworlds members' relations are 'stretched out' along thin and brittle social networks. It is no surprise then that many have a desire to entrench what meaning their online identities do have in buildings and memorials – artefacts that are immune to the speed of online social interaction – maintaining a permanent bond to the Cyberworlds community. Similarly, due to the ephemerality and speed of encounters and the non-permanence of avatars, members also feel 'lifted-out' of the community. As networked communication can disembody social relationships (Castells 1998), members of Cyberworlds go to extremes to embody their identities in online artefacts. The existence of 'ghost towns' provides evidence to suggest that artefacts built by absent community members (prolonged absence is considered 'virtual death') do embody meaning and identity, fulfilling the inadequacies of non-linear and lifted-out textual interaction.

Cocteau: I was struck by Remy's discussion of death and the memorials that are constructed in Cyberworlds and other places on the net. Another side of this issue is virtual death or disappearance. One of the things that has always intrigued me about Cyberworlds is all of the NAC (Not A Citizen) property. I will occasionally go wandering the virtual countryside and it is like going through a ghost town. I always wonder what happened to those people who put so much effort into building something only to abandon it or perhaps they themselves have perished. A lot of times the buildings are empty and devoid of personal touch but sometimes there remain traces of the previous owner. Although, I know, that people build to have others view their efforts, I often feel that I am intruding somehow, committing a trespass. I find this an odd sensation and one that is not engendered viewing traditional web pages. I don't know if other people have this sort of feeling or not. In real life people would sell their property and new people would move in but in Cyberworlds it just sits there. Its like some sort of testimonial, but to what? Where did those people go and why? If there are real friendships made in virtual places then why have so many left?

Bella: I know the eerie sort of feeling that you are talking about. Sometimes, when I go back to a town I helped build over a year and a half ago, I still remember the people I was building with, the conversations we were having. Now it's as though those buildings hold total irrelevance, but when I go back, the people come alive again for me. I haven't really talked to those people since.

Linda_k: Of course ghost towns bring us feelings of intrusions! Not only are they someone else's work, they are someone else's time in history as well! They are the modern Pompeii! Perhaps this is why after building so long in one place we decide to move on. Who wants to thrive around their past? A deserted town is not a symbol of a virtual friendship gone bad. It is a symbol of time moving on. Virtual friendships are about that – we grow, we change, and we move on. In our virtual world, we all come to terms with the fact that that is the way it works. We seek out the information, and even the people, that are right for us at any given time.

There is clear indication that individuals recognise that both public and private space exists within Cyberworlds. The expressions used by Cocteau establish this distinction. 'Intruding' and 'trespassing' evoke a vivid imagery of someone stepping on private ground. There is no doubt that many private spaces, whether populated or deserted, are saturated in meaning and significance that is recognised by community members. Bella's narrative is steeped in nostalgia, showing how old friends are given life once again by the buildings they built together. These feelings of intrusion and nostalgia highlight the point that buildings are private and often very personal artefacts. They embody individual personalities, histories of friendships and associations and are a continual reminder of the ever-shifting nature of online social life. The existence of ghost towns is also evidence, for some, of the interfering nature of commercial interest. The removal of rights from tourists with the introduction of registration fees meant that many buildings and towns became deserted overnight.

```
Amber: Many will loudly proclaim that NAC was only created when
COF began the registration fees. While it is true that 'NAC' never
happened before that time, it is naive to believe that the fees
actually caused all of the NAC to appear or rather disappear. Ghost
towns were, pardon the pun, alive and well long before fees were
ever considered. I've been a citizen since November 1996 and the
first thing I noticed were the empty places, not the areas devoid
of building but the built up areas that were abandoned or so they
seemed to me. I too felt the sense of being an intruder trespassing
some boundary with every step I took. This sense only deepened
when I could actually tell whether property was NAC or whether the
builder was still a citizen. Many people left when the fees came
about, true, but many more had already come and gone long before
that and many continue to do so. As Coctaeu asks, 'Why? Why do
they leave?' I think that the reason lies in the fact that most
objects built in Cyber Worlds are built by individuals and as such
are built as ghost towns from the very start with the exception
of one location. Why? Because no one but the builder even knows
that the place exists. Areas with multiple and/or joint builders
may seem to have more life but even they become ghost towns the
moment those builders leave. We are social creatures by nature and
wandering into a completely unpopulated area is more often than
not very unnerving. That is why the only location in any world
with a true chance of remaining alive is GZ.[7] Other areas may flare
into life when two or more people come by to visit but they still
remain ghost towns for most of the time and I think that is the
reason that so many have come and gone. They have built a place of
their own and no one comes to visit or so it seems to them. Why?
Because when I visited it was abandoned or so it seemed to me.
Only on rare occasion do builder and visitor meet and even rarer is
the chance meeting that becomes a friendship. Unless that builder
loves the atmosphere of GZ, loves to build for no other reason
than the sheer joy of it, loves to explore the far reaches of the
Cyber Worlds or wants to make a statement with a world of his own,
then it is unlikely that he'll remain and he too will add to the
ranks of NAC. I believe that it is the very vastness of the COF
worlds that both contribute to the unimaginable variety in which
we revel and the countless numbers, be they tourists or citizens,
that come and go.
```

The understanding that towns become relics of the past from their initial conception draws on an earlier point that interaction within VR, be it interpersonal or with objects, is far from the ideal that seems to be epitomised by physical face-to-face modes of communication. Degradation in textual communication due to the presence of burdensome visual stimuli within VR interactive environments goes further to highlight these shortcomings. In its attempt to accomplish the nuances of face-to-face communication it seems to fall short. Merely imitating corporal immediacy cannot compensate for the non-linear and lifted-out nature of textual communication within Cyberworlds. The imitation of presence can only achieve so much, as one respondent eloquently describes:

```
Aphex: In 'real life' both law and morality recognize the physical
body as something of a fence, an absolute boundary, establishing
and protecting our privacy. Cyberworlds simply brackets the
physical presence of the participants, by either omitting or
simulating corporal immediacy. In some ways this frees us from the
restrictions imposed by our physical identity. We are more equal
on the net because we can either ignore or create the person that
appears in cyberspace. But in another sense, the quality of the
human encounter narrows. The stand-in body reveals only as much
of ourselves as we mentally wish to reveal. The avatar self lacks
the vulnerability and fragility of our primary identities. It
can never fully represent us. Without the directness of a human
face, ethical awareness shrinks and rudeness enters. One can feel
insulated and protected from people if you're not looking at them-
nobody can take a swing at you. Without direct human presence,
participation becomes optional. Without directly meeting others
physically, our ethics languish.
```

In the absence of an adequate representation of self, VR can only hope to approximate real life encounters. The unique characteristics of CMC still remain, only altered by the increasing level of stimuli. Reductions in social cues and disorganised exchanges remain a central feature to CMC, barriers that prevent online encounters from achieving the same level of social immersion as face-to-face encounters. However, this is not to say individuals cannot, and do not, become attached, involved and committed to online community. Clearly some community members feel avatar representation creates new avenues for online expression, while others see it as a distraction and a mere imitation of corporal immediacy. The fact seems to remain that VR environments provide different opportunities to text-based interaction, allowing for community to be shaped in different ways. Indeed, this may be the ultimate point, that online community need not imitate offline community in order to achieve validity. In the same vein as Jones (1997) agues that face-to-face communication may not be an ideal form of interaction, the same can be said about offline community. Pseudo-physicality is only one of several ways in which Cyberworlds users create their online community. More traditional terrestrial social relations exercised online also help forge complex social networks and interdependencies.

Friendship, trust and community bond

Bola: If you're new to the net, sure online interaction is like a game. You probably won't feel comfortable telling people all about you. After all, that's the purpose of a nickname, to keep your anonymity. You can lie as much as you want, re-invent yourself. Who are you ? Hey, call me Bond, James Bond! It doesn't matter, you're there just to have fun, you don't care at all for anybody but yourself. That attitude changes as you keep coming back. You begin to notice the same people, the same avatars, same buildings, streets and surroundings. You begin to feel at home. You stop insulting people and start paying attention to what they are saying. Well, you even engage in a chat with them. At this point you realize that there is a person on the other side, a real person, maybe someone as cool as you (let's not forget you're 007!). The more you chat, the more common ground you find. Suddenly, you see yourself coming back on a regular basis and you're even considering calling them ... friends!!

Recognising virtual presence as a feature of experience within Cyberworlds, detailing how representation of self through avatars, buildings and memorials creates a 'permanent' bond to the community, rationalises how individuals relate to a virtual or online environment. Another dimension of a bond to the Cyberworlds community is friendship. Friendships and more intimate relationships are an integral part of the maintenance of a social group. Without these couplings and groupings it is questionable whether online community could be sustained. Bola's narrative is a depiction of a process, a journey from 'newbie' to 'old timer'. An analysis of this process allows for a more considered understanding of how community members use Cyber-worlds technology differently, and how some, through time, change their view of the community.

The development of online friendships and relationships puts in question the ways in which community members use computer-mediated communication. For some 'newbies' Cyberworlds is a way to make random acquaintances for a short period; relations quite devoid of any significant meaning or trust. These non-linear and lifted-out encounters are characterised by what Miller and Slater (2000) term *frissons* of gambling. Interactions are characterised by intense exchanges, fuelled by disinhibition (Lea *et al.* 1992). Conversations can be identified by their openness and degree of intimacy at early stages. Bola states how newbies are 'there just to have fun', without a 'care at all for anybody but yourself'. Newbie encounters are a form of mutual entertainment, the mode of communication itself becomes a 'play thing', where any relationship is characterised by non-permanence and ephemerality. Most notably, as Bola states, it is the anonymity experienced by these newbies that prevents the ossification of interactions; there is an initial desire 'to keep your anonymity'. These online relations have resonance with Sennett's (1998) conception of the decline of long-term, sustained deep relationships, and Wittel's notion of network sociality (2001). It is within these types of relations that any bond to community is at its weakest.

While it might be tempting to use such evidence to support the more dystopic visions of late-modern interactivity, the ubiquity of these 'thinned out' and 'brittle' social relations within Cyberworlds is in question. 'Old timers' consider their encounters to be more meaningful. These interactions are seen as part of a series of encounters which span a 'significant' period of time allowing each exchange to build upon the previous, forming relationships and even friendships. This process is captured in Bola's narrative. People 'keep coming back' and begin to notice familiar faces. An important aspect raised in this narrative is the importance of the physical environment to sustained and meaningful relationships, the 'buildings, streets and surroundings'. Building is considered an integral part to forming and sustaining relationships in this environment. While the technological failings of text-only communication may reduce social immersion, creating non-linear and lifted-out interaction, the ability to build counteracts these failings. Buildings embody the identities of individuals and the memories of friendships. These artefacts are permanent, thickening out and forging the once fragile and insipid relations mediated by text. In contradiction to most of the literature on interactivity and CMC, these 'old timers' begin to lose sight of the anonymity they once held so precious. The increasing frequency of interaction results in the inevitable creation of an identity. Old timer identities are recognisable as they are more permanent and less flexible than newbie identities. With forged online personae communication becomes more 'serious', and community members 'start paying attention' to what others are saying. Ultimately they realise that there is 'meat in the machine', recognising that 'there is a person on the other side' of the online persona. Finally, a key point raised by Bola is cessation of derisory speech; community members 'stop insulting people'. As newbies become old timers, through a process of bonding to one another and to the community, they gradually reduce their deviant behaviour.

In an explanation of this disparity in relations of newbies and old timers, Miller and Slater (2000: 61) propose that 'people tend to experience the Internet as a battery of related but separate possibilities for pursuing relationships, which they assemble in different ways according to their particular preferences'. The following narratives indicate how community members' expectations differ and how some have learned to reframe their experiences of friendship within an online environment:

Cocteau: Online interaction is whatever you want it to be. You may or may not be interested in making friends, etc. It depends on the individual.

Isan: I come from a time and place where relationships if not friendships, once lasted a lifetime. Since going online however I've changed the mould of how I view friendships, you have to.

Yet I find the ease of moving on is sad. I wonder if there is any
difference in how friendship is defined or will be defined as we move
more and more into the age of the virtual.

Varying strength in online friendships may be dependent upon several
social variables. These include levels of involvement in conventional lines of
activity within the community, such as building; the amount of commitment
an individual has to building a positive reputation in the community;
the degree of attachment to peers and institutions within Cyberworlds;
and finally the extent of belief in the validity of community social rules.
Aggregated these factors constitute a bond to community. As Hirschi (1969)
outlined how a strong bond to community would result in low levels of
deviation, it is contended that a similar bond results in meaningful and
long-lasting friendships. The narrative below begins to show how different
Internet communication mediums are being delineated by users in terms of
interactivity and immersion, affecting the bond an individual might have to
a social group online.

Cocteau: The interaction on Cyberworlds is different from online
chat rooms. One has the ability to meet people in common, because
the area of a chance meeting are so diverse. As in real life i have
a chance to meet a person at the art gallery because i frequent
the art gallery, rather than a chat room (albeit some chat rooms
have a 'theme') where people gather seemingly haphazardly. In the
community type situation that Cyberworlds affords, one has the
ability to see how another person reacts to various situations
emotionally. One seems to have a chance to get to know a person...
slowly as in real life. Visiting buildings they have built,
watching them interact with others and seeing how they deal with
situations of varying or no responsibilities gives insight into
their personalities and they're dreams. Patience can give insight
into a persons persona. Imho, chat rooms for some reason, avail
a person to a disguise if so chosen. The community atmosphere of
Cyberworlds 'forces' the use of one's self.

Haphazard encounters seem to characterise online environments that
are devoid of community or bond to a significant group. Chat rooms that
lack an underlying community foundation, such as the opportunity to build
structures, reputations, attain membership to organisations and the like,
might prevent interlocutors from forging long-term friendships. While this
may not be exclusive, the argument is that meaningful friendships that have
some sense of longevity are more likely to emerge when individuals are
encouraged to immerse themselves into an online community or social group
that 'forces the use of one's self' and allows and encourages individuals to
take part in more than just textual exchanges. This is based on the premise
that levels of attachment, commitment, involvement and belief are low
within online environments devoid of an analogous community structure.

Friendship, liminality and trust

Online friendships are more likely to flourish when individuals are absorbed in an online context organised around a community or group structure that exhibits properties that encourage greater immersion and group participation. While these types of friendships can be explained by the strength of bond to a social group or community, there are other factors that shape the dynamics of these relations. Levels of liminality and trust also influence the way in which relations manifest within different online contexts (Turner 1967). A full discussion of the liminal effect of online interactions has been outlined in Chapter 3. Briefly, liminality derives from being in a transitional and temporary position on a marginal threshold or similar position resulting in a state of disinhibition (Turner 1967). Given the increased levels of interaction, both positive and negative, within online contexts, it is recognised that interlocutors are interacting with decreased levels of inhibition. The following extracts illustrate how the formation of friendships is influenced by states of liminality:

> IDM: Online relationships form in a context which is largely unidimensional in the sense that you see text written by the other without all the elements associated with individuals in RW such as height, weight, ages, gender, occupations etc. Consequently conversation moves from social chit chat very rapidly. Consequently it is possible to establish a relationship that surpasses in quality and importance many RW relationships.

> Remy: Online interaction is probably the most meaningful communication possible. You get to know a person, without being influenced by any of the senses other than the mind. You can't see, smell, hear or categorise the person. You get a sense of the real person without physical characteristics to influence your judgement.

> Brainiac: As with a person who loses the sense of sight, the other senses become more acute to make up for it. The online experience allows us to get to know the person BETTER in some ways, because we are not distracted by physical things.

> Amber: My serious online friendships have proved more stable and lasting then those in RL. Perhaps because again, you are not influenced by any physicalities, but 'get' the true essence of the other person's personality. I think you can tell a great deal about a person in VR, perhaps even more when they are lying and you are aware of it.

It can be interpreted from these narratives that a lack of 'actual' presence and physicality within online settings is a precursor to the rapid development of friendship. It seems that while a 'virtual' presence may increase interactivity and bonds to a community, 'actual' presence may thwart the rapid development of friendships online. Removing 'actual' presence precludes interlocutors from relying on body language and other social cues to interpret situations and interactions. The majority of respondents noted how the lack of 'actual' presence increased the immersion of relationships formed online, stating that they 'surpassed' relations in their offline communities. If a lack in physical presence can enrich social relations then it might be considered that the relationship between presence and levels of social immersion may need to be re-evaluated. It might be the case that both levels of intimacy and immediacy, purported to rise when interlocutors are present, are replaced by anonymity and liminality when interlocutors are absent online, maintaining, if not increasing social immersion. To further explore this the narratives below show how anonymous interaction increases the likelihood of more open and frank discussion:

> Kid606: Talking to people online is different. You cant see what they really look like, you can't tell if they are fat or thin, tall or short, or even male or female sometimes. Its like you don't really know who you are talking to, and I suppose they don't know if you really are who you say you are. I think this makes people behave differently. I've noticed people get very friendly within minutes of meeting each other, telling each other stories about personal things. In the same way I've also seen people get into arguments. Its as if not really knowing who you are talking to makes it easier for people to either become intimate very quickly or fly off the handle.

> Bola: I was talking to this girl once (or at least I thought they were female) and we were getting on really well. We ended up talking about quite personal stuff, relationships, break-ups. But then I found out that she was really a he! Even though we had got on really well I just cut off contact all together. We had a quite a big blow out online.

While anonymity allows for more open interactions, arguably maintaining and/or increasing levels of social immersion, these extracts show how its disinhibiting effects also increase the likelihood of negative encounters flavoured by abuse, slurs and general defamation. This darker side of anonymity forces community members to question their trust in others while online. Trust can become an integral part to feeling one belongs in a social group. Knowing that others' identities, their histories, their opinions and judgements are genuine becomes essential if an individual is to maintain a bond to a group. The anonymity inherent within online encounters, however, removes the certainty often imbued within offline encounters, replacing it with doubt over the true identity and intentions of others within the social group. Turkle (1995), in her study of Internet use, found that increased levels of anonymity affected her ability to write about her research participants in an authoritative and authentic manner. Correspondingly members of social groups online often find they have to re-evaluate trust in others, as exemplified in the following narratives:

> Rocketscientist: Humans now have a way to have pure mind to mind conversation without regard to each others' 'physical status', ie: Gender, Income, Race, Sexual Preference, etc. Of course those traits can be expressed in varying levels even in VR but it always comes down to this: Is the information I am receiving from this person about themselves really true? Of course, there's no way to verify 100 per cent via VR contact so we are forced to either accept everything they tell us and hope it's accurate (which can lead to the aforementioned romantic pitfalls) or just make note of what's said and not worry about what we can't confirm and just enjoy the exchange of ideas! For me, it has been the latter! I've discovered that warm friendships CAN be had in VR as long as both parties realise this.

> Deb: when I first started really chatting online it was through a game, and I enjoyed acting like I was someone else. However, it didn't take long before I started tiring of that and changed to acting like my true self. Although I like to think I am wary of the fact that people play roles online, I tend to trust most people I meet on cyberworlds for what they say they are. It is hard to live a lie and get away with it for long, and I think you only really fool yourself.

> Carreg: We do have to exert a great deal of trust in the VR context because as Rocketscientist stated we only know what ppl are prepared to tell us.

Members of Cyberworlds report having to take a 'leap of faith' when interacting with others. The uncertainty over the true identity of others within Cyberworlds has to be nullified by this 'leap of faith' if any sense of group cohesion is to be maintained. If there is constant doubt and suspicion over the intentions and identities of individuals then relations and friendships could neither be forged nor sustained. This kind of trust can be associated with the notion of 'active trust' discussed by Giddens (1994). These kinds of trusting relationships are based less on the knowledge of someone's character and more on the knowledge of his/her immediate position in a social field (Wittel 2001). Alternative online identities are more often associated with the gaming genre that the virtual reality technology of Cyberworlds mimics. While some aspects of Cyberworlds are based upon fantasy, the majority seem to retain their offline identities, often finding it difficult to do otherwise. However, the realisation that 'faking it' can be more difficult than it first seems, and that it can lead to some unexpected consequences, is something that is learnt over time.

> Croft: The best yet, was a real macho navy guy who called one night asking me how he should get rid of a guy following him around

in VR. He didn't want to admit he'd been faking it and posing
as a woman to trick the man, because he didn't want to hurt his
feelings. It took him 3 days, but he finally managed to break off
with the guy. LOL.

In order to form bonds to the social group old timers, often of citizen
status, learn that 'faking it' prevents them from forging any serious
commitment, attachment, involvement and belief within the Cyberworlds
community structure. However, for some the issues of anonymity and trust
are too invasive and infect relations to such an extent that true friendship
can never be achieved online:

Andysa: The balance between online and offline friendships must
be kept. I need to have RW friends who I know I can confide in
in absolute privacy. I am not saying that I would not trust a
Cyberworlds friend. But my RW friends would know who I really was
(up to a point) where as a Cyberworlds friend would only know what
I told them.

These individuals, and many like them, form a group within Cyberworlds
that believes any community structure that may have once existed has
been eradicated by the ephemeral nature of online encounters, shaped by
anonymity, liminality, mistrust and non-linearity (Lash 2001). The time
and effort that it once took to engineer and maintain social relations online
is no longer being invested as many believe that little reward will follow.
While some citizens argue that from its very inception Cyberworlds was
flawed due to the ephemerality of online encounters, labelling them 'limited
interactions' that could be severed by an on and off button, others, who in
contradiction, believe in the richness of online encounters, report having
feelings of hopelessness in relation to the future continuation of any form of
online community. The following narratives tell stories of a dystopia, both
of a world that promised rich forms of interaction but failed to deliver, and
of a community under threat due to a lack of any bond to individuals and
structures:

Hopper: Well, here's the thing. I suppose you can post it if you
like, but I'm very depressed about Cyberworlds. I'm a 3D modeler,
and it used to be an exciting place to create and interact with
other creative ppl. I've about completely given up on the program.
I feel a sense of hopelessness there, and I've hardly gone in
anymore since about the beginning of April.

Croft: Because machines provide us with the power to flit bout the
universe, our communities grow more fragile, airy, and ephemeral
even as our connections multiply.

Bella: I have been struggling with this one for a while now because
Cyberworlds really isn't a community any more. Any community that

```
was there has long since broken up into splinter groups and died
off. While at any time there may be a few hundred people online
you are sometimes hard pressed to find a dozen who are actually
communicative at any one time, not to mentions that for a multi-
user environment on the Internet, a 'few hundred' is a pathetically
small number. This may be a perfectly natural thing to have happen.
Nothing lasts forever, as the saying goes.
```

While these bleaker experiences are far from abundant, their existence begins to help explain levels of disruption within Cyberworlds. The liminal aspect of the Cyberworlds environment in tandem with anonymity, while fostering positive disinhibited interactions, also holds the capacity to promote antisocial behaviour. Those individuals who have a weak bond to the community structure are seen by many members to be at most risk of being influenced by this liminal environment and adopting disruptive behaviour.

Summary

At the outset of the research it was to be my argument, in contradiction to cyber-dystopians, that the term community can be applied to the Cyberworlds environment. This chapter has highlighted, through several stages, how community can be, and is sustained within an online social space. First, the notion that a lack of presence in online encounters reduces social immersion was challenged. Via new broadband technologies, online encounters have moved on from primitive text-only interaction. A simulacrum of presence is enabled via three-dimensional representations of self and surroundings. Cyberworlds users become dependent upon these graphical representations to enrich their online encounters. Online artefacts, such as buildings, memorials and homes are integral to maintaining meaningful relationships and friendships online. It is the presence of these icons that allows individuals and friendship groups to hold a permanent bond to Cyberworlds. Second, online friendship was explored to identify the presence of complex social networks within Cyberworlds. Detailed narratives distinguished newbies and old timers, showing how both used the technology very differently. The key point made was that over time, the Cyberworlds environment forced users to present their real identities online, divesting themselves of anonymity. This evidence is used to reject the notion that all online encounters are fettered by their non-linearity and their lifted-out character (Lash 2001). Finally, the effect of liminality on trust and friendship was addressed to show how the absence of presence might increase, as opposed to decrease, social immersion in online encounters. Contrary to this, however, liminality was discovered to be a double-edged sword, in that it also eroded the trust in online interaction. While many within Cyberworlds still view the environment as a community, there is clear disenchantment amongst some tourists and citizens. These individuals are either less likely to form a bond to the community, or have had their already established bond subjected to atrophy. The next chapter will begin to explore the relationship between antisocial behaviour, the liminal environment and individuals' bonds that are forged within the Cyberworlds community.

5 Online deviance

Carreg: As on-line culture grows geographically, the sense of community diminishes. And when the size of the user base on-line increases, the spirit of community diminishes, villains begin to appear. Its exactly like when civilizations reach a certain degree of density, the barbaric tribes return, from within. A large community coupled with insulating anonymity is the perfect environment for riotous disruptions.

Fischerspooner: Online communities, like all other organizations, have cycles of growth, maturity, decline, toxicity, and renewed growth. The decline and toxicity phases can be dangerous, because feelings can escalate to a high pitch quickly due to the multiplier effect, resulting in some people invading the privacy of others and harassing them just because they can.

Narratives depicting the atomisation of self and space within the Cyberworlds environment echo the disenchantment experienced by other online community developers, members and cyberspace authors. The far more positive depictions of online life in the previous chapter highlight the discontinuity of opinion regarding the feasibility of maintaining any form of online community. A similar rift can be identified in academic discourse surrounding the subject. Kolko and Reid (1998: 223) in their analysis of dissolution and fragmentation in online communities write:

> Virtual spaces more often than not are precisely this – locales where participants … move through the surface of virtual worlds, unable to burrow into the layers of the community and experience the idea of action and consequence. What evolves, then, is a case of temporary connections that do not hold any tangible consequences for those who are touched by such fleeting bonds.

While there is conjecture on both the positive and negative aspects of networked technologies to facilitate online community, there are, however, some certainties. No matter how 'dystopic' online environments become, their members continue to visit. Despite all the negative narratives both presented in this chapter and in other texts, Cyberworlds citizen subscriptions increase on a quarterly basis, while over 1,000 individuals continue to visit the environment each day. Similarly, other online communities, such as LambdaMOO, that have experienced degrees of social turbulence, remain highly populated (Mnookin 1996). These increasingly populated 'dystopic' environments form a breeding ground for deviant and antisocial behaviours. The narratives of Carreg and Fischerspooner detail how the Cyberworlds environment, having reached a state of 'critical mass', is subject to atrophy. Individuals begin to feel abstracted from structures and activities as the user base increases, and as a result bonds to community are more difficult to maintain.

The fragmentation of online community and the dissolution felt by many of its members form the central argument of an aetiology of online deviant behaviour. This chapter focuses first upon a typology of deviant behaviours, providing statistical information on the prevalence of certain acts. Second, an aetiology of online deviant behaviours is discussed. Negative narratives written by community members are used in an attempt to establish the premise that weak bonds are a precursor to an increased likelihood of deviant activity.

Typologies of online deviance

The prevalence of high-tech crimes, along with their definition and impact, continues to be controversial (Levi 2001). The myriad of criminal and sub-criminal acts that come under the umbrella term high-tech crime means that their incidence remains deeply imbedded within a dark figure. One of the advantages of researching a specific online environment is that a focus can be maintained, allowing for a detailed analysis of deviant cyber activities specific to that online arena. Breadth of understanding is then sacrificed for depth, allowing for a more informed theoretical approach to the aetiology of some deviant cyber activities. Ascertaining the range and prevalence of deviance within Cyberworlds was aided by the existence of a regulatory body. The Peacekeepers were established to monitor online behaviour and to enforce the community charter (see Appendices 3 and 4). Since their inception a record of all ejections[1] resulting from deviant activity has been maintained. A discussion of the methodological issues relating to the collection and analysis of this offence data is delineated in Appendix 2. The graph in Figure 5.1 shows the distribution and prevalence of deviant activities over a six month period as classified by the Peacekeepers.

The data on offence rates was collected over this period by the Peace-keepers. Recording practices were standardised where the time, nature and severity of the act were documented. All cases involve the ejection of an offender from the community for an action deemed unsuitable by the Peacekeepers. However, as with official crime statistics, due care must be taken in interpreting the data (Maguire 2002). It is highly likely that

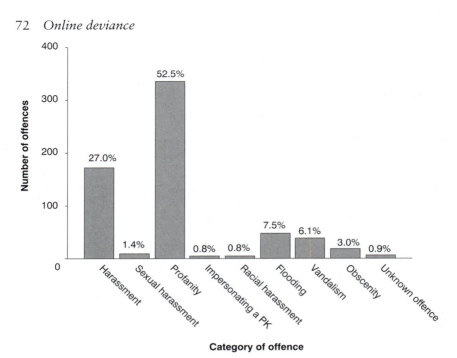

Figure 5.1   Rates of ejection by offence category

not all offences are recorded due to a lack of reporting and low resources. Peacekeeper discretion may also influence the way in which offences are both recorded and categorised.

Of all recorded offences profanity is most prevalent (52.5 per cent). While not being an offence *per se* the use of bad language is frowned upon within the community due to the presence of children, amongst other concerns. The second most prevalent is general harassment (27 per cent), which includes behaviours such as threats, verbal abuse, and stalking within the community – somewhat higher than its occurrence offline (3.4 per cent of all recorded crime in 2004/5, Nicholas *et al.* 2005).[2] This activity is commonly mediated via Internet Relay Chat, email and telegrams (community specific email). Specific forms of harassment such as racial and sexual seem markedly less common online compared to other offences, a pattern which is mirrored offline – racial harassment accounts for 0.4 per cent of crime offline in the UK (Nicholas *et al.* 2005). Both flooding (repeated unwanted messages over IRC) and virtual vandalism (the destruction or defacement of private or public property) are less common in the overall pattern.

The data seem to indicate that deviant acts involving text and the abuse of others (flaming) are most common within the online community, while other non-textual behaviours, such as impersonating a Peacekeeper (spoofing), obscenity and vandalism, are markedly less prevalent. Most other research in the field has also concentrated on *flaming* due to its apparent ubiquity. However, it is the non-textual acts that prove more difficult to conceptualise and rationalise. The instances of non-textual deviant acts, such as vandalism, vary from other computer-related offences, such as cyber theft and cyber obscenity, in that they are born out of and are a product of the online community being studied. Instances of vandalism are enabled due to the graphical visual elements of the community, while impersonating a Peacekeeper or spoofing is enabled by the existence of three-dimensional avatars. In short, unconventional forms of deviance are more likely to be found in online environments which are unconventional themselves. These environments and the organisations that function within them not only have to tackle 'conventional' cyber deviance, but also the more unconventional forms that are bred from the technology of mediation.

Patterns of offending and community status

Offence rates and patterns of offending by community status show marked differences. Crosstabulations of offender status and deviant category were generated to determine relationships and patterns of offending within each group. It was found that citizen and tourist involvement in certain deviant activities was significantly different.[3] For example it was found that the status of the offender is significantly related to the prevalence of harassment (from the sample 41.2 per cent of citizens commit harassment compared to 20.6 per cent of tourists). Further differences were found for the offences of vandalism and obscenity where citizens were significantly more likely to engage in these acts. Conversely tourists were significantly more likely to commit acts of profanity and flooding (see Figure 5.2).[4]

Citizens are both more likely to deviate from group norms and to commit more serious online offences. The offences of harassment, vandalism and obscenity are often policed by the Special Response Team (SRT) – a group of Peacekeepers trained to deal with more serious online incidents (see Appendix 8). Both profanity and flooding are considered misdemeanours due to the potential low levels of harm they can inflict upon individuals and property, and the ease with which they can be regulated. Given that control theory posits that those with weaker bonds to community are more likely to deviate, and the assumption that tourists are naturally less bonded to community than citizens, these findings provide a contrary account. At first analysis control theory may be rejected given these findings, however, upon closer examination these patterns of offending might be explained by weak bonds to community among some citizens of Cyberworlds. Weak connections to the community might result from dissatisfaction with the way organisations are run, the way in which social control is maintained, or just general disenchantment with the system as a whole. To ascertain the link between deviance and offender status the following sections discuss in detail two manifestations of online deviant activity. Both harassment and vandalism

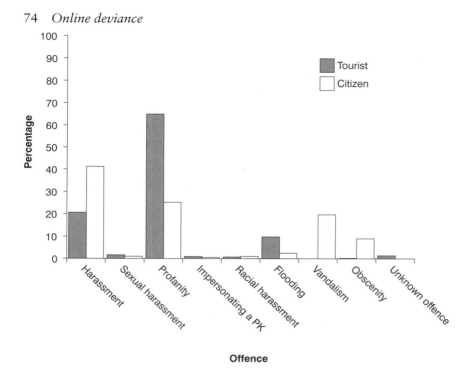

Figure 5.2   Types of offence by offender status

are considered most threatening to community cohesion. Harassment, and associated behaviours, such as profanity, creates a hostile and unwelcoming environment, reducing membership and severing established relationships. Likewise the unsanctioned destruction and defacement of property in Cyberworlds slowly erodes the history and memory embodied in virtual artefacts, ultimately threatening the community.

Online harassment

Online harassment can be compared to Wall's (1998) conception of cyber violence. This categorisation covers a multitude of deviant acts, both criminal and sub-criminal. It relates to the sending of unwanted emails which are obscene, threatening or abusive (Ellison and Akdeniz 1998). It may involve the posting of personal details on publicly accessible message boards resulting in unwanted forms of contact, both Internet-based and in the physical world. It involves the imitation of a victim's online persona (spoofing) and the commission of deviant acts in their name, ruining online reputations and jeopardising friendships and business relationships. It also involves various forms of textual violent acts that are often sexual in nature, which can manifest themselves in emails, chat rooms and VR graphical communities.

To reiterate key points made in Chapter 2, the Internet allows communication with another person unconstrained by social reality, thus creating a certain psychodynamic appeal for the perpetrator who chooses to become a harasser or cyber stalker (Meloy 1998). In the majority of cases only written words are used, and other avenues of sensory perception are eliminated; one cannot see, hear, touch, smell, or emotionally sense the other person. Yet some concern surrounding harassment and cyber stalking is based on the idea that it might be a prelude to physical stalking (Reno 1999). In general Wall (1998: 81) describes these acts of cyber violence in terms of:

> the violent impact of the cyberactivities of another person upon an individual or social grouping. Whilst such activities do not have to have a direct physical manifestation, the victim nevertheless feels the violence of the act and can bear long-term psychological scars as a consequence.

The kinds of harassment that occur within Cyberworlds are equally wide-ranging. Community members talk of acts of violence, derision and spoofing as everyday occurrences. Reports of blackmailing and stalking also featured amongst the gamut of potential harmful activities. The following extracts paint a vivid picture of how harassing acts manifest and harm individuals within Cyberworlds:

```
Laika: 'It' is stalking and harassment via telegrams which cannot
be muted. 'It' is a rapid and horrendous, verbal rape (from a
fast-moving and well hidden avatar) done in whispers so a 2.2 user
cannot mute the person. 'It' is also the petty things, like the
spammers and blatant cursors at GZs ... the bigots and harassers.
These petty problem-makers from yesterday are today's hackers,
stalkers and black-mailers.
```

```
Mark…a: online harassment is people coming up to you and whispering,
'I want to fu*k you' as their first and often only greeting, and if
there is more, it is worse.
```

Individuals with little experience of Cyberworlds can rapidly utilise its communications technology to harass other members. Telegrams (private messages to other members, much like emails) are an effective way of stalking and harassing individuals asynchronously, while the whisper commands (private synchronous messages, similar to Internet Relay Chat) allow for more immediate violent and lucid exchanges. While temporal co-presence in CMC can be considered the most effective vehicle for violent exchanges, temporally distanciated exchanges harbour the ability to sustain an attack (Williams 2001). The location of a victim in co-present encounters allows for violent exchanges to be delivered instantly, but the longevity of an attack is jeopardised by the ability of the victim to either 'mute' the perpetrator or simply avoid them. Harassment via asynchronous, or temporally distanciated methods, such as telegrams which are delivered directly to your avatar, have more of a chance of sustaining an attack, given that it is more arduous to change one's persona. It is clear that modes of harassment online can vary, meaning attacks can come from 'all sides' simultaneously. Narratives that tell of online victimisation give evidence that shows inventive and thoughtful premediated attacks upon individuals. Both synchronous and asynchronous methods of communication are used to effectively track and attack victims:

> M@tt: I was friendly with a person (Internet only) who was clever enough to get personal information about me from a friend who was not knowledgeable about computers. The stalker then sent me email stating my real name and address and stating that he would be coming to visit at a time unknown to me. I then obtained his personal information by legal means and sent them to him with a strong letter from my attorney and also sent a copy of that letter to the police dept of the city where he resided. (he had not physically threatened me at any time or broken any actual law) I received a letter of apology from him and also from his attorney. I have never heard from him again.

> IDM: Some of the name calling and accusations has become brutal, leading to threats of violence, threats of legal action, web pages shut down by one group making complaints against another to sponsors of free web services, and all manner of name-calling and slander.

> Rocketscientist: My sibling was spoofed the first 30 seconds in Cyberworlds by a cusser which caused her to not return and CW lost a huge Real Estate Universe Server sale because of it. (I lost the job as world builder/caretaker for it obviously.) My opinion based on the examples above and many others not mentioned is: spoofing is more dangerous to reputations than cussing is to the community.

> Moog: I had a stalker once. I reported him and after the third report he was gone for awhile. He's back now so, I seldom go to CW anymore. CW has degraded rapidly with lax enforcement of rules and sometimes an absence of rules on private worlds. It's a damned if you do and damned if you don't sort of issue for Cyberworlds policy makers.

Online harassment, while initially manifesting online, can migrate to the offline environment of the victim. Name calling in emails and chat can turn into threats literally on victims' doorsteps. In many cases legal remedies are available to some individuals, namely under specific cyber stalking legislation in some American states,[5] and the Telecommunications Act (1984) and Protection from Harassment Act (1997) in the UK. The severity of online harassment varies and is dependent on whether the attacks eventually manifest in the victim's offline world. Most accounts of online harassment within Cyberworlds usually entail no more that petty name calling and sexual advances, however, a distinction is made between profanity and harassment by the Peacekeepers. This is an important distinction given that the above findings show significant relationships between harassment and profanity and community status. Profanity is considered to be a less serious offence than harassment. However, the point at which an individual who is being profane becomes a harasser is difficult to ascertain, and is often based on the subjective judgement of a Peacekeeper. Harassers often use profane language, while those being profane can be considered harassing. Peacekeeper discretion is then pivotal to whether an offender is categorised as serious or petty.

If we take for granted that Peacekeeper discretion is well founded then the figures for harassment and profanity are an accurate reflection of reality within Cyberworlds. The positive relationship between the prevalence of harassment and citizen status, and of profanity and tourist status, is also accurate. At one end of the spectrum harassment has been identified as a premediated deviant act and profanity, in its most frivolous form, as an impulsive reaction. Long-term members of the community are more equipped to plan a harassing crusade, given that they have more knowledge of the community and its technology, and that they have had more time to make relations with their victim. Short-term members are less likely to have formed relations meaning they are unlikely to have identified a potential victim. Further, their lack of technological knowledge in comparison to long-term members means they are less likely to be able to utilise the tools of online harassment.

'Toto, I don't think we're in Kansas anymore'

The reciprocity between online acts of deviance and the offline world are exemplified in a number of stalking cases (for examples see Ellison and Akdeniz 1998). The most notable case during the course of this research extended beyond harassment and stalking, taking a more sinister and serious turn. During the course of administering the focus group questions a lull was experienced in responses. As a precaution an email was sent to the discussion group commenting on the reduced frequency of exchanges. The response proved to be both insightful and disturbing:

```
M@tt: There might be a bit of a state of shock going on right
now. This is a message group that deals with such things as online
rules, and the consequences of online crimes, and the discussion
seems to be within the context of Cyberworlds. No doubt you have
all seen that we have very recently become aware that a woman
was found dead in Kansas, the victim of an online stalker. She
was also a citizen of Cyberworlds. There was a brief period of
name calling, and accusations, and some finger pointing, because
both victim and accused are members of an online community within
Cyberworlds known as Gor, which does seem to condone and encourage
```

sadomasochistic behaviour, albeit in a fantasy, or even sexual-
fantasy context.

IDM: Some of the name calling and accusations has become brutal,
leading to threats of violence, threats of legal action, web
pages shut down by one group making complaints against another to
sponsors of free web services, and all manner of name-calling and
slander.

John Robinson, also known as 'Slavemaster' within Cyberworlds, was
arrested by Kansas state police for the suspected murder of five women
during June of 2000. Suzette Trouten, John Robinson's last victim, was a
member of Cyberworlds known as 'Faith'. She frequented Gor worlds to
practise fantasy sadomasochistic rituals with other like-minded members. It
is within this world that she embarked on a relationship with her eventual
murderer. Following several exchanges within Cyberworlds Faith decided
to forge an offline relationship with Slavemaster. This relationship led to
her eventual demise. Reports during the time of the investigation stated that
Robinson was known to have solicited sadomasochistic sex over the Internet
several times (CNN.com 2000). What ensued within Cyberworlds was a
fervent debate about the appropriateness of this kind of online behaviour.

The doctrine of Gor worlds is based on the books by John Norman,
which advance the belief that women were born to be slaves to men. Active
participants of these worlds advocate, in their 'fantasy' lives, beating their
women and, if necessary, even killing them. Of the 1,000 plus worlds that
have been set up within the Cyberworlds environment, Gor worlds make up a
small proportion. However, when the population of each world is examined,
Gor environments often boast large numbers. The presence of these worlds,
and the fantasy acts that occur within them, have been long-standing issues
of contention for other members of Cyberworlds. The association of the
murder of Suzette Trouten with Gor and Cyberworlds added volatile fuel to
this debate, resulting in more acts of online violence:

Bola: When we received news of Suzette Trouten's demise, many of
us posted, men and women alike, our feelings about the murders and
the Gor lifestyle. A female member of Gor started posting to the
Forum and opened up a debate. She then encouraged several male
Goreans to post to the Forum. Last Saturday, these male Goreans
started posting entries designed to educate the 'male bashers'
on Xav's forum (Cyberworlds associated web-page and newsgroup),
many of whom are male, of the superiority and dominance of men
over women, bragging about their real life 'slave' hunts, etc.
They started a war, in which mostly the men rather than the women
who regularly post to Xav's participated; and they barraged the
forum with scathing unintelligent and unintelligible insults and
threats that were coming so fast they were disappearing off the
bottom faster than one could read them. Several of them then wrote
emails to Bravenet (ISP), leading to the closing of Xav's forum.

Xav's forum is back up on a new and, unfortunately, secret site -- no longer an open forum because of the way the Goreans handle open forums and opposition to their principles. Furthermore, the computer of one of the regulars on Xav's Forum was hacked into yesterday while she was parked at the Gorean Forum (webmasters of forums can read the IP addresses of visitors). She came home to the sound of her computer hard at work and investigated only to find her email program and several of her emails open, new wallpaper on her desktop, etc.

Brothomstates: I DO NOT LIKE that Cyberworlds, a program of advanced technology, a program that's leading the way into the future of the Internet, a program where censure and banning is justified in the name of the 'family', has become a primary vehicle for this very dangerous brand of backlash to the inevitable evolution of humankind and has become 'home' to these societal misfits. Right now, I'm just hoping that the plummeting CWLD stock will soon lead to Chapter 11 or a buyout of some sort, so that someone with some sense will buy it and put it back on track. I'm not an old timer, but I've been there over three years. I was there before the guys in Boston bought it from the original developers. I've watched this steady decline on so many levels in Cyberworlds, and this latest development, I fear, is not even the bottom of the barrel yet. When you think it can't get any worse... Well, that's where I'm at regarding Cyberworlds. It's a farce and the 'law' there is the pinnacle of hypocrisy.

The reciprocity between online violence, be it consenting or not, and the offline world increases the severity of these acts in the eyes of Cyberworlds members. The murder of a member of Cyberworlds and the subsequent emotive debates, the threats of violence and the hacking of members' machines are clear examples of how online acts of violence can escalate into 'real' world problems. However, the prevalence of online deviance that leads to serious offline repercussions can be easily overstated. It does not take in-depth analysis to recognise that the majority of deviant acts that occur within Cyberworlds are minor in comparison to terrestrial world events. In the majority of cases individuals who become victims of online deviance suffer minimal harm. It is only in extreme circumstances where people are physically or psychologically traumatised. The following extract shows how community members recognise these distinctions:

Bart: Now we must weight the rights of the Goreans to have any sort of worlds, themes, and sexual practices that they choose, against the rights of society to protect vulnerable individuals from psychopaths who would do harm. Then we must consider the severity of the crime, and make definite distinctions between such things as, flooding the screen, which annoys us, insults and foul language which may upset us and make us angry, viruses, hacks, theft of intellectual property which may cost us money. They all seem very insignificant when we are faced with the reality and finality of murder.

A distinction can then be made between conventional acts of deviance which have migrated to the online world, and new forms of deviant behaviour that are born of new online communities. Conventional acts of deviance, such as theft and violence, have found new vehicles for their implementation. However, it would be a mistake to argue that these conventional acts have fully migrated. Often the outcome manifests in the real world, where the stalker gathers information on a person online and then pursues them offline, and where the sadomasochist master turns online fantasy into reality. Pure online deviance, or as Bart puts it, more insignificant acts of online deviance, have little reciprocity with the real world apart from potential psychological trauma. These acts include, amongst others, spoofing, flooding and online vandalism. These distinctions are important if we are to understand the repercussions and risks involved in using computer-mediated communication.

The relative risks and possible harms that individuals face when logging on to Cyberworlds are only fully realised when the community is faced with the extreme and the unthinkable. Before the murder of Suzette Trouten, community members were willing to overlook the existence of Gor worlds, to protest in silence. Acts of profanity and minor harassment were considered everyday occurrences, part of the fabric of Cyberworlds. Feelings and thoughts about safety online, while present, were never at the forefront of Cyberworlds members' minds. Rocketscientist explains how the effects of extreme acts within online communities can alter members' perceptions of risk and increase levels of anxiety:

```
Rocketscientist: Perhaps if there is a lesson to be learned from
this, it is that people need to be careful. Maybe one thing that
Cyberworlds or the community could do is to have some sort of
Internet self defence course for it's citizens. Laika outlined
a number of offences that happen in Cyberworlds some of them I
was not aware were going on in Cyberworlds, although , I knew
they happened on the net in general. Information on net safety is
probably out there somewhere, I just never bothered to go looking
for it and probably not many other people do either. I have fooled
with firewalls and repeaters and that sort of thing. The problem
with them is that I start to feel a little paranoid and anxious
when I go to the lengths that are really needed to protect one's
Identity and end up not bothering with security measures at all
because I don't like that feeling. I guess security or insecurity
on the net just reflects our feelings about the world in general.
There are at least a dozen gated communities within a ten mile
radius of where I live and this is not a very dangerous area of
the world. It seems to me that one of the reasons people use the
net to interact is in part their fear of real world crime. The
unfortunate thing about this is that the facade of anonymity the
net allows causes one to let their guard down, and it is in just
such an environment that predators like to hunt. The net isn't the
safe haven we once thought it was.
```

The murder of Suzette Trouten exemplifies how modes of computer-mediated communication can become entangled with serious criminal acts. It also helps delineate the range of violent acts that can occur online. We are able to distinguish between offline deviant acts that merely utilise online technologies to gather information about and to groom individuals, and activities that have little reciprocity with the offline world that are born out of and wreak their havoc in virtual spaces. This distinction is synonymous with the levels of harm experienced by victims. Conventional deviant acts which use CMC as a vehicle often result in higher levels of harm than pure online deviance. The harm inflicted by having one's online home vandalised is arguably less significant than the potential harm inflicted by an online stalker.

Virtual vandalism

While it may be clear to most that levels of harms to individuals vary by offence type and their manifestation online or offline, the potential harms some activities have on online community are quite unique. Discussed in some detail in the previous chapter was the importance of buildings and more general surroundings in Cyberworlds to the maintenance of relationships, and on a wider scale, the sustenance of online community. Yet the permanence of these artefacts is under constant threat. Virtual vandalism features as a constant concern for those who wish to maintain the integrity of their artefacts, both semantically and aesthetically. Some community members decide to use their programming skills and knowledge of Cyberworlds architecture to sabotage others' efforts, and in some cases undermine community bonds embedded within Cyberworlds culture. Online vandalism, more commonly understood as the purposeful defacement or destruction of web pages, takes on a different manifestation within Cyberworlds. Instead of two-dimensional web pages being re-written to misrepresent their creators, vandalism within Cyberworlds involves the hacking of its computer code, or bypassing of password security systems, for the purpose of destroying or defacing members' homes, public buildings and memorials. The following extract is taken from the community archives, detailing the existence of an organised group of vandals in operation when Cyberworlds was in its infancy:

```
Rookie's Report - Dec. 12 1995:

I became increasingly appalled at the reported incidents of
vandalism to property in Cyberworlds and rumors of a gang of some
sort forming. I have seen the leader of this gang, 'King Punisher'
as he calls himself, in action trying to promote his 'order' and
recruiting members from a crowd. If anyone questioned him he would
respond with profanities and threaten to put them on 'the list'
to become a victim of the order's vandalism and destruction of
```

```
property. I was repulsed by the leader of this gang and his tactics
and decided that I would work to undermine his efforts and his
attempts to bully my fellow CyberWorld citizens.
```

While vandalism was accepted as an already present feature of Cyberworlds even in its infancy, the evolution of such antisocial behaviour into an organised deviant group was unprecedented. The systematic destruction of virtual buildings and memorials and the defacement of virtual billboards left behind a trail of incivilities that shook the Cyberworlds community. It became evident that virtual communities were not isolated from the kinds of criminal and deviant activities that harassed many offline communities. As in other online communities where instances of antisocial behaviour brought about social consensus (see Dibbell 1993; Reid 1999; MacKinnon 1997a), a police department was established via the combined efforts of Cyberworlds users to tackle any further online deviant activity. This, among other occurrences, was seen as an important milestone in the increasing civilisation of Cyberworlds, and served to increase citizens' bonds[6] to the community:

```
Builderz: Yep, I remember King Punisher and his 'posse' back
in 1995 very well. could never forget the Cyberworlds Police
Department, either. ;) And the New World Times brings back memories
as well. Not to worry though; all of the bugs and vulnerabilities
Punisher and his group exploited in the Cyberworlds software have
been fixed. It is indeed an interesting story and captures a period
of time when Cyberworlds was in its infancy. I encourage all
citizens that immigrated from 1997 on to look at the screen shots
of the Cyberworlds Browser on that website. THAT is what us 'old
timers' had to use way back when. They didn't even have telegrams
back then (which could either be a good OR a bad thing, depending
on how you look at it ;). It is my personal view that King Punisher
and his fellow members have left Cyberworlds for good (I doubt
he ever registered a citizenship when now Cyberworlds started
charging for them). But I do believe that Punisher paved the way
for all of the other 'hacker groups' and 'vandalism groups' that
existed/still do exist in Cyberworlds today. It is an interesting
part of Cyberworlds history.
```

The passing of time within Cyberworlds creates an historical framework within which 'old timers' and 'newbies' can create narratives of times past, allowing for the imagined creation of and a reflection upon the 'good old days'. It is within this historical framework that narratives of community crime prevention and reduction can be passed down from 'older' to 'newer' generations. Yet even with technological advancements and changing environments citizens and tourists still find avenues to deviate. Even though the likelihood of a new organised group of vandals is low, given the enhanced technological safeguards of the new environment, sporadic and *ad hoc* incidents of vandalism still plague the Cyberworlds community.

One respondent expresses their concern over recent trends in deviance, highlighting their alarm by comparing the attacks to real world events:

```
ReyemNiffirg: It seems that Cyberworlds has been under attack by
terrorism as well as the world. Some of us remember 1998, known as
the summer of vandalism. Eternal Drifter roamed Cyberworlds, and
until he was finally ridden of Cyberworlds was a scary unsafe place.
Nowadays, its true that things have gotten better, but terrorism
and vandalism still affects Cyberworlds as we speak. Radon is the
big one right now, and he should be ridden of as soon as possible.
Its funny, because i used to know him, in fact it literally grew
up in his old world Utopia. Cyberworlds needs to melt together
like America has. People need to stop fighting and bickering, and a
group of some kind needs to be supported by CyberworldsCorp to rid
of terrorists/vandals of Cyberworlds. If CyberworldsCorp cannot
do this, we need to resort to new leadership (program ownership),
or someone needs to create a universe independent of Cyberworlds
with a supportive leadership. This is the dream of Cyberworlds,
and we need to bring it about! Let Cyberworlds unite as one and
create a virtual Utopia for all. Just an idea, a base on which
Cyberworlds should become.
```

The effects vandalism has on the Cyberworlds community become clear when citizens begin to use expressions such as 'unsafe' and 'scary'. Some of the debilitating effects fear of crime has on community life in the offline world can also impact upon citizens of an online community. The adoption of avoidance behaviour, as in the offline world, can create hotspots of deviance, increasing the opportunities for vandalism. The lessening of social interaction as a result would mean a reduction in social presence, and ultimately the atrophy of bond to the Cyberworlds community. At another level the defacement of buildings and memorials may harm others due to the relevance of these artefacts to meaning, identity and belonging within the community. Buildings function as a representation of self, and any attack on them can be considered an attack on the owner's identity. Having been a victim of vandalism Frasier describes the harm suffered to him and his friends and the avoidance behaviour adopted since the attack:

```
Frasier: You dont think it will happen to your place, you think
passwords and the peace-keepers are enough. About four of us spent
a summer building a place about 100 meters away from CW central
only for it to be completely decimated in one afternoon. It felt
like our home, we spent at least over three hours a day around
that place, talking, laughing, adding extensions and frills. The
place was like us. Bits of us were part of the building. I haven't
built anything since, I don't see the point. I don't really visit
Cyberworlds much anymore anyway. It's a shame, we had fun times
back then.
```

While the individual harm of online vandalism may be negligible, the effect it can have upon the integrity of friendships and the wider community can be significant. Frasier states how the building was essential to maintaining their relationships, how it was functional in bringing people together, and how it became symbolic of the group. Its destruction by vandals not only symbolically destroyed these friendships, but it also led to their actual demise. While the harms of these acts may not directly manifest in the offline world, their negative consequences cannot go understated. If, for so many within Cyberworlds, online life and relationships are as important to them as offline equivalents, then these online harms should be similarly weighted.

Aetiology of online deviance

The majority of the acts outlined in the previous section escape legal rationalisation. It is possible, however, to understand these acts and their aetiology by applying certain criminological theories that consider control as a pivotal factor in crime causation, or more appropriately prevention and cessation. Hirschi's (1969) control theory, much like self-control theory (Gottfredson and Hirschi 1990), lends itself to the understanding of these sub-criminal acts because it is not a theory of crime but of 'imprudent and risk taking behaviours' (Marenin and Reisig 1995: 516). The theory then allows for an analysis of both criminal and analogous behaviours. While vandalising online property, online harassment, using profane language and a range of other antisocial behaviours may not be considered criminal they may have enough in common to justify treating them as the same thing. Individuals responsible for such acts online are not criminals, but they are risk-takers, as their acts have real consequences. Ejection, account cancellation, group shaming and to the extreme extent external regulatory involvement, are all costs a virtual deviant may have to face. The likelihood of an individual taking the risk to contravene social expectations and the rules and regulations of Cyberworlds is dependent upon the strength of the bond that individual has to the community, and the extent to which they can neutralise their deviant activity (Sykes and Matza 1957). The following section takes each element of Hirschi's (1969) bond and applies it to the Cyberworlds setting.

Attachment

Attachment is the first aspect of a bond to community (Hirschi 1969). Primarily attachment to significant others leads to the internalisation of norms and values. Without such a bond individuals are abstracted from the core group and find it difficult to adopt and rationalise the group's conventions, rules and regulations. While the previous chapter highlighted significant levels of attachment to community by several members, indicating that a social group exists that shares common norms and values, the negative attitudes held by other members cast a shadow over this utopian landscape.

The following narratives, in emphasising the fragility and playful aspect of relationships online, echo the disenchanted views concerning the demise of community in Cyberworlds:

Bart: For me, my closest friends happen to be people I know offline. However, people who I know from online hold a special kind of position of importance to me that is similar to that of actors on a show. The dramas and personalities are intriguing. It's almost like a soap opera you can participate in.

Tim: Most people either opt for the RW interaction/relationships or the Other Reality that only online can bring to bear. The pity is that if people just realize that the characters that come across the screen, in most cases, are coming from another set of hands or lips, and that they might be neighbours (in a global sense they are), then the thinking might change.

Smint: In my experience online (I have been online in one form or fashion for nearly 20 years now), I have known many whom treat interactions online as just a game.

M@tt: Quake (TM) and other similar games are situations where chaos rules and rules are chaos; when gamers 'play' Quake (TM), murder is 'okay'...so, when those people who feel Cyberworlds is a game play Quake (TM) or other killing games, enter this pseudo reality...online, there tends to be some 'carry-over' which cannot be expressed in an environment without killing and mayhem. I feel this confusion is expressed by a few trouble-makers through their violent or sexually abusive verbal attacks.

Alison: I have a psychotic family member who at first would not believe CW was not a game. After a year, this family member conceded that CW was not just another 'computer game' (referencing off-line games here only); but, that people were NOT who nor what they said they were. Said family member still (to this day) insists that all (or 99 per cent) of the CW members are males. Now, there are a lot of people in CW who think like my family member. This mentality level is most common in the trouble-makers; though, I have witnessed this mindset in a rare few nice people as well.

The understanding that online activity is not 'real life' leads some individuals to play out scenarios in virtual arenas as games. Interactions and events are thought of as divorced from what some individuals would consider 'real'. This distance and escapism leads to a reduction in the ability and willingness of individuals to form any kind of attachment to others, preventing the transmission of common values and norms. Bart considers his experiences and encounters online as a drama, a work of fiction. While finding the characters he is familiar with 'important' to him, there is no sense that he considers these 'real' people, or indeed his encounters 'valid' social experiences. Tim mirrors this state of mind by emphasising the need to move beyond the online character, similar to Turkle's (1995) unease with interacting solely online, wishing also to interact with the 'offline' personae of her interviewees. Whether or not this means Bart, and others like him, fail to internalise the 'drama's' rules and regulations is questionable. However, it can be assumed that from such a viewpoint the ways in which consequences of action and of risk-taking are perceived by these actors are re-evaluated in light of the 'virtuality' of their social experience.

A similar perspective is held by others in the three remaining narratives, but instead of considering their online experiences as a fictional drama they rationalise their behaviours by associating Cyberworlds with the role playing fantasy gaming genre that has been so popular, both on and offline, for decades. Danet (2001) in *Cyberplay* explains the tendency of some to treat social experience online like a game by emphasising how online communication lends itself to the activation of a 'play frame'. She continues to state (2001: 8):

> Because identity is disguised, participants enjoy reduced accountability for their actions, and can engage in 'pretend' or 'make believe' behaviour of all kinds. In this frame, process is more important than outcome.

The idea that it is the process of interaction which is important, and not the outcome, means that individuals can disregard accountability and ignore the consequences of their actions. Gottfredson and Hirschi (1990) note how low self-control, a precursor to deviance, is defined as the failure to consider the long-term negative consequences of one's acts. This resonates with the point that those who treat online interaction as fiction or a game detach themselves from the group's norms and values. Any antisocial or deviant activity that may result is then neutralised by the individual, and considered as a valid course of action, due to the way they perceive a dissociation between action and consequence online.

Attachment also becomes a problem when online relationships fail. The formation of intimate relations online has become a pastime for many individuals, most notably teenagers (Clark 1998). However, the ability to forge long-lasting and 'serious' relationships online for some seems difficult. This has ramifications for levels of attachment to significant others within Cyberworlds, and can ultimately lead to a weakening of one's bond to the community. The following extracts give examples of how individuals have tried and failed at maintaining relationships online:

```
Mark…a: If we are talking about romance, then I certainly agree. I
cannot conceive of a time where total online contact can substitute
for the primal cues, body language, synergy needed for couples to
fall in love. I have seen others who were certain that they were
meant for one that they met in VR only to have that dream shattered
and their egos severely damaged by revelations they or others in
```

VR discovered or even in some cases by meetings arranged in the RW. Romance requires positive confirmation that both parties are really who and what they claim to be. How could that be otherwise, at least in romance.

Moo: Many of the ppl I counsel are also those who have formed what they perceive as deep and intimate VR relationships only to find their partner in one or another lets them down - usually it seems to me by a lack of commitment to the time needed to maintain such a relationship.

Farrar: Of course this can happen in off line as well, the famous 'I'll call you tomorrow' line. But generally when you have to deal with someone in person, you have to tell them you don't want to see them anymore. On line you can just ignore or even filter them out of your life. I've also noticed women seem to be more prone to this behavior online then off line overall.

Ascom: I am always mindful of the fact that Internet relationships are one-dimensional, that we don't really know each other, and that there is a need to maintain discretion and to preserve privacy.

PAM: I believe that anyone who seriously assigns more importance to cyber-people than to the people in his/her real life could use some counseling. I realize that these friendships can be intense, and that time passes differently online than in real life. However, the intimacy that is created is illusory, unless one actually knows the person, not a mere representation of the person or electronic persona, with whom one is interacting.

While the Internet has been touted as the new dating arena, actually maintaining relationships online is problematic and even arduous at times. Previously it was noted that relationships were pivotal to the maintenance of online community, without them there could be no trust or attachment. Narratives indicated that many within Cyberworlds were able to forge meaningful relationships with others, allowing them to become part of a group. However, not all individuals found this process effortless. These narratives exemplify this disenchantment by isolating two main detrimental factors. A lack of commitment to others and the inability to become intimate both ensured that, for some, online relationships were nothing more than fleeting encounters. Clark (1998) finds similar trends in her analysis of teen dating on the net. She notes how relationships formed online were very different from offline relationships due to shifts along the axis of intimacy. Ultimately Clark (1998: 180) concludes that 'Internet dating…is in actuality more frequently employed for fleeting, 'fun' relationships that hold little consequence in … 'real' lives'. The inability of some to forge more meaningful relations leaves them in the same state of abjection as those who consider online life a game.

Other members have less specific but more fundamental attachment issues. Some believe that communications technologies in general reduce the attachment individuals can forge with each other:

```
Bola: More and more, interactions are done electronically either
by phone, e-mail, video/audio conferencing and the like. It is
easy to 'turn off' something one does not like, or that makes one
uncomfortable...lessening the impact of a true relationship.

Amber: A relationship that can be abruptly terminated by the simple
acts of turning off a machine and walking away is not a true
relationship, but a series of limited interactions. It is healthy
to keep that in mind.

IDM: I am nonplussed by the tendency of some netizens to take the
online environment far too seriously, and to let online events and
online people affect them emotionally. I am also mindful of the
fact that an online relationship ends whenever one of the parties,
for any reason or for no reason, leaves the chat room, game, or
other online environment for a different online environment, or
simply turns off the machine and walks away.
```

The fact that technologies can be 'turned off' at a whim prevents individuals from entering potentially awkward or overly intimate scenarios, reducing the opportunity for attachment-forging encounters. This perspective can be associated with those in Markham's (1998) study who perceived CMC as a tool, as opposed to others who were far more entrenched within the online environment, who considered their interactions more meaningful and comparable to offline relations. The longevity of online relationships is also questioned. Some respondents feel that relations can only be maintained when interlocutors are actually online; when the machine is turned off, these relationships come to an abrupt end. This perspective is in clear contrast to earlier discussions surrounding the function of building in Cyberworlds as a forging feature and permanent reminder of social relations and histories.

Varying levels of attachment arguably result in varying levels of majority group norm and value adoption. Those detached from the majority group run the risk of rule and regulation infraction. Those detached who consider their experiences online game-like or fantastical are more likely to partake in risk behaviour due to their perception of a dissociation between action and consequence online. Therefore those who have not adopted the group norms and values and believe that online experience is not socially 'valid' are more likely to neutralise their deviant behaviours, viewing them as acceptable, than those who have online attachments to significant others. However, weak attachments alone cannot account for all deviant behaviour online. While it may account for the majority of tourist deviant activity, as these are less likely to have had the time to form relations, it cannot account for all citizen deviance. Commitment, involvement and belief are the remaining factors that help further explain the deviant activity of those more entrenched within Cyberworlds.

Commitment

The second element of Hirschi's (1969) bond is commitment.[7] Those committed to a particular line of action within Cyberworlds, such as forming a good reputation, have a stake in conformity. Becoming known as an accomplished builder, and taking steps to become involved within community events and organisations are activities that involve a degree of commitment and deviating from these lines of action have consequences. The pursuit of deviant activities would jeopardise reputation and access to certain organisations and even the Cyberworlds community itself. It is usually citizens, who have paid to join the community, that have such a stake in conformity. Primarily their payment ensures some degree of conformity; breaking community rules could result in account cancellation and a loss of money. However, as the following narratives show, it is the reputation-forming activities that prevent the majority of citizens from rule infraction:

> M@tt: A long time member of a virtual world community will not misbehave, because he has his reputation to loose.

> Hopper: On the other hand, the only reward you get for behaving well and working on projects is the reputation you get and maybe a thanks, but this seems to work.

> Compton: I've worked hard over the years to become a Peacekeeper because I see the need to stop the abuses that happen online in this world and others. I believe I'm doing an important job and wouldn't want it taken away from me.

The pressure to conform to acceptable lines of activity bonds certain citizens to the community. Those both attached to others and who have a stake in conformity are less likely to deviate than those who have had little time to form relations or don't feel the need to develop a positive reputation. These latter individuals, who consist of both tourists and citizens, form part of the disillusioned group within Cyberworlds. Both community members below provide differing examples of how reputation formation can influence behaviour within Cyberworlds:

> Skeel: Physical relationships in the real world depend on jobs, food, and sex more than on social needs. In RL we are agreeable socially to obtain physical necessities. In VL, the social contact via text is the important factor in itself and for itself. There is no pressure to obtain physical benefits.

> M@tt: A new member in an online community has no reputation, has (in general) not invested any money or other object of value in

```
being able to access this community, and therefore, to the eyes of
this new member, he has nothing to loose and his acceptance in the
community is not worth anything.
```

In the first extract Skeel notes how interaction and existence via CMC only requires a textual performance, and is not dependent upon material needs that tie down individuals in the offline world. The only commitments one has online are social. The relative freedom individuals may feel by being untied from material commitments of the offline world may account for increased levels of deviant activity online. The second extract focuses more on the community structure, highlighting how tourists and newbies are less likely to value a reputation within Cyberworlds. With almost nothing material to lose, those who enter online communities are able to break rules and regulations without consequence.

Concern about online reputation was also voiced within the focus groups in response to several vignettes.[8] Several hypothetical scenarios were put to respondents in order to elicit reactions to different levels of online deviant activity. When, in some vignettes, a community member behaved without propriety respondents fervently reacted voicing how such action would irreparably damage the member's online reputation. Loss of or damage to reputation was a major deterrent to deviant activity. Official punishments in comparison were perceived as less deterring. A possible explanation for this disparity is the ineffectiveness of technological modes of punishment. For example, the sanction of ejection being quickly subverted by altering an IP address by using another computer, minimising the duration of punishment. In contrast there are lasting repercussions of having one's reputation tainted within the community. These findings resonate with Braithwaite's (1989) theory of reintegrative shaming, explained in detail in Chapter 7. The following responses illustrate how reputation and a commitment to maintaining a good name are considered important to existence within Cyberworlds:

```
Moog: If you're asking if harmful to Laika...yes....harmful in the
sense that her reputation would be known as an antagonist, and
would be hard for her to have wonderful relationships that could
only add to her enjoyment in Cyberworlds.

Remy: I also explain to them that harassing others is not taken
lightly in CW, and if they are citizens, the consequences they may
face it they continue to cause trouble.

Tim: My opinion? A common spoof. A friend of mine, Draxen was
spoofed, which looked similar, last Winter or so which ruined his
reputation amongst those who did not realize it was a spoofer. The
person or persons made Draxen appear as a child molester.

Rocketscientist: spoofing is more dangerous to reputations than
cussing is to the community.
```

Reputation formation and maintenance become far more problematic and challenging within the online environment. This is in part due to the over reliance on the technology of mediation. The ways in which individuals interact are governed and constrained by technological innovations and limitations written into Cyberworlds architecture. Reputations, along with other forms of social capital, are at risk of being subverted due to errors and oversights in programming. Spoofing, the act of assuming another's online identity via hacking, repeatedly arose in focus group discussions in relation to the fragility of one's reputation online. It was noted how impersonating another character had the potential to seriously damage a reputation. In Tim's example his friend's online persona was adopted by another community member in order to maliciously incriminate and undermine the character. Spoofing is then considered a 'danger' to one's reputation, and such fear is an indication of how valued online reputations have become within Cyberworlds.

Commitment to forming a good reputation for the purposes of becoming a builder, to join the Peacekeeper core or a myriad of other reasons ensures to some extent that people will behave with propriety when interacting within the Cyberworlds environment. The anxiety expressed at the fragility of online reputations is a further indication of the importance placed on maintaining a good name. Conversely a proportion of the Cyberworlds population place little importance upon reputation formation reducing the controlling effects of this bond to community. These individuals, both citizens and tourists, are more likely to deviate from conventional lines of action and drift into deviant activity.

Involvement

Positive involvement within the community is dependent upon pre-occupation with legitimate forms of activity (Hirschi 1969). The straightforward notion that those who take up positive activities do not have time to partake in deviant enterprises has formed the nexus of many youth crime initiatives. Providing opportunities that disrupt deviant behavioural trends, such as youth centres, has seen the success of many crime reduction initiatives. Similar distracting activities are in abundance within Cyberworlds. Building, volunteering for community organisations and organising events are all legitimate forms of activity that prove time-consuming and function to divert individuals from drifting into deviance. The mode of communicating online is also considered very involving and time-consuming. Online interaction requires a great deal of attention. Disentangling disrupted adjacency and multiple threading requires sustained concentration and a willingness to learn the intricacies and nuances of a new digital dialect. As the following extracts indicate the process is often so involving that members of Cyberworlds have to divorce themselves from offline activities in order to communicate effectively:

```
Bearcub: Actually online relationships can be quite invasive, I
find that I have to be quite abrupt sometimes simply because for
example, my children need immediate and urgent attention. Being
online and conversing is an activity that is consuming, it is hard
to do anything else during this time, and conversing, or otherwise
interacting with a group of people can be overpowering in terms of
the intensity and the time consumed during which one can do little
or nothing else.
```

```
Bola: As Aria stated in the VR context you need to concentrate and
that means being tied to the keyboard for some time.
```

While the process of interaction is involving it cannot solely account for the displacement of deviant activity online. Many online deviant activities require intense concentration. Hacking for the purposes of vandalising property and impersonating another character requires a great deal of time and attention. What are more important than simple time commitments are the kinds of legitimate activities members of Cyberworlds take part in while online. Individuals have different agendas and as a result visit Cyberworlds for different reasons. Some consider it a place of refuge, to escape the pressures of the offline world; others see it as a creative medium where they build and experiment with digital art forms; while some consider it a space for intellectual stimulation and broadening experiences:

```
Smint: We would exchange ideas, share general life experience
(always interesting when you meet somebody grown up in so different
culture) etc. For me it was not meaningless at all. On the contrary
- the discussions I would have there would often be more serious
and engaging than the real life one's.
```

```
Laika: The people on Cyberworlds tend to be more creative and
intellectual types than on the standard online chat or game, and
they tend also to take the time to help others out using their
own areas of expertise, whether through building, object/avatar
development, or bot programming.
```

```
Brainiac: I work online in large part and the online mode can
become demanding - some even say they cannot bear to be online
when not working - however, I find it immensely freeing, friendships
formed, relationships developed explorations undertaken of the net
and CW and people all within the safety of my home. This freedom
feeds into my work tremendously.
```

Using Cyberworlds as a space to meet new people, form relations and take part in stimulating discussions is one way in which Smint engages in legitimate involving activities. The time and effort that are required to form meaningful relationships online are substantial. As a result little time is left for individuals to think about, let alone engage in, deviant activities. On the more technical side Laika discusses other legitimate pastimes including 'building, avatar development and bot programming'. Taking part in these legitimate activities not only benefits the online community but it can also prove to have positive effects upon life in the offline world. As Brainiac states, engaging in purposeful legitimate action online actually benefits his offline working environment. However, not all visitors and members of Cyberworlds invest their time so constructively. Some lack the enthusiasm to invest time in forging online relations, while others simply have no interest in developing their technological skills:

```
IDM: Offline (real life) romantic relationships are more important
and significant than online. Although it's easy to fall in love
with a person's mindover the net, and there's something to be said
for loving the mental before the physical aspect of a person, I
couldn't settle for a strictly Internet romance. I need to be in
the here-and-now, eye-to-eye flesh-on-flesh with the object of my
desires. I want real intimacy and involvement.
```

```
Fischerspooner: It is true that many people are less invested
in interactions taking place in this medium. And thus their
interactions have less meaning to them. It could be stated that
any interaction is as real to the participants as they are invested
in it...
```

Those individuals who lack the interest in legitimate forms of involvement are more likely to have a weaker bond to the Cyberworlds community. Having no avocation to take up one's time while visiting Cyberworlds can increase an individual's propensity towards deviant activity. Citizens who feel disenchanted with the Cyberworlds environment and tourists who have had little time to get involved in community activities are more likely to deviate from the rules and regulations.

Belief

Control theory posits that a universal belief system exists in any given society (Hirschi 1969). Little weight is given to the argument that subcultural formations result in the impulse to deviate. It is more the point that there exists a variation in the extent to which people believe they should follow the rules of society. Within Cyberworlds there is clear variation in beliefs regarding the moral validity of social rules. Several themes developed out of the data which showed how individuals simultaneously accepted the laws of Cyberworlds while neutralising them, regarding them as irrelevant to their conduct. By becoming a citizen, or by simply visiting Cyberworlds, individuals accept the rules of conduct as written in the community charter (see Appendices 3 and 4). In doing so they also agree to abide by the laws as interpreted and enforced by the Peacekeepers. However, while the rules and regulations are not exhaustive, disagreement on their applicability to all members of Cyberworlds causes degrees of contention, undermining a common belief system. Primarily, concern over the universality of rules and regulations has ensured that certain groups within Cyberworlds are able to discount certain beliefs allowing for the neutralisation of rule transgression.

The regulation of behaviour within online environments is challenging. The immediate problem is one of transnationality. Cyberworlds is a global forum, unrestricted by national boundaries and accordingly attracts a variety of individuals from disparate and distant cultures. This cultural mix, while a source for rich interaction, proves problematic to regulate. However, if we are to accept that communities and nations are actively constructed, with finite boundaries, in which the face-to-face mode of interaction of oral communities has been displaced by an imaginary simultaneity of existence, then the laws of the online imagined community are as valid as the laws that govern a member's offline community or nation state (Anderson 1983). Yet there is little agreement over what form online regulation should take, and what should influence its development. The main contentious point expressed in the focus groups centred around the 'Americanisation of regulation'. Many Cyberworlds community members, both Americans and non-Americans, felt that the arbitrary application of Cyberworlds law, which is clearly an adaptation of American norms, values, idiolect and regulatory ideology, was inappropriate and fundamental to the demise of the community. The narratives below exemplify the disdain felt by community members regarding law formation and application in Cyberworlds:

> Skeel: there are laws, rules, regulations, morals and mores. When mores (localized folkways determining what is considered proper or moral behavior, though not the same as the definition of morals) are enforced on a worldwide medium; that is wrong and there will be problems. What is 'wrong' behavior in one country is totally acceptable in another and visa versa. Since this is a worldwide medium, I feel you should consider separating Cyberworlds 'specific' rules and regulations which are occasionally mere extensions of American mores from those which are Universal. The rules and regulations in Cyberworlds ARE decidedly American, with American mores defining what is proper and what is improper. One example: ONLY American cusswords are taboo. If we added all of the words that are not cusswords in America, but, are cusswords in other countries...talking would be impossible! We can say bloody and shag.

> Moog: The rules and regulations in CyberWorlds are generally 'Americanized' and it's obvious why America is certainly NOT the world leader on 'good behavior'. A truly INTERNATIONAL group should make the rules...both serving and getting input from their constituents. Constituents should have the right to petition for removal from office if they find they have a 'corrupt' by their terms Representative.

> Carreg: Wow -- I sooooo concur with Moog. In fact, I think the CW guidelines are so presumptiously 'American,' I'm a tad embarrassed

at times in Worlds to admit I'm an American. Moog, fyi, though
I know many of us do (including several of the PKs), not ALL
American's believe that the American way is the right way and the
only way. And, furthermore, some of us believe that if we Americans
weren't so ethnocentric, we could learn a thing or two from our
global neighbors in Worlds.

Bella: CW is an American company exhibiting American Imperialism
whether you agree with it or not.:-)

The universal application of one set of rules and regulations based
upon one culture ensures that behaviours considered deviant by some
are sanctioned while behaviours considered appropriate by others are
prohibited. This non-commensurate interpretation and application of rules
and regulations causes resentment. This coincides with a reduction in the
belief in the social validity of the norms, values and laws of Cyberworlds.
Furthermore, the disdain held for 'American' values distances groups
of Cyberworlds members away from the universal belief system. Some
not only consider the lack of a poly-cultural approach to regulation as
inappropriate, but also recognise the sexist and ethnocentric modes of
representation within Cyberworlds:

Kid606: As far as the CW community being 'Americanised', I think
we might be more accurate in saying it is 'white male-ised' or
a reflection of western populist culture to a high ethnocentric
degree. A small example are the avatars used in CW and the gateway.
There are no black men in business suits. There are no orthodox jews
who must cover their heads. The only women in dresses are scantily
clad, there are no children at the gateway nor are there Asians.
And not a single avatar is roundish. I also find it abhorrent that
we have a North Americanised Bot governing language usage at the
Gateway. If we are to govern language usage then let it be all
languages or none at all. It wouldn't take much work to fix that
bot but then we all know the cultural inclination or climate of
our small governing body doesnt give much priority to its minority
community members.

The definition of an avatar is the incarnation or embodiment of a particular
quality of a being. Reflecting Kid606's account it seems inappropriate for
this term to be used in relation to Cyberworlds characters. In very few of
the cases do the bodily manifestations mimic those of the user. On one level
this might not be considered problematic; many use Cyberworlds as a means
of escape, and adopting an avatar that misrepresents the user (be it thinner,
sexier or another sex) is part of the fantasy. On another level the limited
range of representations offered in Cyberworlds ostracises many individuals
both personally and culturally. The lack of variance in characteristics such as
skin colour, age, body shape and clothing restricts modes of representation,
reducing the ability for some to embed themselves within the community
and hence the belief system as a whole.

The use of bots (robots) to regulate language within Cyberworlds environments also means that only certain forms of dialect are controlled. Each bot is programmed by its designer and accordingly reflects their beliefs and values. If the designer is American it is more than likely that a language monitor bot will only be designed to identify American profanity. This automated form of regulation has clear shortcomings and will only reflect those who design the system. Marginal groups have little representation within this system, and as a result are able to subversively neutralise any deviant activity by ascribing little moral validity to the social rules.

Groups of individuals who feel left in abjection by a belief system that reflects a culture quite distinct from their own are more likely to break rules and regulations. A belief system that seems alien to some breeds confusion and contempt, allowing individuals to drift into rule breaking by neutralising their acts as either non-deviant or justified in the face of an unjust system of governance.

Summary

Bonds to other individuals, organisations and rules facilitate the internalisation of group norms and values heightening a consciousness of other members' opinions and expectations. Conversely those with weak bonds have a tenuous attachment to group norms and values becoming ignorant of community evaluation. It follows that those who deviate from rules and regulations are likely to have a weak bond to the Cyberworlds community. This analysis is helpful in accounting for the deviant activity of both tourists and citizens. Tourists are more likely to embark upon certain deviant activities, such as using profane language and flooding, because of their general lack of all four conditions of a bond. Contradictorily they are also unlikely to engage in the more serious deviant acts as a result of their weak bond. Acts of vandalism and harassment require individuals to have invested time to become familiar with Cyberworlds technology and to identify potential victims. This level of bond is present in some citizens within Cyberworlds, however, not all use their contacts and technological skill to deviate. Those who consider their reputation important, who engage in building and who have internalised the Cyberworlds belief system are predominantly conformist. It is those citizens who feel disenchanted with the environment who are more likely to drift in and out of deviant activity. Such individuals are more likely to take the risk of deviating from group norms and values as they gradually begin to invest less in community life. However, armed with the esoteric knowledge only citizens appropriate, they are more than capable of committing the more serious acts of online deviance. Deviant behaviour can be neutralised allowing for its proliferation (Sykes and Matza 1957). It is clear from the levels of deviant activity within Cyberworlds that certain aspects of the online environment create a social space where the integrity of bonds is in constant flux. Levels of attachment, commitment, involvement and belief in online community life are influenced by the liminal and ephemeral nature of cyber encounters (Turner 1967). Those who are in transient and temporary positions are far less likely to form a bond with the Cyberworlds community.

Those with little commitment to achieving or maintaining a reputation online are more likely to deviate from group norms and values. Because commitments online are less constraining than those in the offline world, less is jeopardised by being deviant. For example, there are fewer material belongings in an environment made up of purely social relations. A lack of legitimate online avocations also increases the propensity for an individual to drift into deviance. Those not involved in building, maintaining friendships or running community organisations are more likely to have time on their hands to break rules and regulations. This is especially the case within online environments where some deviant acts, such as vandalism and other forms of hacking, require a great deal of time and concentration. Variations in the extent to which members believe they should follow the rules of the Cyberworlds community impact on levels of deviant activity. Those who consider the law of Cyberworlds to be culturally biased, sexist, ageist or racist are less likely to accept aspects of the belief system, allowing harmful acts to be neutralised. Finally, lacking attachment to significant others, peers and friends might be the most significant indication of bond atrophy. Those who consider life online as game-like or playful, or who consider it to be akin to the plot of a fictional drama attach little significance to online encounters. As a result, process becomes more important than outcome. The act of doing something becomes important, while its effect goes unrecognised. Individuals begin to identify a dissociation between action and consequence, allowing for the neutralisation of deviant activity. Mitigating comments such as 'online life isn't real' and 'it's only words' allow individuals to justify their deviant acts. These neutralising techniques are addressed in the following chapter. First, neutralising harm on the basis that online experience is virtual is addressed. Second, the rationalisation that because the medium of communication is purely text driven, any deviance is mitigated due to the harmlessness of words is theoretically challenged. The chapter then highlights how words online do have the capacity to wound a victim.

6 The mechanics of online harmful activity

The language of cybercrime

A theoretical model which explains the *modus operandi* of online textual deviant activity forms the beginning of this chapter. The model is intended to be general in its application in that it can help in the understanding of online deviant activity in a myriad of online settings, including Cyberworlds. The model also helps in understanding the potential harms that may come from derisory textual performances. The first sections outline the main theoretical components of the model and relate them to both offline and online settings. Examples of derisory discourse and virtual violence are taken from the literature to demonstrate how the model operates. The later sections address harm both within Cyberworlds and more generally. Narratives from the focus groups help illustrate the feelings and opinions of community members towards harm online.

As with offline communities, online populations are subjected to a myriad of quasi-criminal activities such as verbal abuse, defamation, harassment, stalking and at the extreme extent 'virtual rape' (MacKinnon 1997b). These forms of online deviance might be dubbed simply as misbehaviour, highlighting the 'virtual' element of these acts, playing down their significance in relation to 'real' world affairs. However, basing assumptions of the seriousness of online deviant acts on the separateness of the 'real' and the 'virtual' only serves to shift accountability away from the online offender. The notion that a deviant act is mitigated due to its 'virtuality' is short-sighted. To argue that an act of racial or sexual harassment carried out within an online environment through text is any less serious than an equivalent verbal act in the offline world is to grant the would-be offender the right to defame and humiliate individuals on the basis that it is simply not 'real'. A contrary position is advanced in this chapter, stating that both the 'real' and 'virtual' are not separate experiences and as such the nature of online communication enables a perpetrator to inflict recognisable levels of harm upon a victim via textual slurs and abuse. It is further argued that due to the unique conventions and modes of 'being' experienced by many online users, certain acts of harassment might be afforded with more 'force' to harm a victim than is otherwise found in offline equivalents. While this chapter does not identify an aetiology of online abusive acts (as Chapter 5 explains), it does convey the way in which forms of abuse online have the ability to harm the objects of derision significantly enough to warrant a closer examination of these acts, and subsequently to consider suitable forms of redress. To accomplish this the chapter delineates the mechanics of abusive acts online, which in turn indicates how individuals are susceptible to harm from these acts. Understanding that abuse online manifests through text is imperative and identifying which forms of abusive text pose a significant enough threat to an individual's identity becomes necessary if any form of redress is to be made possible both on and offline.

'Real' and the 'virtual'

As a precursor to understanding how offenders harm their victims through text within online environments, it is important to understand that events within online settings are not wholly separate from those in the offline world. Such a strict dichotomy between the 'real' and the 'virtual' must be rejected if the consequences of abusive acts online are to be fully acknowledged. Social scientists frequently compartmentalise cultural phenomena into opposing, interrelated or complementary forces, a process which allows for a clearer understanding of social practices. Yet some may argue that oversimplifying what might be a far more complex and interactive social process for the sake of a presumed theoretical, methodological or philosophical predisposition can lead to unfounded and hasty conclusions. Writers such as Baudrillard (1998) and Jameson (1991) have been criticised for their claims of the separateness of the 'real' and the 'virtual', as they pay little attention to the reciprocity that exists between these two states (Miller and Slater 2000). If online arenas were to be viewed as places apart from offline life, one would expect to find behavioural patterns, such as deviant acts, that were abstracted and alien from offline interactions. In practice some crimes carried out on computer networks seem to be extensions of everyday crimes in the real world. Crimes are then re-engineered to function in the online environment, utilising the technologies they are faced with. It is then important to understand that both acts of deviance and experiences online are inexorably linked to the 'real' world. As such the consequences of online abuse and harassment can manifest in the terrestrial world even if the act was performed in a 'virtual' setting. To better understand how online abuse harms individuals in the offline world an examination of how language both constitutes and de-constitutes the victim's identity is required. Recognising that language is a sustaining force behind 'being', utilising it as an abusive tool may result in the victim experiencing degrees of ontological precariousness.

'Being' through language and text

The need to deconstruct online deviance in order to understand its consequences requires an examination of the vehicle through which derision is made possible – the speech act. Althusser (1971) gives an account of the constitution of bodies through language that proves useful in the analysis of online deviance. The argument made is that language is one of the sustaining entities or forces behind individual identities. The social existence of the body is made possible partly by being interpellated within the terms of language (Althusser 1971). In short, a non-defined body is called into existence, or being, by language. In Althusser's example of interpellation a policeman calls out 'hey you there' in a crowded street, and everyone who hears him turns around, ready to be recognised. The answer from any member of the crowd does not pre-exist the policeman's call, so the passer-by turns precisely to acquire an identity. In short, the address animates the addressee into existence. In this sense language fundamentally constitutes the 'self'. The outcome of the address may either include the body in the language system, or marginalise it outside of the system, in abjection. In summary, individuals come to recognise themselves as individuals with an identity through their objectification by others in language; this objectification places them in a hierarchy of the social/language system where relationships with others are recognised through difference.

Speech acts – illocution and perlocution

If the body is constituted through language, then it follows that language can also de-constitute an individual's identity. Butler (1997) examines the ways in which language can be used as a weapon to wound individuals through 'verbal assaults', which can help in understanding the potential harmful effects of similar acts within Cyberworlds. When individuals claim to have been injured by an insult they are ascribing a certain agency to language, a force that allows it to harm an individual in similar ways to physical acts. Indeed, to claim that language injures is to combine both linguistic and physical vocabularies. The choice of title in Matsuda *et al.*'s (1993) text *Words that Wound* suggests that 'language can act in certain ways that parallel the infliction of physical pain and injury' (Butler 1997: 4). Indeed, the psychological and physiological battering from racial and homophobic slurs can mirror that of a physical assault; 'it's like receiving a slap in the face, it's instantaneous' (Lawrence 1993: 68). The ability for language to harm with such force draws on the body's reliance on the language system. A verbal insult draws on that initial process of interpellation, recasting and subordinating the individual within the social/language hierarchy. So the essential point remains that the contemporary address recalls and re-enacts the formative ones that gave a priori certification. As Butler (1997: 5) summarises, 'If language can sustain the body, it can also threaten its existence'.

Yet before any analysis can be made of offensive or harassing text from within Cyberworlds and the general online environment, it would be prudent to ascertain what speech or text could be deemed as offensive. Yet, as Becker *et al.* (2000: 36) note in attempting to define hate-speech: 'in constructing a definition … one is really crafting unspoken rules regarding discourse'. Any attempt to map the pains of verbal or textual performances, in terms of content, individual susceptibility and the multitude of contexts derisory speech can take, would be fruitless. For this reason a broader mechanical approach can be adopted to identify wider frameworks of derisory speech, theorising the mechanics which allow for such agency in language. Here the 'form' injurious speech takes is examined, not the 'content'. By adopting a broader approach it is possible to identify a bifurcation in forms of language, particularly speech or text of a derisory content. Austin (1975) delineates illocutionary and perlocutionary speech acts. Although a clumsy dyad, with a substantial 'grey' area between them, this way of proceeding can be beneficial in understanding forms of online derision. The illocutionary speech performance is one where at the same time as what is being said, something is also being done; the policeman stating 'I am charging you with assault' is not saying something which has a delayed consequence, the consequence is immediate. The speech is the act of doing, where a certain 'force' is acted upon another. Perlocutionary acts, however, have a delayed effect; what is said at one point in time may have a consequence that is temporally distant. Austin gave the examples of 'warning' (I warn you) as an illocutionary act and 'persuading' (I persuaded him) as a perlocutionary act. The speech act of warning has an instantaneous effect, where the act of warning occurs at the same time as the utterance. Persuasion itself implies that the consequences of a persuasive speech act are temporarily removed from the utterance. The reason for the disparity in speech acts derives from social and linguistic conventions. The illocutionary speech act is only so due to its ability to refer and draw from convention and ritual in society at points in time such as the wedding ritual (I do) and the naming of a ship. Indeed, instances of failed speech performances can help explain the illocutionary act's reliance on the temporal social milieu.

It is the illocutionary performance that harbours the force to effectively harm an individual in a derisory context. The possibility for the abusive illocutionary act to simultaneously convey action in speech means that it does more than represent violence; it is violence. The forceful utterance 'reinvokes and reinscribes' a relation of domination (Butler 1997: 18). For Matsuda *et al.* (1993) this relation of social and linguistic domination provides a site for the mechanical reproduction of power.

Illocution and computer-mediated communication

Illocutionary performances also exist within synchronous forms of computer-mediated communication. Synchronous (such as chat) as opposed to asynchronous online communication (such as email and newsgroups) allows for temporal co-presence, an effect that intensifies online interactions, creating an atmosphere where discussions can flourish. The immediacy of synchronous communication online makes it akin to that of offline spoken communication. This heightened sense of immediacy in chat leads to the expression of more emotional and heated exchanges. Emotion can be readily expressed within synchronous forms of communication, due to the realisation that IRC (Internet Relay Chat) is more oral than literate – the latter being characteristic of asynchronous communication. Even though temporally co-present online communication is text-based, its characteristics reflect those of speech. For example, the use of emoticons and phatic communication, such as '*swoon*' or '*gag*', and the use of the uppercase to denote a raised voice ('SHUT UP!'), are more typical of verbal and visual interaction, not writing (Sternberg 1998). It is within this medium that injurious illocution can flourish.

Injurious illocutions online can appear in two quite distinct forms. The first is a textual adaptation of the spoken illocution, so what would have been a vocal insult now appears as text on screen. This type of injurious speech has already met with legal rationalisations and proceedings in the terrestrial environment (for example Stratton Oakmont, Inc. v. Prodigy Services Co. 1995; Cubby v. Compuserve, Inc. 1991; California Software, Inc. v. Reliability Research, Inc. 1986). Internet Service Providers or bulletin board operators who regulate online discourse can be held liable as publishers of defamatory material. Users of CMC could also be found liable for defamatory online statements (Davis 2000). The second form of injurious illocution online differs from the first in that it draws on several textual conventions that have emerged from within the virtual environment itself. Reid (1995: 167) notes how 'language [offline] does not express the full extent of our cultural and interpersonal play. Words themselves tell only half the story – it is their representation that completes the picture'. In contrast, words and text are the only form of interpersonal play within many online environments, recasting, if not reducing, the opportunities for modes of representation. This opens the door for a form of illocution that allows for traditional forms of violent behaviour (i.e. forms of physical or actual violence within an offline environment) to be re-engineered as textual violent performances online. The very nature of interaction inherent within computer-mediated communication has forged a convention that allocates more 'functions' to text than is usually granted to the spoken word. Where speech partly functions as dialogue, description and emotion offline, text online is solely responsible for these functions. Online text allows for 'physical' performances to occur in a virtual environment and is the only vehicle through which individuals can create an online context. Consequently online text carries a heavier burden than offline language in sustaining individual identities.

As Markham found, many individuals in her study conceptualised CMC as a 'way of being', emphasising how they and others were able to express self through text, talking of experiences 'in or as the text' (1998: 85). The example of 'virtual rape' can be understood from this perspective, where text is the sustaining force behind the body's identity online, and where 'physical' performances are expressed textually (MacKinnon 1997b). When, in the case of 'virtual rape' described by Dibbell (1993: 240), the assailant Mr Bungle forced his victim to 'eat his/her own pubic hair' by typing in a detailed description of the process in real time, the textual act bore a twofold performance; the act of 'eating pubic hair' occurred at the same time as the assailant's utterance. Virtual perceptions of time and environment (where what is said often has no temporal lag to what is done) mean that such textual performances have immediate consequences. Such a burden and reliance on text arguably leaves it susceptible to misuse, being employed as an effective vehicle for derision.

If this act of 'virtual rape' were to occur in the actual environment, in a vocal or a printed form, the consequences would possibly be less harmful. Arguably individuals are more ontologically secure in the offline world in comparison to those online whose identities are made vulnerable through an over-reliance on text (Turkle 1995). In order to understand why acts of textual violence lack illocutionary force outside of the online environment, two of the three requirements needed for a successful injurious illocution can be drawn upon. The initial success of any kind of illocution depends on what Austin called 'securing uptake' (1975: 118). This process is best explicated by a reciprocal process between two interlocutors. For example, once A utters a potentially injurious illocution to B, the object of potential derision, B, must be open to the idea that A might be telling B what in fact she means to tell him/her. At first one might assume that a verbal expression of 'virtual rape' in the offline world would be possible if the criteria of reciprocity were met between two interlocutors, essentially the offender and the victim. Indeed, a harassing telephone call ensures reciprocity by evoking a convention between the caller and the called. The called performs the convention by greeting the caller, who proceeds to deliver a verbal account of 'virtual rape', whereupon the called understands that they are subject to a harassing telephone call. If the victim decides not to continue with the exchange, reciprocity can be severed by a refusal to respond or responding in an unconventional manner. However, the argument made here is that such an exchange differs from the second type of textual illocution online in that the effects are likely to be less harmful. The online illocution is able to involve and invade the potential victim to a greater extent due to their over-reliance on text as the sustaining force behind their identity. While vocalised language has the role of sustaining the body in the harassing telephone call, the burden on verbalised language is less. Essentially, while reciprocity between two interlocutors offline can be secured in order to perform a 'virtual rape', the absence of the online context reduces the illocutionary force to harm.

To reiterate, the role convention has in securing uptake has already been detailed (e.g. the statement 'I do' in the wedding ceremony), yet neither convention nor reciprocity can account for the success of an illocutionary performance alone. When an injurious illocution is delivered there must be a conducive context. Taking the above example, it is noted that the second type of illocution found in the virtual arena could not secure a successful uptake in other offline settings. This is precisely because the illocution would be used in a non-conducive context – the convention of text as description, emotion and action within the online environment allows for the mechanical reproduction of physical violence in text; the same cannot be done offline as the conventions and contexts do not apply. In his performance of 'virtual rape' online Mr Bungle secured a context that would allow his victims to know they were about to be the subject of an attack by his unmistakable entrance into the community, described in text as 'A fat, oleaginous, Bisquick-faced clown dressed in cum-stained harlequin garb and girdled with a mistletoe-and-hemlock belt whose buckle bore the quaint inscription "KISS ME UNDER THIS YOU BITCH!"' (Dibbell 1993: 239). Clearly the assailant's intentions were made clear from the outset with the creation of a sexually oppressive and insidious social context. To clarify, an example of a non-conducive context in the offline world might be a judge saying 'I sentence you to life imprisonment' outside of the courtroom. The object of the illocution would clearly question the utterance and hence both reciprocity and uptake would be at fault creating an unsuccessful illocution.

The final ingredient to a successful illocution is subordination. The feminist claim that the female voice has gone unheard, overshadowed by male dominance and its replication in language, highlights the way in which powerful groups in a community determine the scope of reciprocity and hence restrict the illocutionary potential of certain groups. This is not to say these groups cannot literally be heard, it is more the case that they can do less with speech than others, they are lacking certain ingredients to secure successful illocution. The same perspective can be applied to the successful uptake of injurious illocutions; someone who is in a privileged position within a language/social hierarchy is able to subordinate another with more success. The use of racist slurs by a white individual would have a more forceful illocutionary effect than another Afro-Caribbean or Asian person using similar language. This is supported by the adoption of once insulting words by these subordinate groups, e.g. the use of 'queer' in friendly exchanges between gay males. Further, research into the emotion humiliation, a possible harm of an injurious illocution, indicates subordination as a precursor to harm. According to Klein (1991), humiliation occurs within relationships of unequal status where the humiliator dominates the victim. Humiliation or injurious illocution is essentially the practice of social control, where an individual's sense of identity is undermined (Silver *et al.* 1986).

The manifestation of subordination and hierarchy within the online environment calls for a re-evaluation of the mechanics behind the illocutionary act. Both on and offline personae harbour differing power relations for the individual, akin to Goffman's (1971) multiple selves; individuals have the opportunity to carry out two distinct lives, both with differing social relations. The question here is what self does a potential illocution draw its power from when performed within the virtual environment. At first thought we might assume the online persona, but one cannot ignore the reciprocal relationship between the real and the virtual, identifying that each influences the other. So in the case of textual insults it becomes less obvious who is delivering and who is the object of the attempted illocution. However, status relations are more apparent in the second type of illocution online. During his act of virtual rape Mr Bungle harboured a unique kind of power that enabled a successful injurious illocution. His knowledge of the technical aspects of the online community allowed him to control and deliver injurious illocutions while his victims were immobilised; arguably without this technological power the objects of his derision may have silenced his illocutions and power relations would have been equalised. With his grotesque entrance Mr Bungle secured uptake by ensuring reciprocity, and his esoteric technical knowledge allowed for both the physical and social control of his victims, while the context of the environment ensured that his textual performances were effective in victimising the objects of his derision.

Misfires

Mentioned earlier was the possibility for illocutionary text/speech performances to fail in their attempts at derision. Matsuda *et al.*'s (1993) argument presumed that a social or hierarchical structure is enunciated at the moment of a hateful utterance. It is an assumption then, that the social structure remains constant. It is at this point that an important issue must be raised in relation to Matsuda *et al.*'s argument. In the analysis of hateful speech Matsuda *et al.* refer to subordination within a social or hierarchical structure that is ignorant of temporal shifts. In order for a hateful utterance to be effective in subordinating its target then a social or language system would have to remain intact and unchanged. However, Matsuda *et al.*'s claim is open to question; is not the social and language structure prone to temporal shifts and changes, and if so would the ability to initiate a hateful speech performance be prone to 'misfire'? It is clear that Matsuda *et al.* take a synchronic world-view of both the language and social system. Indeed they may be correct in thinking that one can only understand a language system by looking at it in temporal stasis, and many Saussurian linguists would agree. Matsuda *et al.*, within a synchronic paradigm, are then interested more in the form hateful speech can take. Yet it is advanced that a fuller explanation of derisory speech acts would develop from a diachronic analysis an investigation that also examines substance in language.

Linguists who take a diachronic stance provide explanations as to how and why language systems are subject to temporal forces. Issues of 'closure' within the work of discourse studies have exemplified the preoccupation with the limits of a linguistic 'system' (see Laclau 1996). Common examples of how the meaning of words can change over time highlight the shifting nature of these 'systems'. The terms 'awful' and 'gay' have obviously been subject to re-signification (awful once denoting one's positive awe or wonder towards an object or action). Similarly, the act of 'talking back' shows how those who are the subject of victimisation can call into operation the language system and take the opportunity to 'fight back'. The revaluation of the term 'queer' suggests that derisory speech can be turned back to the addressee in a different form. In essence, the re-signified term allows for a reversal of effects, and points to the flexibility of power in terms of speech acts that have an origin and end (in terms of meaning) that remain unfixed and unfixable (Butler 1997). Parallels can be drawn here between the arbitrariness of the sign – that the signifier and the signified have no solid or relational bond – and the arbitrariness of the derisory speech act – that what is said and the meaning have no necessary bond or consequence. This loosening of the link between act and injury opens up the possibility for counter-speech, as exemplified above. This way of theorising has certain consequences for the mediation of online deviance. With the current paucity of legal remedies to aid the mediation of hate-speech online, and the reluctance shown by some online communities towards 'external' interference (MacKinnon 1997a), other non-legalistic forms are needed to reconsolidate 'inappropriate' behaviour (also see Chapter 7).

Social practices and remedies have to be put in place that ensure the possibility of counter-speech, along with other technical mechanisms such as ejection. Examples of counter-speech have been seen in the mediation of 'virtual rape'. After the failed efforts of technological mediation (e.g. ejection from the community) in the case of Mr Bungle, textual methods were employed which aimed to disempower his actions. These textual performances involved the community 'shunning' the assailant and ultimately 'shaming' him. These acts, which were textually and socially performative, secured the social ostracism of the offender. Similar instances of vigilante justice have emerged in other cases of sexual harassment online. Reid (1999) recounts an instance of 'virtual rape' in the Multi-User Domain named JennyMUSH, an environment created for the purpose of counselling women who had suffered offline sexual abuse. The harasser taunted and verbally abused several of the online visitors, while performing acts of sexual violence through text. Given the nature of the environment the assailant's actions were considered exceptionally harmful. Members of the community were encouraged to textually harass the assailant in an attempt to deliver punishment. Female sexual victimisation seems to have even permeated the safe haven of the virtual arena, where perpetrators invade the sanctity of the home and cause further harm to their victims.

Illocution and harm within Cyberworlds

In order to examine the effects of derisory illocutions within Cyberworlds it is useful to examine their non-computer-mediated form and their ability to harm in an offline context. The effects of injurious hate-speech offline have been well documented. Richard Delgado (1993) remarks in 'Words that Wound' that immediate mental or emotional distress is the most obvious direct harm caused by a racial insult. Without question, 'mere words, whether racial or otherwise, can cause mental, emotional or even physical harm to their target, especially if delivered in front of others or by a person of authority' (1993: 94). Delgado (1993: 94) is so emphatic on this point that he continues 'the need for legal redress for victims also is underscored by the fact that racial insults are intentional acts'. As already mentioned, humiliation may be an intentional outcome of an injurious illocution. For the purposes of clarity, humiliation is defined as 'the deep dysphoric feeling associated with being, or perceiving oneself as being, unjustly degraded, ridiculed, or put down – in particular, one's identity has been demeaned or devalued' (Hartling and Luchetta 1999: 264). The debilitating effects associated with humiliation, such as social and physical withdrawal, behavioural constriction, and isolation, further indicate the harmful nature of some verbal attacks (Hartling and Luchetta 1999). There are further similarities between the deconstituting effects of injurious illocutions and experiences of disconnection, an associated outcome of humiliation, which can have 'profound and negative consequences' on an individual's identity (Hartling and Luchetta 1999: 261). While it is clear that injurious illocutions can harm individuals, the unintentional effects on the wider community are less well documented. In the context of humiliation and similar emotions such as embarrassment and shame, those who witness the injurious illocution, while escaping the direct harm caused, may become anxious and adopt avoidance behaviour within the community. Even those who deliver the injurious illocution may develop a fear of humiliation and associated emotions (Klein 1991). In sum, it is believed that certain forms of insults, delivered in a conducive context by an authoritative individual not only harm in similar ways to physical acts, but can also have a debilitating effect on the community as a whole.

How these harms manifest within Cyberworlds is a key question if forms of online injurious speech and textual expressions of violence are to be fully acknowledged. Individuals who use CMC often express themselves through 'online personae' (Turkle 1995). The construction of online personae and the psychological attachment an individual has to their 'virtual self' become important issues when assessing the risk of harm and victimisation online. At what 'self' an injurious illocution is aimed (the online persona or the offline self) might at first seem an important consideration. When Legba was sexually assaulted by Mr Bungle, it was the online persona that was victimised and 'physically' assaulted through text. However, the psychological effects and harms were experienced by the creator of the Legba persona (Dibbell 1993). Similarly, when a Cyberworlds member harasses another it is the online persona that is targeted, but the effects of the injurious illocution are inevitably felt by the persona's creator. Reid's (1995: 178) analysis of online interaction shows while 'the physical aspect of MUDs may be only virtual … the emotional aspect is actual'. It seems clear that any injurious illocution online strikes at the identity of the computer user in the offline world. The anonymity of an online persona or its difference from the offline self that created it are nullified in face of deconstituting and debilitating textual acts. Successful injurious illocutions within a textual environment (those that secure context, reciprocity and subordination) can harm with an effective degree of force to mirror that of offline injurious illocutions. Essentially, the accepted convention of text within the online environment leaves individuals susceptible to harm. The permanence and visibility of text within 'chat' constantly reminds those who were injured of the act, which gives a certain longevity to injurious text. The following narratives show how individuals perceive and experience harm within Cyberworlds:

```
Teamdoyobi: ppl always suggest that verbal abuse is far less
harmful than physical abuse however I think each is equally harmful
just in different ways. So in terms of how ppl see themselves,
their level of confidence and self esteem there is risk of harm; in
terms of the public image of the 'chat room' there is also harm.
All such behaviour is harmful - even to the perpetrator.
```

```
Oliver: A bad selection of words and you can hurt your virtual
friend the same way you would a real one. And just like in real
life, you can make friends and enemies in CW.
```

```
Billgatessux: what is said in the commmunity of the online world
can have quite an impact, if you're an active member of the
community in particular the thing said can carry down into your
personal life.
```

All these narratives compare and contrast the effects of derisory illocutions in on and offline settings. The majority of Cyberworlds members recognise that forms of derision are evident within their online community. Many citizens and tourists recognise that verbal abuse, on and offline, can have significant negative effects. Teamdoyobi highlights that a verbal attack online can affect the way in which a victim 'sees themselves', reducing their 'level of confidence' and 'self esteem'. These feelings resonate with the literature on humiliation discussed earlier (Hartling and Luchetta 1999). Teamdoyobi goes as far as to state that even the perpetrator of these acts suffers harm. It is likely that an offender would be labelled as deviant by the group, harming their reputation and weakening their bond to the community. This process either results in ostracism or recidivism. Billgatessux continues with the assertion that the more an individual is bonded to the Cyberworlds community the more likely that they would suffer harm from a derisory illocution. Further, the harms felt by derisory acts can even manifest in one's 'personal life'. Drawing a link between on and offline life, Billgatessux acknowledges that both personae are connected and co-dependent, meaning harms are actual. These rationalisations are not uncommon and go some way to reject the techniques of neutralisation which rely on the belief of the separateness of the real and the virtual, sometimes employed by perpetrators. However, not all community members were convinced that online encounters could result in recognisable levels of harm:

> Gescom: Well I am not the rough and tumble type who goes to seedy bars and breaks bottles over people's heads like in the Hollywood westerns. On the other hand, I really can't understand what all the concern is about a little 'bashing'. There are what... 30,000 usenet newsgroups? I don't think I have found one yet where there is no bashing, trolling, spamming and all sorts of other bad behavior. Not once have I been traumatized by reading something in a newsgroup.

> Buxton: There are incidents where someone can flood the screen or block someone's view or bring a bot to GZ, but it is not going to change the outcome of someone's life because you have to scroll up a few lines on the screen. Burglars and murderers and such can definitely change the way someone's life swings.

> Wilde: I agree with Buxton here. But if you take the reverse angle on all of this, and say compare racial or sexual harassment at GZ with pickpocketing or littering offline then more harm can be done online. Its swings and round abouts really. It become harder when you try to compare the same crimes, like harassment. I couldnt say which would be more serious, it would depend on the circumstances I suppose.

> LFO: Any harm done online, as far as I've experienced, is usually only hurt feelings on the part of the recipient of the taunts if they happen to know one another or, probably more likely, anger at the breach of common etiquette or simply for being on the receiving end of said abuse. I don't see any real harm being done to the community by this, any more than I'd see harm done to a RL community by one unruly citizen throwing a fit in public.

Some citizens and tourists emphasise the 'virtuality' of encounters to deny that any significant harm can be experienced while online. In an attempt to legitimise their point of view Buxton compares less serious online deviant acts, such as flooding, with the heinous offline crimes of burglary and murder. While this is a clearly biased example, it does provide an insight into the perceptions of many online users. More comparatively Wilde considers the flaw in Buxton's rationalisation and problematises the issue. It becomes very complex when attempting to ascertain the level of harm done when comparing the same deviant act in both settings. As opposed to making generalist statements about levels of harm being mitigated by the 'virtuality' of online experience, the context and minutiae of the deviant act have to be considered if an accurate judgement is to be made on the levels of harm induced. The issue of harm and community is addressed briefly by LFO. While it seems that individual harm online is in question, there seems to be little disagreement over the effects of derisory illocutions upon the community:

> Autechre: If this sort of behavior is allowed on a very frequent basis, I think it likely that people will start to stay away from this community. I think this can cause harm to the people who put in money and effort to develop a community. I don't think it is likely to cause much harm to the individual who was attacked if they were a healthy adult and understand the difference between the virtual and the real world. A child might be more vulnerable to internalizing such attacks and could suffer in terms of ego development and distortion of self image.

> Aphex: Online there can be no real harm to individuals other than the sense of embarassment or unease that many of us get when attacked like this for no real reason or when we witness such an attack. Possible real damage to the community if members begin to drift away due to discomfort or bad behavior begins to elicit similar behaviors from others.

> AlderandElias: I think in a offensive situation, unless the people had known each other for a while, the group could break up. I know if I were a new or relatively new visitor and this happened I'd write off the whole experience and not come back.

> Xcite: Most people don't like to be called names and be treated with disrespect, so if nothing else they are emotionally hurt. It also makes the community more paranoid, and closed. Basically we learn not to trust and not to communicate.

> PJ: It harms the community yes. Think of my answer in the following context...real life. If you went to a shopping mall and saw a group of people arguing, using vulgar language in a loud manner, or just generally being obnoxious...would you consider returning to that mall in the future if you had another close by with the same stores?

Autechre rejects that 'adults' could experience significant levels of harm online, but in contrast recognises the potential for the community to be damaged via derisory illocutions. All narratives talk of the threat of deviant acts to the stability of the Cyberworlds community. Witnessing these acts results in feelings of 'discomfort', 'distrust', and 'paranoia' which echo Klein's (1991) observations of the wider effects of humiliation. Derisory illocutions not only have the potential to harm the targeted victim, but also have negative consequences for witnesses, and wider still, the community at large. As AlderandElias states, groups begin to break up, fragmenting the community. Individuals stop coming back to Cyberworlds for fear of victimisation. The disjunction between the perception of individual and community harm may be indicative of personal experience. While the prevalence of harassment was relatively high compared to other offences within Cyberworlds, few of the respondents reported being a victim. It would be expected that individual victim accounts of harm would tell a different story. It is also reasonable to assume that those who were victimised are less likely to return to the community, resulting in their exclusion from the research. Those who did comment on harm within Cyberworlds were far more likely to be witnesses of derisory illocutions. This would account for their preoccupation with the harm these acts have on the community as a whole.

Summary

Most forms of abuse online manifest textually. Their force to harm is dependent upon the context of the utterance, a reciprocity between interlocutors and differing power relations and that they draw on analogous verbal and physical acts from offline settings. The notion that 'real' and 'virtual' phenomena are inexorably connected indicates that these online abusive acts impact upon 'actual' lives. The ability for online injurious illocutions to convey physical violence in text affords them extra-performative muscle, where 'traditional' forms of violence are re-engineered to function online. The individual's reliance upon text online to sustain an identity makes it vulnerable to such attacks, resulting in levels of harm that may have psychological repercussions that are similar to if not more serious than consequences of offline verbal abuse. Within Cyberworlds, members made a distinction between individual and community harms. While harm to the community from derisory illocutions was considered more pertinent, it is acknowledged that personal experience of victimisation would increase the perception of harm done to the individual. In acknowledging these harms, forms of redress must be instituted if basic cyber rights are to be upheld. The following chapter traces the development of Cyberworlds regulatory mechanisms from non-structured forms of redress to more systematic modes of social control.

7 Order in cyberspace

Punishment, shaming and mediation

Bob B. Soxx: Some of these may seem trite but when ppl fail to understand the word 'no' and keep pestering you by their presence of telegrams or messages of one sort or the other there must be recourse to something to settle the matter. Stating that I or others can choose to log out is to punish the victim of such harassment and is not effective – perpetrators of harassment simply move on to another victim.

Moby: I am here to tell you that as a co-world owner for several years, we have tried it both ways, and all degrees in between. Ejecting people for bad behaviour not only doesn't work, it makes matters worse, MUCH worse. This is one area for the moment in which the REAL WORLD is far ahead of the online hi-tech world. In the real world, bad people can be put away, for as long as necessary to keep them from doing more harm to society. The debate about whether such people can be rehabilitated will go on forever. You cannot however 'jail' a Cyberworlds user. You can inconvenience them for a few minutes at best. And then, like a bee they just come back at you madder than before. You can block their Cyberworlds userid or even IP address or even block everyone from their ISP. This has the effect of blocking all other family members and countless others who may be totally innocent and may simply think that Cyberworlds is 'down'. The bad guys are not stopped for long though. They can change their name, they can change their IP address, they can come back 50 times before their mothers tell them its time for bed, and there is nothing anyone can do about it.

Cyberworlds has a history of control and regulation. From its inception members would misbehave in a variety of ways. The proliferation of bad language, the disruption of conversation, vandalism and harassment, amongst a myriad of misdemeanours, led to calls for a system-wide response. The previous extracts show how users have become increasingly concerned about methods of behavioural control. If and when presented with a disturbing scenario online the inexperienced user may consider the 'off switch' a viable avenue of escape. Indeed this is often the assumed response of individuals who have rarely, or never, experienced and lived within these online communities.

However, as users become increasingly bonded to the online community this way of dealing with troublemakers becomes unsatisfactory. Primarily this response jeopardises community cohesion and development. The need to tackle troublemakers online becomes a fundamental part of community growth. This has been evidenced in many cases, most notably in the online community LambdaMOO (Mnookin 1996). Further, if a community is to exist online then its citizens must have rights. The provision of a safe environment would be one of the most basic of these rights. However, establishing effective regulation within online environments is complex. As the second extract shows, while technical measures prove temporarily satisfactory, troublemakers often find ways back into the system. For this reason other methods of regulation have been introduced which are more dependent upon processes of mediation and shaming. The shifts in modes of regulation within Cyberworlds form the focus of this chapter.

First this chapter outlines the development and maturation of regulatory mechanisms within Cyberworlds. The tensions between those who advocate informal modes of regulation, such as community vigilantism and processes of shaming, and those who consider official methods of control more appropriate, shape this first part of the chapter. The second part of the chapter focuses upon the opinions of community members regarding the impingement of offline regulation upon life online. Third, the effectiveness of regulation within online communities is discussed. The chapter concludes with a discussion of the application of Braithwaite's (1989) theory of shaming to the online environment.

From oligarchy to vigilantism

From the inception of Cyberworlds its governance was oligarchic. Primarily the commercial arm to the venture had total control over the development of the worlds. Key individuals, called world owners, had complete control over each environment. What could be built where, how many buildings could be erected, who could visit and what they could and could not say came under the sole governance of a select group of individuals working for the corporate arm of Cyberworlds. During these nascent years membership to Cyberworlds was small. A small membership base meant regulation and control was easy to maintain under this oligarchic system. Increasing financial pressures resulted in the expansion of Cyberworlds citizenship. In tandem Cyberworlds was also being advertised as an exciting place to visit, increasing its tourist intake. These moves added an additional burden onto the oligarchic modes of governance. Increasingly community members and tourists began to self-regulate, forming their own set of rules and standards. World owners began to take a back seat in regulating their worlds as populations dramatically increased. Oligarchic governance slowly shifted to modes of community and self regulation, evidenced by the adoption of vigilante style justice. Rachel, Cavan, Farral and Buxton, all 'old timers', explain how community members would deal with deviance before more formal methods were introduced:

```
Rachel: Online punishment, rules and the breaking of them, ponderous
topics. No one has brought this up and it may be that there aren't
any other 'old timers' around who remember, so I'll do it. There
used to be no set rules other than no encroachment when building
in Alpha World. Gate was the world everyone dropped into and only
'Grays' lived there. All of the same problems in the Gate then
exist now but they were handled in a much different manner. If
someone started to badger another user, multiple people would
begin badgering the badgerer until the offender either left or
stopped the badgering, while others would tell the badgeree to mute
the badgerer. Because users were so vigilant with this vigilante
style enforcement of common decency, there was rarely a need for
the greater power of eject that we now have. That being said, there
were definitely times when eject would have been a good thing but,
as indicated, those were rare. Common decency ruled supreme.

Cavan: Actually when you really get into chats, there are many
unspoken or unwritten rules, that you just don't break. What I
meant about being careful not to offend, is that if you accidentally
offend, then the other members are quick to defend the offended
party. The offender always loses. I won't begin to go into the
numerous ways offenders can be stopped, booted or banned.

Farral: There was rarely a problem with users stepping over the
bounds of what would be considered appropriate chatting behavior.
If there was a problem, peer pressure was an effective means for
stopping the inappropriate behavior, whether it was scrolling
chat, excessive profanity or other harassing chat tactics.

Buxton: I believe the key word here is 'conduct'. During the Cy
Awards Ceremonies (where awards are given to the best builders in
CW) we basically have expectations of all attending that they show
'respect' for others during the event. If they don't show that
and conduct themselves as they would at an irl event ceremony,
we are faced with asking them to leave. We don't 'post' these
expectations...we just expect everyone to have manners and courtesy
for others. I think if everyone conducted themselves as they would
irl...then there would be no need for posted regulations.
```

In these early days until a citizen or tourist had acclimatised to the tacit rules and conventions of Cyberworlds they may have considered the virtual environment as chaotic, a place where the controls and bonds that constrain behaviour in the offline world are temporarily suspended. Buxton highlights how 'newcomers' often perceive the environment to be liminal and how this can be problematic for maintaining social order at certain Cyberworlds events. Both Rachel's and Farral's accounts show how modes of social control in the early days of Cyberworlds were devoid of any due process. Forms of vigilante justice, peer pressure and ostracism maintained order in an otherwise chaotic environment. Reid (1999) notes how the medieval practice of charivari in thirteenth- and fourteenth-century France has similar characteristics to modes of informal regulation within online communities. Charivari involved the public ridicule and physical taunting of an individual who had transcended community rules. Similarly the mediation of deviance within online environments often involves the use of shaming via textual performances. Even after the introduction of technological mechanisms to curb deviant behaviour these modes of regulation are still employed. Very often technical means of regulation can fail if the aggressor has access to esoteric knowledge such as inside information on the programming language that created the community (MacKinnon 1997a). Even if banished from the community the anonymity experienced by each community member allows for an avenue where the deviant can re-enter as another avatar. It is for these reasons that the community turns to modes of public ridicule that are intended to humiliate the virtual offender.

A common example of ritual shaming can be seen in the practice of 'toading', often found in Multi-User Domains. The process usually involves the system administrator, or the person at the peak of the community hierarchical scale, altering the appearance and/or description of the offender's persona into something shameful (commonly a toad, which can be traced back to fantasy gaming and the Dungeons and Dragons role-playing genre). A process of public ridicule then begins with the victims and other sympathetic community members venting their anger upon the offender via derisory speech. This way of controlling deviant behaviour is well established in many online communities and discussion groups (Reid 1999). However, the outcome of the shaming process is not clear. While in some circumstances the aim of the shaming is to ostracise the wrongdoer permanently, in some online communities the outcomes are more reintegrative. Within Cyberworlds many citizens reject overt crime control methods, preferring methods of reintegrative shaming and mediation:

Rocketscientist: Now, there is another way that this does work if you exclude the word 'punishment' and replace it with 'rehabilitation' though that word is too clumsy for what I mean. In other words, treat the offender as a human, determine why they are acting the way they do (often it is merely young teens who crave attention but do not know positive ways of getting attention), and meet them on level ground as an equal. This paragraph does NOT apply to older persons though. With older persons, it's often socially acceptable behavior in their country and not in ours, or, a few are just plain head-cases.

Buxton: Nothing except communicate with them. Get through to them that first time, before they get mad. It works. I've done it, and I have seen it done far more times than I have seen ejection work. The sad thing is that Cyberworlds and its volunteers are no longer about communication. Some of the Peacekeepers don't begin to have the communication skills needed to do this even if they wanted to.

```
Remy: When I have tried to mediate problems where people are being
abusive to each other, I first talk to the ppl involved separately.
Then, if I feel that it will help, I get them together and try to
help them work through the problem. I try to get them to open up
about why they were friends in the first place. Often that can be
helpful. Also, I try to find positive aspects of each. For instance,
if their builds are nice, complementing them may help to get them
talking civilly. Sometimes I have managed to get them to part on
speaking terms. In most of these cases I feel that is the best
outcome the can be achieved. However, if they cannot get past
whatever caused the trouble, I try to get them to build/chat in
different areas/worlds. If one wants to build elsewhere, I point
them to several locations where open land exists. I also explain to
them that harassing others is not taken lightly in CW, and if they
are citizens, the consequences they may face it they continue to
cause trouble. I let them both know that if they have any trouble
in the future (from each other or anyone else) they can always call
on me and I will do what I can.
```

```
Billgatessux: I most cases of abuse I'd first send a message
requesting that the perpetrator behave themselves as their language
and action where offensive to others. If they continued to attack
the given avatar I'd contact the chat rooms administrators and
inform them of the offensive person. (Most systems will boot that
person from the room at least. Some will boot them from the whole
system.) If the system administrator refused to do anything I'd
recommend the avatar being assaulted move to a system that will
help. I'd also move, recommending to others they do so as well.
If the offender logs on again as a different avatar and begins
misbehaving again, I'd repeat the same process again.
```

Rocketscientist adopts an amateur therapeutic approach to punishment. Instead of ejecting or negatively shaming the wrongdoer, a more liberal neo-rehabilitative approach is taken. Challenging the deviant's behaviour and addressing the 'root' of the problem forms part of this online therapeutic discourse. However, a distinction is drawn in relation to eligibility. Rocketscientist and others only consider this process suitable for 'young teens' who 'don't know better'. The rationalisation of deviant behaviour exhibited by 'adults' is less sympathetic. Deviant adults are either considered culturally 'alien' or suffering from a level of sociopathy. This distinction seems to work well in practice as it is believed the majority of those embarking on deviant behaviour are indeed adolescent. Continuing the therapeutic theme Buxton emphasises the value and effectiveness of communication. Condemning the Peacekeepers Buxton has recognised how a crime control model is being implemented at the cost of more therapeutic and due process methods. Both Remy's and Billgatessux's narratives of how they would deal with an online harasser illustrate how the zero tolerance policing employed by the Peacekeepers is considered a last resort, maintaining the therapeutic rhetoric. However, moderate levels of disquiet were unlikely to influence high level decisions to introduce more systematic methods of regulation, especially in light of the virtual crime wave Cyberworlds was facing.

The emergence of formal social control

While informal social control proved effective in protecting individuals and the community in the majority of cases, the increasing sophistication of the deviants within Cyberworlds called into question the effectiveness of vigilantism and shaming. As the technological architecture of Cyberworlds rapidly dated, mischievous citizens and tourists were able to find loopholes and errors in the computing code. These oversights, normally corrected with system upgrades, allowed individuals to subvert the efforts of other community members. Committing acts of vandalism and harassment became less complex, increasing their prevalence. Individuals could easily masquerade as other characters, taking on hijacked personae, or gaining access to other users' passwords, allowing buildings to be vandalised and deleted. The most prominent example illustrating how increases in deviant activity lead to the institution of official regulatory mechanisms is that of King Punisher and his 'Order' of virtual vandals.

The Order of King Punisher

During the summer of 1995 a community member was seen to rapidly change his persona (switching between King Punisher and Pharaoh) demonstrating his ability to hack into the architecture of Cyberworlds. As his abilities grew King Punisher turned to vandalism, targeting individuals who criticised his activities or who attempted to remove him from Cyberworlds utilising the established informal vigilante methods. Gradually an 'Order' of vandals emerged, led by King Punisher. Their activities became more pronounced and frequent, creating an environment that the citizens and tourists of Cyberworlds found unpredictable and 'scary'. Screen shots of King Punisher's recruiting activities can be seen in Figures 7.1–7.3. In Figure 7.1 Atomic Jello is attempting to verify the identity of monster byte, an infiltrator to the Order whose intentions are to expose their illicit activities. During the questioning King Punisher emphasises his superior technical skills by stating his ability to adopt multiple personae allowing him to escape apprehension.

Following the verification of monster byte's identity he is welcomed into the Order. Figure 7.2 depicts the inauguration of the new member. The organisation's structure is outlined by Atomic Jello, while King Punisher attempts to secure allegiance to himself and the group. A description of the current activities of the Order are given in Figure 7.3. Atomic Jello is quick to boast that the Order already attacks properties near Ground Zero, an extremely public and busy environment, while King Punisher gives details as to how the Order maintains its element of terror by delivering threatening messages to local residents.

The emergence of an organised deviant group roaming through Cyberworlds causing havoc was never an anticipation of the environment designers or the world owners. As a result of short-sightedness there were no adequate regulatory mechanisms to deal with deviance on such an organised scale. As the Order rapidly expanded and its pattern of victimisation spread to other areas, senior community members, world owners and the corporate arm to Cyberworlds began to consider a response that was equally as organised as the criminal activity they were facing. As a direct response to the threat King Punisher's Order posed to the citizens and tourists of Cyberworlds a formal policing body (Peacekeepers) was established to phase out the informal vigilante modes of regulation that proved ineffective against deviance on such a large scale.

Patterns of policing and crime prevention

The patterns of policing vandalism, amongst other deviant activities, within Cyberworlds can be neatly rationalised by using Gill's (1994) model of societal policing. Before King Punisher's organised attack on the community in 1995, social control was organised around a *community involvement* model, in that the community took responsibility for the policing and introduction of crime prevention measures on a non-structured basis (Gill 1994). World creators would monitor behaviour when they were online, forming regulations that were specific to their environment. If and when an 'incident' occurred community members could either log a complaint with the world creator who would then decide how to deal with the offender, or resort to vigilantism. Implementation of these forms of regulation was *ad hoc*, and there was no formalised method for dealing with troublesome individuals.

In a response to the organised vandal attacks engineered by King Punisher, it was recognised that an equivalent organised response had to be developed if the community were to maintain integrity. As a result the Peacekeepers were established. This was seen by community members as an important mark in the increasing civilisation of Cyberworlds, and served to increase the commitment, involvement and attachment of citizens to the community. These developments can be considered a progression to Gill's (1994) *volunteer community policing* model where the community provides some limited structure to policing. The Peacekeepers are essentially an organisation of volunteers who are formally trained to deal with rule breakers within Cyberworlds. They are a structured organisation which consists of a Peacekeeper Academy for training new recruits, and teams of Peacekeepers who work on a shift basis. A Special Response Team is dedicated to the investigation of complex and serious cases of vandalism and harassment (see Appendices 7, 8 and 9).

Figure 7.1   Atomic Jello attempting to verify the identity of monster byte

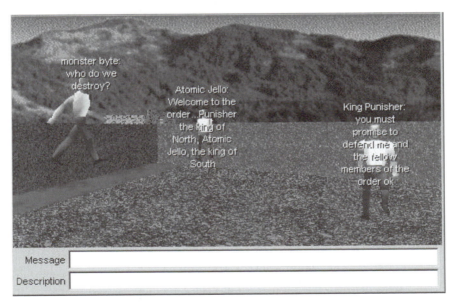

Figure 7.2   Inauguration of the new member

Figure 7.3   A description of the current activities of the Order

Tertiary crime prevention

The ability of Peacekeepers, as capable guardians (Felson 1994), to punish offenders 'on the spot' exemplifies how tertiary crime prevention developed under a more structured mode of policing. Ejecting offenders from the environment, and locking down and removing accounts are several methods employed to deter and prevent recidivism (see Appendix 6). However, these efforts to formalise social control are only marginally effective at reducing instances of vandalism, and more general acts of deviance. While the Peacekeepers may be effective at policing and reducing organised forms of deviant activity, the more sporadic acts remain prevalent. Groups of deviants are easier to identify reactively, especially if they develop a group identity. King Punisher's so-called 'Order' was recognisable by their overtly public presence, in order to 'recruit' new members, and their use of a unique marking (the use of mailboxes) left behind on all vandalised properties. The group was easily penetrable, allowing their organisation to be exposed and subverted. In contrast, random acts of vandalism by individuals are more difficult to detect. Reasons for this are twofold: first, vandals working alone may be one-time offenders meaning no pattern of offending can be identified; second, anonymity is easily maintained if individual vandals do not have an established bond to the online community.

Primary crime prevention

The method by which individuals vandalise property online is governed by their levels of technical knowledge which enables illegitimate access to other community members' building rights. To be an effective vandal within Cyberworlds you have to be a good hacker. Hackers look for weak points or loopholes in computer code which they use to gain access to secured areas, akin to Wall's (2001) categorisation of cyber *trespass*. It follows that a change in code to make it more complex and secure would have the beneficial result of reducing the ability for hackers to gain access to private areas. The code or architecture of Cyberworlds goes through this process several times a year due to advances in technology. While this process is not a direct response to the need to reduce general online deviance, it does create a *diffusion of benefits* (Pease 1997) in a routine and systematic way. One respondent demonstrates how technological advances are most effective in protecting the citizens and tourists of Cyberworlds:

```
Bilbo: CW themselves have provided us with everything we need to
censor unacceptable behaviour and/or chat, namely, Mute. What an
awesome idea! You don't like chat scrollers? Mute them! You don't
like what someone is saying? Mute them! You've told someone you
cannot or will not answer anymore questions and they continue to
ask anyway? Mute them! What is so difficult with the concept of
Mute? Our sole format for socialization in CW is the typed word.
All of the 'bad' behaviour outlined to the initial responses to
this survey question (and the vast majority of complaints from
others I've heard in my two years of citizenship in Cyberworlds)
can be remedied with a simple click, either on that person's avatar
or, if you are running CW3.0, you can simply click on that person's
chatline in the chatscreen. Once muted, when the offending words
can no longer reach your chatscreen, what else is there to do? One
of the best ways to stop that kind of behaviour is when ppl stop
responding to the perpetrators. After all, that's why they do that
in the first place. They want attention without having to spend the
time needed to establish the respect that's generally required for
civilized socialization. I don't accept the line of reasoning that
ppl in CW need to be 'protected' from bad words. If they can't take
on the responsibility of enabling a simple option in the browser,
they need to find something else to do. We already have too many
superfluous agencies, groups, etc charged with our 'protection'
where none is really needed if we just use a little common sense
and a minimum of initiative. I have never seen a compelling reason
for the existence of groups like the PKs here in Cyberworlds.
Protection of others' copywrited files? Use Digimarc if you feel
you must keep it all to yourself and password your zip files while
you're at it. Aggressive 'hackers' trying to nuke ppl's PCs while
in Cyberworlds? Get a firewall and keep it updated!
```

Advances in system technology can be considered as a form of primary crime prevention. More secure technologies increase the perceived effort for individuals to commit acts of online vandalism through a process of target hardening (Clarke 1997; Newman and Clarke 2003). Increasing the complexity and security of the code reduces the opportunity for vandalism, especially amongst opportunistic or one-time offenders. The situation within which virtual vandalism is committed is altered. It is this form of online crime prevention that allows for a systematic eradication of vandalism and other forms of online deviance. Tertiary forms employed within the community are reactive, labour intensive and have a limited scope. Primary forms, however, are relatively non-labour intensive, take immediate effect and implementation is system-wide. However, in tandem with advances in technology there are advances in hackers' abilities.

Hackers often have the ability to develop and to keep up with advances in technology. The aptitude of criminals to keep up with advances in target hardening technology is well known. For instance, safe crackers developed new methods to break into safes during a century-long technology war between the *cracksmen* and the manufacturers. This hi-tech war was eventually won by the industry – because it simply became too difficult, time-consuming and therefore too risky to break into the newer safes. However, computer code, no matter how new, complex or secure, can be compromised given time. It remains to be seen whether the hacker will go the same way as the safe cracker. However, given the insider knowledge hackers are able to acquire through their subversive employment within the information security profession, with over one-third of US corporations willing to employ hackers as security professionals (Richardson 2003), it seems unlikely that their abilities will fall short in the foreseeable future.

However, technology alone cannot regulate. Code writers or the architects of the Cyberworlds environment are ultimately responsible for creating the new technologies which eventually act as social and behavioural constraints. Regulation can then be seen as a product of the interface between the architects and available technologies. Further, these architects are constrained by the rules, norms and values of the Cyberworlds community and terrestrial laws. Regulation is then a product of the networking of these constituent parts, and can only be understood in relation to these parts. The influence that both offline and online laws have on the shaping of these technologies, and the actions of other tertiary modes of regulation, are significant and are a site of contention for many Cyberworlds citizens.

The emergence of virtual law

> Suppose you wanted to witness the birth and development of a legal system. You would need a large, complex social system that lies outside of all other legal authorities. Moreover, you would need that system somehow to accelerate the seemingly millennial progress of legal development, so you could witness more than a mere moment of the process. The hypothetical system might seem like a social scientist's fantasy, but it actually exists. It's called the Internet.
>
> (Wittes 1995: 8)

The introduction of regulatory mechanisms within Cyberworlds ensured that forms of power, control and governmentality formed part of the everyday life of citizens and tourists. In the form of community charters, bodies of law systematically replaced and embraced the tacit understandings, expectations and rules which underpinned previous methods based on vigilantism (see Appendices 3 and 4). Some rules were informed by conduct that was deemed appropriate in the 'real' world, while others were more specific to the nature of the online community itself. However, the very nature of the tacit rules and the expectations about social practice, that were existent when vigilante modes of regulation were dominant, is that they are unspoken and unwritten. The ossification of these bodies of knowledge and understanding, during the introduction of the Peacekeepers, proved complex and controversial. The key advantage to less explicit rules and regulations was their diversity in time and space. While a specific set of unstated rules operated at the Gateway at any one time, a distinctly different set of rules could operate a few hundred metres, or days away. Formalising these diverse rules proved unfeasible, leaving the community no choice but to institute a centralised body of law, lacking in degrees of variation. The extracts below show how community members often disagreed on this centralised law formation within Cyberworlds:

Bola: Now when we speak of CW, we are talking about a different matter. The laws there should come about as needed by the community and will no doubt be entirely different than RL laws. In the past vigilante law worked pretty well when citizens banded together to get rid of offenders. If you get down to it, all laws come about as needed to protect society.

Aphex: Of course, rules that don't reflect the needs of that given community will just condemn that community to fall apart. And since we exist in both online and offline communities the needs of the online community will have similar needs from the off line communities.

Autechre: As far as I know laws of real life *DO* and should apply to online activities. Anyone who thinks that when they go online that 'anything goes' will have a rude awakening eventually. Enforcement of these RL laws online is seriously lagging due to the explosion of technology. But wherever there are people involved there will eventually be laws. Hopefully those crafting those laws (and their means of enforcement) will have a bit of common sense and will have learned from experiences in real life. Such was not the case with CW.

Cocteau: If more people had a say in what goes on, I think that more people would be inclined to obey the normal rules of courtesy. This is one reason I am interested in self government for CyberWorlds, the Peacekeeper's are a dictatorship, world government should not be, it should be an iteratively interactive

consultative process, I'm trying to avoid saying 'democratic'
because that has overtones associated with the US that I'm trying
to avoid, but essentially, the nature of the technology means
that each and every citizen can be consulted about all matters
that they are interested in. This process in itself is not
necessarily healthy as 'democracy' becomes the tyranny of the
many rather than the tyranny of the few, i.e. there is no really
good government, (which is why I'm an anarchist), but I'd rather
have the chance to talk about things than not, and the chance to
input to rules imposed on me, and in fact I'm apt to ignore rules
arbitrarily imposed from above.

The primary note of contention between citizens is the application of
offline laws to the online world. A key distinction can be made between
the feelings of 'newbies' and 'old timers'. Bola's feelings towards external
regulation are typical of other 'old timers' within Cyberworlds. There are
strong feelings that the online environment is so different from offline
counterparts, in terms of physicality, demographics, geography, and
sociality, that any form of external regulation would fail to recognise the
minutiae that distinguish them. Bola states the success of the vigilante mode
of regulation was due to its embeddedness within the community. Formal,
centralised modes of regulation prove less entrenched, almost 'lifted out'
of the community they seek to regulate. MacKinnon's (1997a) notion of
'virtual just adjudication' resonates with the feelings of many 'old timers' in
Cyberworlds. The notion emphasises the importance of the 'virtual context'
and how it is often perceived to be separated from the 'offline context'.
This separation of jurisdiction calls into question a universal jurisprudence.
MacKinnon (1997a) argues that a suspect's actions should be evaluated
and judged in the local context via due process. However, contrary to this
belief, Aphex's and Autechre's viewpoints embrace the understanding that
on and offline lives are inexorably connected, a view common to 'newbies'
and a constant hurdle for those who seek to establish social, economic,
demographic and political independence from the 'real world' (see Barlow
1996 and Appendix 1).

Given these mixed opinions a hybrid set of rules and accepted ways of
conduct are in operation within Cyberworlds. The collective that exists
is phantasmagoric, a 'space penetrated by and shaped in terms of social
influences quite distant' (Giddens 1990: 19). Individuals who break rules are
subject to whatever means the community deems necessary to reconsolidate
the inappropriate action. This may take the form of reintegrative shaming
(Braithwaite 1989) or more punitive measures such as expulsion from the
community or legal proceedings in the offline world. Online deviance is
then classified as the breaking of rules, and/or ignorance of values, norms
and morals set out by the community. More generally, methods of curtailing
deviant instances are dependent upon and specific to each online community.
Online collectives can then be seen as virtual gated communities, with their
own methods of control and government.

Other examples of deviant activity online help to paint a more holistic picture of the mixed employment of offline and online regulatory mechanisms. One of the better known cases of a computer-mediated act of deviance is that of Jake Baker, a young man who posted a lurid and salaciously graphic depiction of rape of a fellow classmate (MacKinnon 1997a). The threatening story was placed on the Michigan University Bulletin Board, normally used for campus wide dissemination of information to students and staff. Resulting from this perceived 'threat' or 'harassment', Jake Baker was expelled from the university and arrested for threatening behaviour over a telecommunications network. Subsequent to the acquittal of Baker, MacKinnon (1997a: 217) contested, commenting:

> Words are never only words, but constitute acts in response to which authorities have an obligation to exercise sanctions against 'offenders' despite the civil protections usually accorded to citizens in real life.

Here we can see two mechanisms of control in operation, the non-legalistic expulsion of Baker from the University, and the subsequent legal arrest. To expand on this dual process of punishment a clearer picture of online community control and punitive measures can be seen in the Mr Bungle case addressed in the previous chapter (MacKinnon 1997a). A number of chat and role-playing sites have been noted for their explicit sexual activity between consenting participants; so called 'cybersex' or 'cybering'. Some participants employ their programming skills, particularly through 'move' commands and aggressive and sexually explicit verbiage, to 'spam' unwitting participants in ways that might be legally actionable in real life. In the most notable case of such abuse, an accomplished programmer with the persona Mr Bungle devised certain commands that allowed him to isolate and immobilise female participants in a MUD in order to spam them abusively. Detailed accounts of the incident revealed not only the consequences of the pernicious form of derision inflicted by one player on another, but also how the community was forced to address questions of standards and to create some form of mediation. As a consequence the physical act of rape had been re-engineered as a textual form, connoting a meaning that represented the relational dyad of offender and victim within the actual, in a virtual space:

> virtual rape ... is defined ... as a sexually related act of a violent or acutely debasing or profoundly humiliating nature against a character who has not explicitly consented to the interaction. Any act which explicitly references the non-consensual, involuntary exposure, manipulation, or touching of sexual organs of or by a character is considered an act of this nature.
>
> (Virtual Rape Consequences 1994)

The linguistic injury drew its vocabulary from physical injury. Further similarities can be found in the metaphor 'words that wound' in Matsuda *et al.*'s (1993) work. 'Wound' suggests that a linguistic inference or text can act in ways that parallel the infliction of pain and injury (see Chapter 6). Subsequent punitive measures involved a combination of expulsion and shaming in an attempt to mediate the deviance and injury. Ostracism and social admonition were available and were generally an effective means for enforcing community standards of behaviour (Reid 1995; MacKinnon 1995). Yet it is important to understand that a virtual punishment, such as non-reintegrative shaming, will only be successful if the existence of the punished persona matters to the computer user who created it. Unlike the Baker case Mr Bungle was not subjected to any legal proceedings. It is very doubtful that offline law could have grappled successfully with this case. Not only is the act of virtual rape questionable in law, but it is doubtful whether Mr Bungle's physical self could be identified and apprehended. Membership of these communities is characterised by a socially fluid and eclectic population, drawn from a global pool of connected Internet users, hidden by a veil of anonymity. Moreover, external interference by the state is often unwelcome within virtual communities, whose citizens prefer their own methods of mediation to curtail deviance (MacKinnon 1997b). It is clear that community members who favour the application of offline laws to the online context are short-sighted. At a slow pace terrestrial laws continue to grapple with novel and evolving forms of online deviance (Davis 2000). It is unlikely, however, given the rapid evolution of online deviant acts and their esoteric nature, that terrestrial bodies of law can increase or even sustain a comparable momentum. As a result online communities are often left to attend to their own problems. However, even the effectiveness of 'in house' regulation is in question.

Perceptions of peacekeeper effectiveness

The case of Mr Bungle can be seen as synonymous with the King Punisher case within Cyberworlds. Both were considered extreme and calculated acts of deviance (given the technical expertise required to engineer such acts) and were followed by seminal community actions. Online community charters (see Appendices 3 and 4) and sets of rules and laws were drawn up in a response to these unprecedented deviant acts in an attempt to curb their reoccurrence. Yet the question over the effectiveness of these new bodies of virtual law, and the likely success of a combined approach of online and offline regulation is still debated within Cyberworlds. The introduction of systematic modes of regulation, while at first considered a civilising advancement by community members, proved to be far less effective at curtailing deviance than previous vigilante methods:

Bola: Forms of online punishment are not effective in preventing and deterring further deviance. One reboot and the offender is off and running again. Should the offender be disconnected at the ISP level, there are plenty of free ISPs they can turn to, re-enter and begin anew.

Fourtet: Online punishments are far from effective, but you can't really do much more. In Cyberworlds The most used punishment is ejecting someone. But what else would you do? Build a Cyberworlds jail or something?

Gescom: I think it will be a while before any effective type of regulation will evolve, so in the mean time we will have to put up with a bunch of stupid, over reactive, and poorly enforceable laws to deal with.

Teamdoyobi: Online communities most severe form of punishment is banishment. For this to work it must be possible to actually identify who a user really is. Fortunately or not, the current technology makes it easy for a user to just re-incarnate themselves as another user and thwart that ultimate punishment.

There are clear levels of disenchantment with technological forms of punishment. An effective techno-mediated punishment is precluded due to the technological autonomy granted to every citizen and tourist of Cyberworlds. Bola and Teamdoyobi clearly recognise these limitations, noting how deviants can easily 're-incarnate' themselves and return with little opposition. Offenders can escape the most severe sanction of 'virtual death', making redundant the deterrent aims of punishment. These technological limitations evidence how tertiary preventative methods continue to struggle against the perpetual desire of some community members to subvert or take advantage of the technological mechanisms of Cyberworlds.

The effectiveness of online punishment is dependent upon the degree to which it brings the actions of personae into accordance with the social priorities of the online community. Within Cyberworlds, and cyberspace more generally, life and liberty are dependent upon frequent and autonomous interaction amongst interlocutors (MacKinnon 1997a). Online sanctions therefore draw their ability to punish from the restriction and disruption of the communication of the offenders (Maltz 1996). Unlike offline environments where the ultimate source of power is the manipulation of the physical and the sovereignty of nation states, the nexus of online power is located in the technological control of communication. When this technological control is not complete, the effectiveness of online punishment is in question.

The punishment options available to Peacekeepers include ejection from Cyberworlds for a short period, a lockdown of the offender's account, account closure and contacting the offender's ISP (see Appendices 5 and 6). While each of these sanctions has a disabling effect upon communication, a troublemaker can easily subvert each one if persistent. Even the most drastic sanction – the closure of account and contacting an ISP – is flawed due to the autonomy granted to all Internet users to reinvent themselves, allowing them to choose a different ISP and open a new account in Cyberworlds under a different identity. These technological shortfalls leave Peacekeepers with a limited arsenal to combat deviant activity. Not only are they ill equipped, they also face high levels of opposition from community members who believe the Peacekeepers are unaccountable and impose justice in an overtly crime control fashion.

> Adult: The very presence of these individuals [Peacekeepers] often incites bad chat behaviour. Anyone who has spent any time at Cyber World Ground Zero knows what I mean. Additionally, I believe the presence of these peace-keeping individuals has led to a general decline in the quality of chat found in public areas of Cyberworlds. Many of the people with whom I formed close online relationships have left CyberWorlds because of their distaste for this form of arbitrary chat monitoring. I have observed that, at almost any given time, CyberWorlds Ground Zero is populated with more Peacekeepers than citizens, and that the citizens/tourists that have remained as loyal, regular users are either teenage children or part of a core group of adults who are almost child-like and naive in their conversations reflecting the type of conversation that is acceptable to the controlling citizens aka Peacekeepers. Free thinking, free speech and creative conversation are things of the past.

> Autechre: So... various forms of punishment both online and offline only stand a chance of being effective if there is some forms process of oversight and review. In the case of Cyberworlds, such processes were promised, but never delivered. So the Cyberworlds community at this point really consists of the 'police', and those few users who don't mind being bullied by them.

> MiraCalix: Its pretty much human nature to resent being controlled. One way to avoid being controlled is to be among the group doing the controlling. Not uncommon for such 'control freaks' to be in police forces and government agencies in real life. Democratic forms of government that tend to work are one's where there are checks an balances on such authority. In Cyberworlds there are none. I think many of us who complain about the PKs would have a more moderate view if there were any evidence of such checks and balances in place. Saying that there are bad things that will happen without PKs in place does not resolve the issue. I maintain that bad things are happening BECAUSE the PKs are in place, and based on my historical perspective (a 4-digit user number) I am quite positive that things were better before they came along.

> Alder: As an adult, I resent being subjected to the moral judgements of a citizen-based organization of power. I have personally observed users warned and/or ejected for a certain behavior by one Peacekeeper/Gatekeeper and have seen the same type of behavior

ignored by another Peacekeeper/GK. I have also observed that these organizations seem to attract a certain type of person. I believe that a large per centage of these officials become almost giddy with the power they perceive they hold, thus, leading to some unpleasant ramifications.

Funkarma: I have little to add to Alder's very articulate comments about the incredibly chaotic inconsistencies in the enforcement of CW's guideline. The PKs are so out of control it's a joke, and not a very funny one. The only thing I want to add is that it's my observation that the selection process and management of the PKs is very poor.

Billgatessux: If the owners of CW had set out to do a case study in pathological forms of governance they could not have done a better job. Unfortunately I don't think this was their intention.

The importation of offline policing styles into Cyberworlds not only introduced the benefit of more systematic regulation, but also brought with it the problems of accountability and discretion. As the quote by Wittes (1995) at the beginning of this section elucidates, online environments, in this case Cyberworlds, are microcosms in a virtual atavistic state. These online communities, in some respects, are the modern ancestors of offline communities. Many exist without regulation, while others struggle to implement nascent forms of governance. It is no surprise to see publicly expressed concerns over the policing of online communities when similar disquiet is expressed offline. Primarily there is a general hostility towards the Peacekeepers due to their influence upon the environment. Many community members are concerned that the presence of Peacekeepers results in a decline in the quality of chat, and a subsequent decrease in community membership. Peacekeepers are seen as antagonising, often inducing the behaviour they are required to regulate. The overarching discontent lies with concern over policing and the abuse of power. Many have experienced Peacekeepers engage in bully tactics, jeopardising any form of due process. Many consider the policing system to be devoid of any oversight or review, evidenced by the selective implementation of Cyberworlds law. This has led many of the respondents, and others within the community, to the belief that Peacekeepers are unaccountable and 'out of control'. While the impetus behind these concerns originates partially from poor policing, the actual root of the disquiet is more attributable to the citizens and tourists' expectations of the online environment.

The online gated community

Such fervent reactions towards the Peacekeepers are not exclusively due to 'pathological forms of governance'. This disquiet is also explained further by more general shifts in modes of regulation. Many online communities have been heralded as 'third spaces', public spheres that replace the sanctity of traditional meeting places such as the public house or the church (Oldenburg 1999). The primary characteristic of these environments is a lack of regulation. The prominence of vigilantism and ritualistic shaming during the first few years of Cyberworlds shaped an environment that was devoid of any formal regulation. While tacit rules were in existence, their manifestation and embodiment were far less visible than offline official regulatory mechanisms. Arguably these tacit rules were effective at maintaining social order even without a clear visible presence. It was this perceived lack of formal regulation that attracted many tourists to Cyberworlds. The breakdown of informal regulation within real communities, where arguably the ability of social norms and values to control individuals is waning, has resulted in the proliferation of systematic and structural modes of social control. The expansion of the private security sector, most notably in the United States, has created social spaces characterised by over-policing and regulation. These modes of social control are embedded in everyday life and are becoming increasingly visible. The expanding infrastructure of crime prevention and community safety calls upon the support of multiple agencies within the community to regulate, police and prevent disorder (Garland 2001). These hyper-regulatory practices clearly impact on the degrees of freedom individuals are granted in their everyday lives. If restriction is not physically experienced, the psychological impacts of these practices have clearly forced some community members to seek freedom in alternative social spaces. Cyberworlds, and its once unregulatory nature, was one such alternative social space that attracted populations who felt over-regulated.

IDM: I asked them why they keep meeting here and not in real Brighton. They couldn't explain. One of them told me that this was the world of their own – they set the rules themselves and no other people (like parents or grown ups basically) would interfere.

Rocketscientist: I remember from my time as a teen and from things I've seen our US society do with teens that can make the VR realm a preferred and/or important source of forming a social group. That is having a place to hang out in the first place. In our offline world we are not friendly to letting others just hang out. Most public places are set up for specific activities. So retailers don't want teens hanging out and not spending money and sometimes when the teens are the business world still shoos them away because the view them as too loud and bothering others.

Bella: At a time when McD. was advertising as a place for teens to meet friends and enjoy some food, our local McD had local police going through the parking lot shooing teens away, and they didn't really want you to hang out longer then a hour inside. This is in a town that didn't have a big teen problem and the store itself was not being vandalized or anything. McD just felt that having a bunch of teens hanging around at 10pm on a Saturday night was scaring away old paying customers. Today Mall of America requires an adult to accompany a teen inside, police actively patrol to stop cruising and hanging out in parked cars. Most business catering to young people, cater to the under 10 and require adult supervision. Long gone are the soda shops, and roller rinks of past generations of teens to hang out. And because of our fear of drugs if teens meet in some out of the way place, like a cow pasture, you can be sure the cops will cruise buy if they know about it. In our homes adults are both working coming home tired, last thing they want is a bunch of teens hanging around. For the teenager VR is a great alternative. No police watching you, no time limits, and no constant questioning of what you are doing with your friend, and no being pushed from one location to another because people find you to be bothersome. In many ways they are correct in saying in VR they can have their own world with their own rules.

Amber: I mean most of them say socializing in VR equals 'normal socializing' which is something I basically don't believe. The sense of belonging to a group reminds me of some youth opposition underground movements that I was once involved in. There's something more in VR than people are willing to admit. I find it hard to verbalize myself. In a sense they(we) are sort of claiming VR and web in general 'independent territory' – we don't want RL authorities to mess around in VR, because VR is ours.

Cyberworlds was considered by its members to be a social arena that was untouched by the constraining regulatory mechanisms that are so pervasive within the offline world. This resulted in the re-creation of offline spaces within an online environment, built to the specification of online citizens, including and excluding whatever characteristics they chose. The creation of a 'virtual Brighton' signifies the importance of terrestrial 'place' to some citizens. Its re-creation in virtual space pays homage to its aesthetic, symbolic and cultural importance. Yet the need for a re-creation in a virtual environment questions the adequacy of terrestrial equivalents. In this particular example the case is put forward that regulatory mechanisms offline restrict the usual residents of the 'real' Brighton. Virtual Brighton, a space seemingly impermeable by offline regulation, nullifies these constraints. Bella notes how the demise of public spaces aimed at juveniles has seen the exodus of youth to the online arena. The notion of 'independent territory', as used by Amber, can be taken further to incorporate general feelings of freedom experienced within VR environments. Not only do individuals use VR to escape from the regulations imposed by agencies of social control in the real world, but also it is increasingly evident that this medium is being used to expand upon other real world constraints.

Croft: Probably being a lot older than most of you and a lot closer to the grave, I find cyberspace and VR to be REAL. Maybe different than real life, but in Cyberworlds, I can still dance. I suffer from post polio syndrome and the physical limitations of real life are considerable. Thank God the Internet came along in time for me to jump in and become young again.

```
Linda_k: In the online context greater freedom is experienced by
ppl. They are able to experiment, to be with each other, to develop
images around them that they want - unconstrained by conventional
factors experienced in offline contexts.
```

Croft describes Cyberworlds as if it is a virtual fountain of youth. Not only are individuals attracted to these online environments because of their lack of regulation, but the very technology itself provides for experiences that are precluded in an offline context. Croft's narrative is only one of many examples, from this research and others, which demonstrates how various online environments are being used as 'escapes from reality', and even as a place of refuge (Reid 1999). The ability to experiment with new identities and to remain anonymous in many online settings is attractive to those who experience over-regulation offline. Themes of escapism reoccur many times in the data suggesting that VR mediums are used increasingly as alternative spaces to the real world. It is no surprise then, to see disquiet emerging when regulatory mechanisms are imposed from above without community consultation. The online alternative 'third space' that was once devoid of overt visible regulation now mimics the very nature of the offline environment community members were trying to escape. The disenchantment felt by many community members manifests in the form of Peacekeeper criticism. The following narrative from a Peacekeeper shows how many online citizens and tourists desire certain levels of regulation, but are not willing to accept the by-product of social control:

```
Sun 0))): Peacekeeper's, like any other form of policing, is
subject to criticism and abuse. I detect the wind of those who
feel that ANY restriction on their movement/activity online and
particularly with reference to Cyberworlds is an infringement
of their 'rights', while at the same time wanting to be able to
punish the person responsible for heinous crimes. I have declared
an interest here, I am a Peacekeeper, and I think that the work on
the whole is necessary. Notice I didn't say 'good', that's not a
judgement I want to bring into play here, I want to say 'necessary'
because I want to point out the fact, as if it really needed it,
that people do not behave humanely or decently to each other if
they think they can get away with it.
```

The systematisation and ossification of rules resulted in a shift in the mode of regulation that objectified power in certain individuals. Previous modes of visceral regulation distributed power more evenly amongst the citizens of Cyberworlds. It is no surprise that animosity was felt both towards the commercial arm of Cyberworlds who instigated the change, and the Peacekeepers themselves. While similar processes may have occurred offline in many societies, the rapid rate of change within online environments ensures the maximum disruption of everyday online life. Such disruption inevitably results in elevated levels of uncertainty and anxiety. Much of the disquiet resulting from these anxieties has created the desire to reintroduce the more flexible distributed forms of regulation that were in play before the introduction of the Peacekeepers. This call for community-led policing is fuelled by the belief that offline modes of regulation remain alien to the online context.

```
Bola: Were punishments effective? Mostly, the offending party
usually left or modified his behavior. Why? Because the offender was
often shamed into modifying his behavior as he was often publicly
ridiculed for his abusive behavior. As soon as the behavior
stopped, so did the ridicule. I think that the current method of
using Peacekeeper's to police the situation actually degrades the
environment as it lends itself to give the malcontents an excuse
to don the rabble rousers' robes and stir the populace against
authority. If the same actions (sans the eject) is taken by one's
peers, then there is no rabble to rouse and one has to admit one's
own shame and guilt at being such a numbskull in the first place.
```

Similar narratives reoccurred in the focus group responses. There is a clear desire for the reintroduction of vigilante styles of regulation which are reliant upon shaming to bring about social control. The relative effectiveness of shaming in comparison to techno-mediated punishments is more than evident to community members. In many respects the advocates of the shaming process reflect the empirical evidence of its success in offline contexts (Ahmed *et al.* 2001). Shame has been considered an inevitable way in which individuals regulate themselves and others. Ahmed *et al.* (2001: 315) concisely summarise the points made by many community members in stating 'since self- and social regulation are necessary to the just and peaceful co-existence of human communities, shame is to this extent desirable'. However, there are questions over the successful application of shame in the online context. Given the unique characteristics of the online environment – anonymity, ephemerality of interaction and disinhibition – it is questionable whether the reintroduction of vigilante style regulation, which is dependent upon shaming (whether reintegrative or disintegrative), will be any more effective than organised forms of policing.

Applying shame to the online context

The vigilante forms of regulation so fervently advocated by many community members of Cyberworlds has resonance with recent moves towards mediation with young offenders in England and Wales. Braithwaite's (1989) notion of reintegrative shaming might be said to be the theoretical backbone to mediation. It has become recognised over the past few decades that an offender's moral conscience may be a far more effective deterrent against further deviance than any formal crime control mechanism. While mediation has met with moderate success in the offline world (Zender 2002), its purported success within online social arenas has resulted in its continued support by many online citizens. However, the distinction still remains –

whether or not the process of shaming results in ostracism or reintegration. While some community members see the usefulness and effectiveness of shaming as ostracism, others perceive its value in the therapeutic rhetoric that it can embody. A closer examination of Braithwaite's theory can help explicate this difference, provide insight into how shaming might operate in an online context and highlight the concordance between shame and control.

At the most basic level, Braithwaite argues that societies which are characterised by communitarianism and complex interdependencies, where the family and community play a significant role in individuals' lives, are societies that have low crime rates. A typical example is Japan, where the family maintains a significant influence on its members throughout life. Forms of informal social control, such as shame and dishonour, that can be brought upon oneself and the family by breaking rules, prevent criminal activity. Further, Braithwaite maintains that these forms of control are far more effective than more official state controls.

The theory relies on the assumption that to be shamed is undesirable, so undesirable as to prevent someone from committing a crime. Shaming can also work on two levels; it can be applied directly by an audience, be it verbal or tacit communication, such as a frown, or it can be internally applied by the wrongdoer. What is important for both forms of shaming to work is the existence of a conscience. Drawing from learning theories, Braithwaite contends that we all have a learnt conscience, or *classical conditioning*, inculcated from early childhood, which tells us the difference between wrong and right, and it is this conscience that allows us to feel the pains of shaming. To go further, Braithwaite argues that internal shaming is far more powerful than shaming by onlookers. First, shaming oneself has the benefit of immediacy – the wrongdoer knows instantly that they have done something wrong. For this reason the pains of shaming are amplified. Second, shame as punishment is more immediate as it can take effect as soon as the wrongful act has been committed. If the offender is caught, state punishments occur at a much later stage. And third, because shaming can be immediate, it has the power of educating the wrongdoer and reinforcing his or her *classical conditioning*. Here we can see clear similarities with both control and learning theories, and from this we could say Braithwaite's theory takes for granted that people are motivated to offend, and have to be pressured socially not to do so. The effectiveness of shaming is then reliant on an individual being bonded to family and wider social structures such as the community.

Following this line of argument, the existence of a bond to family and community allows for the effective use of shaming in the prevention of offending. Shaming is regarded as undesirable within the community and as a result becomes a deterrent, on both an individual and at a general level. Several studies have provided evidence to suggest that shaming is in fact more of a deterrent than more formal criminal justice sanctions.

A British government social survey asked youths to rank what they saw as the most important consequences of arrest. While only 10 per cent said the 'punishment I might get' was the most important consequence, 55 per cent said either 'what my family' or 'my girlfriend' would think about it (Zimring and Hawkins 1973). Similarly, Schwartz and Orleans (1967) carried out a deterrence study on taxpayers. Two groups of taxpayers were interviewed prior to the tax declaration day. One group were told of the penalties of income tax evasion, while the others were lectured on the moral reasons for tax compliance. The results of the study revealed a significant increase in the tax paid by the moral appeal group, while the deterrent threat was associated with no increase in tax paid compared to the control group. It seems evident then that people are far more deterred by what their peers may think rather than the punishments the criminal justice system can dispense. However, Braithwaite (1989) does not advocate a system where the state remained outside of the shaming process; he argues that the role of the state is important in further developing individuals' *classical conditioning* by taking it out of the family arena and exposing it to other, more extra-familial acts of deviance.

Braithwaite devotes considerable attention to distinguishing between shaming that is reintegrative and shaming that is not. Drawing from labelling theory, he states that shaming that is disintegrative can result in stigmatisation. Braithwaite continues to note that if shame is applied without forgiveness at a later stage then this may lead to secondary deviance, and possibly abjection in a criminal subculture. It is Braithwaite's contention that if the current 'disintegrative' shaming process in Western societies was to be replaced by 'reintegrative' practice, the result would be a reduction in recidivism. But at this point, we might want to ask the question, is not stigmatisation more of an effective deterrent than the generous liberal rehabilitationism of reintegration? Braithwaite argues no, because the point of deterrence is not the severity of the sanction but its social embeddedness; shame is more deterring when administered by persons who continue to be important to us, whether in the family or the wider community. Stigmatisation would mean being removed from your peers, whereas shaming that was reintegrative would involve a more omnipresent punishment. This line of reasoning bears many similarities to Hirschi's (1969) control theory. Citizens and tourists that are less likely to deviate due to their online significant attachments are also more prone to being shamed by these peers. These individuals place themselves in potentially harmful relations if they deviate from community expectations. Not only do strong attachments make it less likely for one to deviate, they also forge social conditions that make very effective reintegrative punishments, further increasing the unlikelihood of deviation.

The next stage in this process is the reintegration of the wrongdoer back into the community. For re-acceptance to work there can be no stigmatisation, so the disapproval must be placed on the wrongful act or the behaviour itself and not the individual as a person. This prevents any criminal label being attached to the person holistically. Once the wrongdoer has been shamed, they are forgiven and it is hoped that the severity of the shame would have re-educated them or built upon their *classical conditioning*, which would hopefully prevent recidivism.

Applying such thinking to an online context, there is little doubt that complex social relationships are played out within Cyberworlds, and similar communities. Reid (1999) and Mnookin's (1996) accounts of social interaction online show how individuals developed complex interdependencies, characterised by social and emotional bonds. It is these online interdependent social networks that provide a fertile ground for the use of shaming in deviance reduction. While the constraining effects of the family are absent within Cyberworlds, the bonds to online community for some are as significant as offline ties. Acts of shaming online invariably draw on these ties, attempting to either humiliate the wrongdoer or draw upon their *classical conditioning* in an attempt to induce feelings of guilt.

The process of shaming draws upon bonds to community in attempting to maintain social order within Cyberworlds. As Braithwaite (1989) contends, it is deterrence that is the key to crime reduction – the fear of being humiliated by your peers or being made to feel the pains of guilt. The ability of online offenders to deliver injurious illocutions in attempts to humiliate victims has already been documented (see Chapter 6). These same methods are being employed by vigilante groups to punish. Offenders are also made to feel discomfort as a result of internal guilt, triggered by a *classical conditioning*, that has expanded to encompass elements of the online social arena. Tourists and citizens that have attachments and commitments, and who are involved and believe in the community of Cyberworlds become subject to the potential pains of shaming, and as such become subjects of social control.

While some online communities have adopted humiliation and hence disintegrative tactics in order to shame wrongdoers (Reid 1999), the earlier extracts show how much of the shaming within Cyberworlds draws on a *classical conditioning*, in an attempt to induce guilt and to reintegrate the offender. Part of the reason for this disparity in approach may be technological. In Reid's example the environment was textually mediated, allowing individuals to alter the offender's appearance via their textual performances. The graphical component of Cyberworlds does not allow for such flexibility. Vigilante groups cannot change the appearance of a wrongdoer, making humiliation more difficult to achieve.

A further explanation for variance in approaches to shaming relates to levels of interdependency. Not all online environments are characterised by complex social networks. As noted in Chapter 5, there are varying degrees of attachment, commitment, involvement and belief in the Cyberworlds community. Braithwaite (1989) contends that internal shaming is more effective at reducing deviance than shame applied by onlookers. The extent to which this can be said to be an accurate portrayal of the shaming process in all online environments is dependent upon the social embeddedness of its members.

The level and complexity of interdependencies within online environments vary and are more likely to be less multifarious than those existent offline. For example, while complex social and emotional interdependencies may exist online, the more significant relationships evident in family networks are absent. As a result, online populations are characterised by varying degrees of social embeddedness in the online community. The ephemeral nature of some online relationships has undoubtedly resulted in the use of humiliation as a shaming tactic. Humiliation is a more effective punishment if the individual has no complex set of online interdependencies. In these circumstances any appeal to the individual's *classical conditioning* would fail to bring about the desired shame due to a lack of online socialisation. Stimulating internal guilt is difficult if the wrongdoer has no bond to the online community. The more draconian rituals of public ridicule then become the only effective way of shaming these less bonded individuals.

The variance in approach to shaming has consequences for the reintegration of the wrongdoer and levels of recidivism. Braithwaite postulates that shaming by onlookers, which often results in humiliation, is fundamentally disintegrative. This is because the deviant label is placed on the individual and not the deviant act itself. In the offline world, the application of the criminal label may lead to deviance amplification and recourse to criminal subcultures, thereby sustaining deviant activity. In the online social arena, it is unlikely that such a label would remain with the wrongdoer for a prolonged period given that identity online is fluid and changeable. For this reason, humiliation as shame has the function of temporary ostracisation from the peer group. Any sustained positive change in the wrongdoer is unlikely unless the offender becomes bonded to the online community. Shaming within Cyberworlds could be said to be more reintegrative (in the case of bonded individuals) because of appeals to a *classical conditioning*, and avoidance of shaming by onlookers. The therapeutic approaches referred to in the earlier narratives are similar to Braithwaite's notion of internal shaming. Offenders are asked to consider their behaviour in a mediatory context, avoiding stigmatisation and fostering reintegration.

However, the question of reciprocity between the 'actual' and the 'virtual' further complicates the online shaming process. Even though the process of shaming seems effective online (whether based on humiliation or internal guilt), the effect this has on the 'actual' person behind the deviant persona is uncertain. If the link between the online persona and the 'actual' person is tenuous, then arguably no form of shaming can have the desired effect of rehabilitation or exclusion. This leaves the question of public ridicule as punishment. In the offline world the mode of punishment as spectacle (Foucault 1986) was successful in the eighteenth and nineteenth centuries due to the offender's constant residence amongst their community peers, allowing the shaming to have a sustained effect. Yet shaming in a virtual environment is short-lived. The purpose of public ridicule must then lie in a justice based on the alleviation of the feelings of those harmed. The chief concern is to protect the community's integrity and to expel anyone that threatens its solidarity, while simultaneously repairing the harm done via a process of retribution. However, this process of justice may have the opposite effect; by encouraging community members to taunt and abuse other members, hatred and derisory performances are given a free and legitimate reign, encouraging a lack of trust and interdependence. Without trust and interdependency a community becomes fragmented where members grow ever more anxious over the possibilities of victimisation and the eventual demise of their online environment.

The application of shaming within virtual communities is complicated by the differing levels of belief, attachment, commitment and involvement to the immediate online context. Where individuals lack complex online interdependencies it is unlikely that reintegrative shaming would be effective in reducing recidivism. Alternative disintegrative shaming tactics may be more effective in humiliating the offender, but the punishment is temporary given the ephemeral and anonymous nature of the online context. In relation to Cyberworlds, vigilante modes of regulation which rely on reintegrative shaming are marginally effective when applied to bonded individuals. However, such marginal effectiveness cannot justify the use of vigilante methods alone. It seems most beneficial to combine both methods of vigilantism and organised policing, relying on techno-mediated forms of punishment where social forms fall short.

Summary

Citizens and tourists of Cyberworlds have seen dramatic system-wide shifts in regulatory practice in a relatively short space of time. What might be said to have taken centuries to have occurred in the offline world, has taken less than five years to occur online. Throughout these shifts in regulation, shaming has remained the favoured mechanism by which to maintain social control. The failure of tertiary forms of crime prevention called into question the adequacy of the Peacekeepers, resulting in a desire to reinvigorate old vigilante methods. In many respects the technology was responsible for the ineffectiveness of the Peacekeepers, yet ironically it is possible that it could also be the saviour of Cyberworlds. While situational crime prevention has been criticised in offline contexts for its micro approach to crime and its limited impact on overall crime rates, its application in Cyberworlds has proved more fruitful. Because online deviance is dependent upon technology as a mediator it leaves it susceptible to disruption. The very technologies that facilitate online deviance can also be used to prevent it. More secure computer code and tighter access control may reduce the opportunity for individuals to use technologies for the facilitation of deviant activity. The main contention is that because developments in technology occur much more regularly and rapidly than changes in online regulations and social practices, it is far more able to deal with and adapt to evolving online deviant threats. Yet technology cannot and should not regulate in isolation from social and quasi-legal modes of social control online. Social methods of control retain their function within Cyberworlds, if only to appease those citizens so fond of shaming and ostracisation. What exists within Cyberworlds is then a multi-modal regulatory framework utilising various crime prevention techniques where and when most effective.

8 Community, deviance and regulation beyond Cyberworlds

With the advent of each new technology concerns arise about its misuse. History has seen the use of technology as a tool to aid in illegal practices, and more recently it has enabled forms of derision, harassment and property damage to migrate to the virtual arena. While knowledge has been generated on how cybercrimes are affecting both social and legalistic practices, this study has provided knowledge on other forms of 'indigenous' deviance that exist within populated online environments. Credit card fraud, computer hacking and the dissemination of child pornography over computer networks are but a few of the cybercrimes already recognised in academic, legal and political discourse. To complement this growing body of knowledge, this study has drawn attention to and examined other forms of deviance that are performed on a daily basis within virtual environments, whose legal status and general acceptance remains unclear. Unlike 'conventional' cybercrimes, both the practice and the consequences of the 'indigenous' cyber deviant acts found in Cyberworlds take place within the virtual environment, complicating our understanding of their aetiology and manifestation. This study accepts 'indigenous' online deviant behaviour as a 'valid' form of inquiry to further develop our understanding of cybercrime. By examining the *modus operandi* and the aetiology of deviance within virtual environments the study has provided an insight into how online community and forms of regulation are intricately linked to its manifestation and prevalence.

Wider online community?

The increased social use of the Internet in the mid-1990s coincided with general concerns at the time over the demise of community in the 'real' world (Rheingold 1993). Social commentators rushed to substantiate their claims heralding the 'virtual' as the new homestead. While some of the claims were considered premature, what did emerge towards the end of the twentieth century was a definable online population, some of whom belonged to social groups which bore characteristics similar to those of Gemeinschaft communities. These online communities manifest in different ways. Some are purely text based and mediate discussion asynchronously, such as newsgroups and discussion boards. Others utilise newer broadband technologies to enrich social interaction, including graphics to complement the text and allow for synchronous exchanges.

This research provided an insight into one form of online community. The study began by challenging current claims that meaningful immersed interactivity is fettered by mediating technologies (Beniger 1987; Healy 1997; Lash 2001; Lockard 1997; Peck 1987). These analyses were directed at all forms of communication, including that which is mediated by computers. The example of Cyberworlds showed a distinct community, exhibiting many of the characteristics used to qualify offline community. Lockard's (1997) criticism that a reduced bandwidth in communication could not allow for a community to emerge was first challenged. In relation to Cyberworlds, individuals were enabled to create a simulation of presence via avatars. What was more important, however, was the opportunity to build within the online environment. Simulated presence, and ownership of surroundings proved to increase levels of social immersion, and enrich interactivity. It was also found that buildings helped maintain community by embedding memory, culture and history within online artefacts. Realising the non-permanence of their online existence, members would build to be remembered when offline, creating a permanent attachment to the community. These attachments served to deepen their connection with the community and other members. Online artefacts also helped maintain friendships. Those friends who shared a building project claimed their relations became embedded in the artefact. Relationships were given an added depth of meaning and longevity. Claims that relations mediated by technology become 'linear' and 'lifted out' (Lash 2001) were refuted in light of the entrenched and rich relations that characterise Cyberworlds.

Despite this, it is clear that not all online social formations or communities provide the opportunity to erect buildings creating a permanent attachment. Newsgroups, discussion lists and Internet Relay Chat are all still primarily text based. However, this does not preclude community from forming. For example, it would be incorrect to state that text-only MUDs, that predated Cyberworlds, were not communities. Text-only interaction can also increase levels of inveracity and social immersion due to the liminal nature of the online environment. Those who interact online are more likely to engage in more open exchanges, free of the social and hierarchical restrictions of the offline world they leave behind. However, while relationships may be formed quickly, they may just as rapidly disintegrate. It is likely that those text-only MUDs that have formed a community-like structure rely upon other forms of artefact to maintain a presence. Instead of building a graphic representation of a home or a memorial, a textual description of an artefact can be left behind, calling upon a passer-by to employ their imagination. Similarly, much like in Cyberworlds, text-only MUDs and other forms of online community, such as some newsgroups, create online artefacts in the form of web pages.

The research also highlighted the importance of understanding the different uses of Cyberworlds, and the Internet more generally. Not every member of Cyberworlds considered themselves a part of a community. Many of those who visit newsgroups and chat rooms feel a similar way. As Markham (1998) highlighted, those who use the Internet can be characterised into those who see it as a site of information and knowledge and those who see it as a new social and cultural space. Often, many use these online environments instrumentally, as tools to achieve a purpose. For example, those who visit a culinary newsgroup for information on how to cook a particular dish are unlikely to consider themselves a part of an online gastronomic community. However, those individuals who run the newsgroup, and regular contributors, may perceive their online social network quite differently. Some may even consider others on the newsgroup friends. This distinction was also apparent within Cyberworlds. Newbies were far more likely to perceive the environment as game-like and playful, taking time to develop fantasy online personae, making fleeting encounters, but with no interest in building. In contrast, old timers had long established friendship networks, were often involved in building, and had a serious interest in the Cyberworlds way of life. Rejecting the fantasy character of Cyberworlds, old timers also divested themselves of their fantasy online personae, removing their veil of anonymity.

When attempting to establish if online community exists, one may first consider what constitutes a community in the offline world. This is very unclear. Sociological accounts conflict, and are in constant flux. We can talk of traditional community ideals, the kind of community governments want to encourage within their towns and cities, but it is unfair to use these as a benchmark against which to evaluate online social formations. To a similar extent it is unsuitable to evaluate online social formations against current manifestations of community offline (if community still exists). The characteristics of cyberspace are quite different and unique from 'meat space'. The expectation that online social spaces need to meet the requirements of offline community to be considered equivalents is the product of one-dimensional thinking. In the same way in which Jones (1997) questions the 'validity' or primacy of face-to-face communication in relation to CMC, it is equally viable to question the primacy of offline community in the face of new emergent online social formations. However, some parallels are inevitable. One particular similarity is the extent to which people feel part of a community. As within both on and offline communities, many of its supposed members can feel abstracted, left in abjection, due to the discontinuity between their behaviours and values and the wider majorities.

Cybercrime, deviance and harm

As the title of this book denotes, the online performances subjected to analysis in this study might be considered 'virtually' criminal in that they are not quite the 'real' thing, deviant acts still to be rationalised within legal discourse, yet to be, if ever, escalated to the status of 'criminal'. Several novel forms of deviance were encountered during the research. Flooding, spoofing, harassment and online vandalism plagued the Cyberworlds community on a daily basis. Via basic statistical analysis and the application of control theory, the prevalence and dispersion of these acts was delineated and explained. Primarily those individuals that are bonded to online community, and regard online social spaces as more than fleeting ephemeral networks, are far more likely not to have a propensity towards online deviant activity. This study found that those Cyberworlds members who considered their reputation important to maintaining friendships, who engaged in building and who had internalised the community's belief system were predominantly conformist. In contrast those individuals who considered the environment game-like, rejecting it as a viable social space, were more likely to have a propensity towards deviant activity. Cyber deviants rejected the reality of their situation and actions, neutralising their behaviours via cognitive scripts that emphasised the virtuality and abstractedness of online encounters. Fuelled by disinhibition and liminality these offenders disassociate their actions from consequence, where process becomes more important than outcome.

The analysis also revealed that acts of online deviance could be distinguished by their severity and technical complexity. Tourists were more likely to take part in less technical and less serious acts such as profanity and flooding, whereas citizens, armed with more technical expertise and larger social networks, were more likely and more equipped to commit the more serious and technical acts of harassment and vandalism. The commission of the more serious acts by citizens, who were more likely to have a bond to community, was rationalised by their feelings of disenchantment, subjecting their bond to atrophy.

Relating these findings to the wider technologies that constitute the Internet requires a consideration of the different types of behaviours that we seek to understand. At the beginning of the book a distinction was made between cybercrimes and cyber deviance and harms. This distinction is based on the current terrestrial legal rationalisation of cyber phenomena. Cybercrimes are acts that contravene specific terrestrial laws in any one jurisdiction, while cyber deviance or harms are activities that contravene social norms and values within any given on or offline community. In some cases these deviant acts or harms have changed their status to cybercrimes, as seen in cases of online harassment. This trend is likely to continue if pressures, whether legal, political or social, come to a point where state intervention becomes necessary. However, in some cases, it is likely that the more esoteric or less serious acts of deviance will remain the problem of online communities.

A key issue is whether anything can be learnt from studying acts of online deviance or harms to further our understanding of cybercrime. If we take the above example of online harassment, the analysis put forward to explain its aetiology and manifestation as a harm would apply equally to its criminal incidence. At a more general level a lack of bond to online social networks or community and the liminal qualities of the Internet used to account for deviant activity in Cyberworlds could also be applied to explain an array of criminal acts, including theft of intellectual property and more general acts of online vandalism. Individuals who visit websites or use peer-to-peer networks in order to download copyrighted materials may disassociate their actions from consequence, neutralising their deviant behaviour by considering the stolen information as merely virtual, bits and bytes that are not physically tangible. Similar techniques of neutralisation can be used by hackers who deface web pages. Altering pixels seems far less deviant than spray painting government property or damaging a building. However, there are limitations to this theorising. The majority of the study was concerned with acts of deviance that manifest within online communities. Outside of these environments the theories put forward risk losing their explanatory power. Nonetheless, as online social formations continue to evolve through cycles of growth and demise, understanding how online community relates to deviant activity and its regulation becomes pressingly important.

Regulating cybercrime and deviance

The regulatory trends found in Cyberworlds relate to wider issues of Internet regulation in two main ways. First, the finding that heterogeneous regulatory approaches are more successful at reducing deviance and maintaining victim satisfaction within Cyberworlds resonates with current thinking around wider Internet governance. The second finding, that technology or architecture is an effective regulator within Cyberworlds, relates to the most current perspectives on Internet regulation. Addressing the first finding, the majority of the research participants recognised the need for both internal and external regulation. While many ardently called for 'net federalism', claiming a distinction between 'real' and 'virtual' space, in the face of extreme deviant/criminal activity facilitated by Cyberworlds, such as the homicide in Kansas, opinions were tempered, acknowledging instead the need for a joint 'online/offline' approach to regulation. This perspective was also mirrored in respondents' attitudes towards Peacekeeper activity and jurisdiction. The disenchantment expressed over the overtly crime control measures employed by the Peacekeepers highlighted the benefits, both in terms of deviance reduction and victim/community satisfaction, of a joint community-commercial regulatory partnership. The combination of the mediatory techniques that once dominated the social control infrastructure and official Peacekeepers was considered to simultaneously reflect the communities' inclusive reintegrative approach while maintaining a more systematic policing service.

This first point is reflected in much of the established thinking behind Internet regulation more generally. A combined decentralised approach to

Internet regulation has been advanced for three reasons. First, cyberspace is resistant to regulation by any particular sovereign (Greenleaf 1998). Its transnational nature makes it too complex for one body of jurisprudence to dominate. Second, the manifestation of cybercrimes, especially 'indigenous' forms of online deviant activity, can escape legal rationalisation, calling for alternative methods of redress. Lastly, a growing body of 'netizens' are claiming independence from the offline world, hence rejecting existing laws[1] that relate to physicality, instead preferring 'decentralised emergent laws' (Johnson and Post 1996). Essentially 'cyberspace does have characteristics that distinguish it from real space, and they make it more difficult for us to develop a coherent approach to how it should (or should not) be regulated by law' (Greenleaf 1998: 600). Taking the first two points, it is useful to sketch out what terrestrial laws are currently applicable to certain types of cybercrime/deviance. In particular, due to recent legal advances, avenues for offline redress for those who have suffered a form of online derision provide an insightful case (Ross 1995).

Given the non-reporting and non-recording of computer-related crime by the police, our understanding of when and where 'it' occurs is very limited. Clearly the prevalence of defamation online is unknown. While there are organisations who aim to monitor incidents of hate-speech and the like online, their efforts seem fruitless due to the *ad hoc* regulatory nature of the Internet. Further, those who have been victimised online may not define it as a crime and hence would fail to report such an incident to any authority, even if they knew what authority to report it to in the first instance. Yet this cannot mean that these acts, however prevalent, can be overlooked in offline law. Kent Greenawalt (1989) states that any analysis of the law in regard to abusive speech offline has to consider the extent to which this language has expressive value. He considers four criteria that might make such expressions criminal: 1) that they might provoke a response of violence; 2) that they may deeply wound those at whom the speech is directed; 3) that such speech causes offence to those that hear it; and 4) that slurs and epithets have a degrading effect on social relationships within any one community. However, grading each of these criteria on what is and is not acceptable discourse is exceptionally difficult – one cannot reproduce the intonations and other verbal expressions at the time of the incident.

There has been some success with the application of these criteria online. In the US for example redress may be available under vague disorderly-conduct or breach-of-the-peace provisions, where the main source of civil recovery may be the relatively novel tort of intentional infliction of mental or emotional distress. Further, with regard to Greenawalt's first criteria, the 'fighting words' doctrine established in *Chaplinsky v. New Hampshire* (1942) prohibits someone being called an 'offensive name' in a public place, 'offensive' being construed by the state court as an expression that 'men of common intelligence would understand would be likely to cause an average addressee to fight'. In the UK provision may come under defamation laws or the enactment of the Public Order Act (1986: section 18) that states:

> A person who uses threatening, abusive or insulting words or behaviour, or displays any written material which is threatening, abusive or insulting is guilty ... if (a) he intends thereby to stir up racial hatred, or (b) having regard to all the circumstances racial hatred is likely to be stirred up thereby.

However, the key question is how applicable are these laws to the online setting? If we can identify that online injurious speech can be as harmful as offline abusive speech then surely these forms of redress should be made applicable. While there are several cases running in the US regarding instances of abusive speech online, it seems as if the legal provisions are still vague. Davis (2000: 44) makes clear the decision that lies ahead:

> Despite the novelty of ... 'cyber-actions', courts face the age-old question of deciding whether to develop a new body of jurisprudence to deal with a novel legal problem, or to identify analogous legal precedents that best fit the facts at bar.

However, it seems unlikely that any current form of legislation could be adapted to deal with more 'indigenous' acts such as 'virtual rape' or 'virtual vandalism'. Recognising the level of harm induced by such acts seems the first milestone to reach. A likely answer to the immunity of these acts lies in quasi-legal methods of mediation online, where communities have their own mechanisms for redress. For example, the opportunities to 'fight back' through counter-speech may serve to prevent and/or mediate certain textual attacks online. Where the technology that sustains an online community is subverted for illicit purposes, such as in the case of virtual vandalism, the controllers of the technology might develop preventative measures, bypassing legal remedies. Ensuring higher levels of network security, and incorporating automated functions that can identify forms of abusive speech and code breaches could prevent cyber criminal/deviant activity.

The second finding, that the technology or the architecture of Cyberworlds was an effective regulator, resonates with the current legal scholarship of Greenleaf (1998), Hosein *et al.* (2003) and Lessig (1999). Regulation was exercised tri-modally within Cyberworlds – through established online values, conventions and regulations, via external bodies of applicable law and via technology. The first two modes, which might be considered sociolegal, exercised their regulation *ex post*. An offender would be punished after the deviant act had been committed. The third mode of technological regulation, which may be considered the 'nature' of Cyberworlds, exercised its regulation *ex ante*. For example, alterations in code, akin to that of situational preventative methods, prevent would-be offenders from vandalising property. The 'tightening up' of code, removing loopholes and weak spots, has the systematic effect of increasing the perceived effort, increasing the perceived risks and reducing anticipated rewards of deviant activity (Clarke 1997; Newman and Clarke 2003). This was experienced on several occasions within Cyberworlds during system-wide architectural upgrades.

The idea that technology is a more effective regulator of cyberspace than laws, norms or markets has been advanced by Lessig (1999). It was Lessig's aim to counter the technological deterministic view that the Internet could not be regulated. Instead he subscribed to a 'digital realism' that recognised the disruptive capacity of technology within cyberspace. Rejecting Boyle's (1997) notion of an Internet Holy Trinity – that regulation was impossible due to the *technology of the medium*, the *geographical distribution of its users*, and the *nature of its content* – Lessig found that the thread that links all of the Internet's characteristics together – code or architecture – could be used to control behaviour. Much in the same way that Cyberworlds architecture restricted the behaviour of deviants, Lessig saw it performing a similar function on a much wider scale.

The effectiveness of technology as regulator can be accounted for in several ways. First, technology can disrupt human action, forcing individuals to renegotiate paths and goals (Latour 2000). Second, technology, code or architecture is malleable; it is easily shaped by actors that have access to its control. Third, the way in which technology imposes constraints on how people can behave is more pervasive and immediate than other modes of regulation. Fourth, technology is more readily and rapidly adaptive than laws, norms or markets to cyber criminal threats, allowing it to control both criminal and sub-criminal behaviour. Fifth, changes to system architecture have a preventative approach. It is far more effective to prevent an online offence as opposed to reactively identifying and apprehending an offender. Finally, it is a native form of regulation making it less contentious. Often the origins of the technology are concealed, and hence its regulatory practice is perceived as less coercive than a state-sponsored regime. Technology is then perceived to be more benign, merely shaping – or even facilitating – individual choices (Boyle 1997). The effectiveness of technology as a regulator then lies in its ability to alter behaviours, its ability to be shaped, its rapid adaptability, its *ex ante* approach, its wide-reaching scope, its sensitivity towards criminal and sub-criminal activity, and its less visible approach to social control.

Examples of the effectiveness of technology as a regulator could be seen in the system-wide architectural upgrades within Cyberworlds that prevented the more *ad hoc* acts of deviance. However, not all uses of technology were so effective. The use of bots – software designed to automatically monitor profanity – within certain cities and towns caused a degree of contention amongst citizens and tourists. The bots were only programmed to identify American expletives, leaving a substantial proportion of the Cyberworlds population free to break its laws. This shortfall in the technology forms the basis argument of Hosein *et al.* (2003) which aims to complicate the role architecture or code has in regulating cyberspace. Instead of being a self-executing benign regulator, Hosein *et al.* talk of technology as a biased cultural artefact, which is embedded with subjectivity. For this reason alone, there can be no certainty that technology will produce a particular behaviour. In the case of the bots in Cyberworlds, the objective to reduce profanity failed because of the technology's reliance upon codewriters. Hosein *et al.* continue to complicate this relationship. Instead of claiming it is the technology that determines freedom and rights, they take a non-technologically deterministic approach, arguing instead that individuals (codewriters) become the alternative sovereign. Concerns are raised about the accountability of these new masked regulators, and the basis or root of their authority is questioned. They conclude by considering technology as one form of regulation that cannot be separated from other modalities. Technology, law, social norms and markets are all intricately connected, and need to remain so if regulators are to make sense of them. Online regulation should then be considered a socio-technical issue, where the nature or roots of regulation are not always made clear and are in constant flux; where its outcome is never certain, and sometimes even autonomous. Clearly further research is required to map out socio-technical relations to better understand under what set of conditions actors are able to regulate technology, and in what circumstances technology autonomously regulates behaviour.

If we are to accept that technology on its own cannot regulate, either within Cyberworlds or the Internet more generally, then reactive modalities, such as community-led and formal modes of policing, are required to regulate where technology cannot. However, achieving the right balance is complex when online community members feel such strong animosity towards external state interference. Yet if our aim is to reduce all forms of online deviance/crime then a continuum of regulation is required (Bonnici and Cannataci 2003). As Grabosky and Smith (2001: 8) note, 'much computer-related illegality lies beyond the capacity of contemporary law enforcement ... security in cyberspace will depend on the efforts of a wide range of institutions'. While it is not realistic to ask for immunity from state regulation, there are clear regions where a sovereign need not become involved. A realistic expectation is that state intervention is likely to remain where economic issues or public concerns are strong motivators. In all other cases, where the cost of intervening is likely to be non-commensurate to the outcome, a sovereign will more than likely devolve regulation to the online community members themselves (Bonnici and Cannataci 2003). This general line of thinking is shared by Grabosky and Smith (2001) who perceive the resource constrains upon governments will force them to enlist the assistance of the private sector and the 'community'.

The latter point draws attention to the policy implications of this study. In relation to regulation, where appropriate, online communities should be left to regulate themselves. Only in instances where deviant activities exceed the capacities of internal regulation should terrestrial bodies become involved. Further, online community regulators and those who create cyber law or adapt current jurisprudence to recognise online deviant behaviour should be made aware of both the power and fallibility of technology as a regulator. Of all the points raised the most significant, in terms of interpreting the Internet and the theoretical understanding of cybercrime and its potential harms, is that online interactions and events are not 'virtual'. If we were to accept them as virtual individuals and governments would be able to turn a blind eye to many cyber deviant phenomena. While this is slowly being realised in legal discourse, there needs to be a wider understanding and recognition that *virtually* criminal acts online harbour the potential to inflict harms analogous to those of *actual* criminal acts offline.

Appendix 1

Statement by the Electronic Frontier Foundation

A Declaration of the Independence of Cyberspace

by John Perry Barlow <barlow@eff.org>

Governments of the Industrial World, you weary giants of flesh and steel, I come from Cyberspace, the new home of Mind. On behalf of the future, I ask you of the past to leave us alone. You are not welcome among us. You have no sovereignty where we gather.

We have no elected government, nor are we likely to have one, so I address you with no greater authority than that with which liberty itself always speaks. I declare the global social space we are building to be naturally independent of the tyrannies you seek to impose on us. You have no moral right to rule us nor do you possess any methods of enforcement we have true reason to fear.

Governments derive their just powers from the consent of the governed. You have neither solicited nor received ours. We did not invite you. You do not know us, nor do you know our world. Cyberspace does not lie within your borders. Do not think that you can build it, as though it were a public construction project. You cannot. It is an act of nature and it grows itself through our collective actions.

You have not engaged in our great and gathering conversation, nor did you create the wealth of our marketplaces. You do not know our culture, our ethics, or the unwritten codes that already provide our society more order than could be obtained by any of your impositions.

You claim there are problems among us that you need to solve. You use this claim as an excuse to invade our precincts. Many of these problems don't exist. Where there are real conflicts, where there are wrongs, we will identify them and address them by our means. We are forming our own Social Contract . This governance will arise according to the conditions of our world, not yours. Our world is different.

Cyberspace consists of transactions, relationships, and thought itself, arrayed like a standing wave in the web of our communications. Ours is a world that is both everywhere and nowhere, but it is not where bodies live.

We are creating a world that all may enter without privilege or prejudice accorded by race, economic power, military force, or station of birth.

We are creating a world where anyone, anywhere may express his or her beliefs, no matter how singular, without fear of being coerced into silence or conformity.

Your legal concepts of property, expression, identity, movement, and context do not apply to us. They are all based on matter, and there is no matter here.

Our identities have no bodies, so, unlike you, we cannot obtain order by physical coercion. We believe that from ethics, enlightened self-interest, and the commonweal, our governance will emerge. Our identities may be distributed across many of your jurisdictions. The only law that all our constituent cultures would generally recognize is the Golden Rule. We hope we will be able to build our particular solutions on that basis. But we cannot accept the solutions you are attempting to impose.

In the United States, you have today created a law, the Telecommunications Reform Act, which repudiates your own Constitution and insults the dreams of Jefferson, Washington, Mill, Madison, DeToqueville, and Brandeis. These dreams must now be born anew in us.

You are terrified of your own children, since they are natives in a world where you will always be immigrants. Because you fear them, you entrust your bureaucracies with the parental responsibilities you are too cowardly to confront yourselves. In our world, all the sentiments and expressions of humanity, from the debasing to the angelic, are parts of a seamless whole, the global conversation of bits. We cannot separate the air that chokes from the air upon which wings beat.

In China, Germany, France, Russia, Singapore, Italy and the United States, you are trying to ward off the virus of liberty by erecting guard posts at the frontiers of Cyberspace. These may keep out the contagion for a small time, but they will not work in a world that will soon be blanketed in bit-bearing media.

Your increasingly obsolete information industries would perpetuate themselves by proposing laws, in America and elsewhere, that claim to own speech itself throughout the world. These laws would declare ideas to be another industrial product, no more noble than pig iron. In our world, whatever the human mind may create can be reproduced and distributed infinitely at no cost. The global conveyance of thought no longer requires your factories to accomplish.

These increasingly hostile and colonial measures place us in the same position as those previous lovers of freedom and self-determination who had to reject the authorities of distant, uninformed powers. We must declare our virtual selves immune to your sovereignty, even as we continue to consent to your rule over our bodies. We will spread ourselves across the Planet so that no one can arrest our thoughts.

Appendix 2

Researching the Cyberworlds environment

The burgeoning of online research over the past decade has seen significant advancements in online social science research methods. Both quantitative and qualitative methods have been re-engineered to function in environments devoid of physicality and sustained on computer networks. The methodological challenges posed by boundless research populations, multiple virtual field sites, anonymous research participants, online disinhibition and reduced social cues, to name a few, have been well documented (see Jones 1995, 1997, 1998, 1999). A detailed account of how these methodological issues were dealt with in this research is beyond the scope of this appendix. However, the author has written extensively on online social science research methodology and detailed accounts can be found in both Stewart and Williams (2005) and Williams (2006).

Both online participant observation and 'virtual' focus groups were utilised in the collection of qualitative data within Cyberworlds. In order to become familiar with the virtual graphical surroundings of Cyberworlds and to begin to understand how avatars interacted and behaved with each other and their environment a period of participant observation was required. Observation was conducted over a six month period within Cyberworlds. Observation was delineated into 'avatar watching' and a detailed examination of the graphical environment (parks, homes, churches, graveyards, monuments, shopping malls etc.). Close attention was paid to interlocutory practices between avatars. Idiomatic forms of textual and visual communication were recorded digitally via Hypercam software (http://www.hyperionics.com/) while detailed fieldnotes were taken at the researcher's desk. Few instances of deviant behaviour were actually witnessed by the observer (apart from mild forms of harassment and the use of profane language). However, there was never an expectation that cyber deviant phenomena would be experienced firsthand. Needless to say, nor is this an expectation in terrestrial criminological research. Both the focus group online and secondary offence data provided the necessary evidence of cyber deviant activity for analysis (for a more detailed discussion of online participant observation see Williams 2006).

The online focus group consisted of 60 respondents recruited from the newsgroups supporting the Cyberworlds community. Unlike terrestrial focus groups significantly more respondents can be recruited due to the ease of mediation afforded by the Internet and the extended length of questioning. In total the asynchronous online focus group ran for a period of 60 days allowing each respondent to engage in the discussion at their leisure. Three sets of discussion starter questions were posed to the group at various stages. These included questions on online community, deviance and regulation. At the end of the focus group stage approximately 70,000 words of discussion data had been collected. These data were subsequently analysed using code and retrieve techniques within the computer aided qualitative data analysis software Atlas.ti (for a more detailed discussion of the use of online focus groups see Stewart and Williams 2005).

During the course of the fieldwork access was gained to offence data collected by Peacekeepers within Cyberworlds. During the nine years the Peacekeepers have been active, offence incidents resulting in the ejection of offenders were recorded on an *ad hoc* basis. Over the past five years a more systematic system for recording offences was introduced. Access was gained to offence records covering a six-month duration (March to August) for the year 2000. In all there were 640 recorded incidents. These data were organised by offence type and status of offender (citizen or tourist). Using the statistical package SPSS, descriptive and bivariate analyses were conducted in order to identify statistical associations between category of offence, prevalence and status of offender.

Appendix 3

Cyberworlds conduct and content guidelines

Cyberworlds Conduct Guidelines

The following constitute the general rules of behaviour while visiting Cyber Worlds in Public meeting areas (areas within 400 meters of ground zero). Please read these thoroughly.

- Please do not insult other tourists or citizens by use of inflammatory or offensive statements or images. We ask that you refrain from expressions of bigotry, racism, hatred, or profanity. Please do not harass other users, including verbal abuse or personal attacks.
- Please do not engage in racial, religious, ethnic, or sexual slurs, lewd comments, or generally disruptive behaviour in public areas.
- Public meeting areas are not appropriate spaces for cyber-sexual behaviour, sexual orientation discussions or activity.
- The use of all caps is considered shouting, please refrain from using caps unless you are intending to shout. Please refrain from flooding (continuous posting of repetitive text) as this can be annoying to users.
- Cyberworlds Inc. or its associates reserve the right to enforce compliance with these guidelines, which may include temporary ejection from the world.

Cyberworlds Content Guidelines

Cyberworlds Inc. has carefully developed the following content guidelines to promote the free-flowing exchange of ideas regarding your interests, activities and hobbies, while maintaining standards consistent with the Internet community and the societies of the world. Cyberworlds Inc. does not discriminate based on sex, age, gender, sexual orientation, ethnicity, culture, religion or socio-economic status.

Please refrain from using Cyber Worlds for the following activities:

1 Displaying material containing nudity, pornography, or sexual material of a lewd, lecherous or obscene nature and intent or that violate local, state and national laws.
2 Providing material that is grossly offensive to the online community, including blatant expressions of bigotry, prejudice, racism, hatred or excessive profanity.
3 Promoting or providing instructional information about illegal activities. Promoting physical harm or injury against any group or individual, or promoting any act of cruelty to animals. This includes, but is not limited to, the following activities: Providing instructions on how to assemble bombs, grenades and other weapons.
4 Covering excessive amounts of land in any of the Cyberworlds public building worlds, including AlphaWorld, Mars, Atlantis, Yellow, or COFMeta, by any means including bots, keyboard macros, or even manual building. Please limit land claiming to land which you can directly use to build on yourself. 'Excessive' land claiming is defined as any area greater than 1 square kilometer, or 100 cells by 100 cells.

We reserve the right to suspend or remove any world, objects or properties from the Cyber Worlds universe which is brought to our attention and which we find, in our sole discretion, violates any of these content guidelines or otherwise is in violation of the law.

Cyberworlds Inc. does not actively monitor the content of the worlds in Cyber Worlds, but we will investigate complaints of violation of these guidelines.

Please submit any such complaints to abuse@cyberworlds.com.

Users who are in violation of the Cyberworlds Inc. Content Guidelines may have their membership revoked, services cancelled and their worlds or properties, or portions of their properties, removed without warning; in which event Cyberworlds Inc. will not return the removed properties or Worlds to the offending member.

Cyberworlds Inc. is not responsible or liable for any loss of data resulting from our deletion of worlds or properties, network or system outages, file corruption or any other reasons.

The opinions and views expressed in the Cyber Worlds Universe do not reflect those of Cyberworlds Inc. The contents of the worlds are not reviewed in any way before they appear in the Cyber Worlds Universe.

Cyberworlds Inc. is not responsible for the content in any of the worlds. Users are solely responsible for their properties, and everything contained in their own worlds. Cyberworlds Inc. does not verify, endorse or otherwise vouch for the contents of any world. Users may be held legally liable for the contents of their worlds.

Cyberworlds Inc. is not responsible for the delivery of any goods or services sold or advertised through its sponsors in the worlds.

Cyberworlds Inc. also reserves the following rights:

To amend or change the Cyberworlds Inc. Content Guidelines or End User License Agreement at any time and without notice. To release current or past member information if Cyberworlds Inc. believes that a member's account is in violation of the Cyberworlds Inc. Content Guidelines or End User License Agreement, is being used to commit unlawful acts, if the information is subpoenaed and/or if Cyberworlds Inc. deems it necessary and/or appropriate. To deny membership to serious or repeat offenders of the Cyberworlds Inc. Content Guidelines or End User License Agreement. To remove members for conduct that Cyberworlds Inc. believes is harmful to other members, to non-members or to Cyberworlds Inc. as a business.

Cyberworlds Inc. makes no guarantee of availability of service and reserves the right to change, withdraw, suspend, or discontinue any functionality or feature of Cyber Worlds.

Appendix 4

Cyberworlds newsgroup charter

Charter of the news.cyberworlds.com/cwcommunity

INTRO:

The need for a moderated group is best explained by taking a casual look at the many off-topic postings in other, non-moderated group. Often times, disputes arise of personal nature or insults are thrown about with no care or regard for the rights or feelings of others. This flaming is not the purpose or intent of this particular newsgroup. We would like to avoid such problems from the start. News.cyberworlds.com/cwcommunity has been set up as a media for dissemination of Information relative to the CW community and the CW software in general. Events of interest to this community and the sharing of knowledge and community discussion will be posted here. Often times COF Inc. employees will respond directly to questions or issues they have special knowledge of or interest in. We invite you all to take an active share in this newsgroup and hope it will be a positive addition to your CW experience. Please join in and have fun.

CHARTER:

news.cyberworlds.com/cwcommunity newsgroup is a moderated newsgroup for the free exchange of information and opinions on CW culture, language, history, economics, science, and other topics related to CyberWorlds. Posts appropriate for news.cyberworlds.com/cwcommunity include, but are not restricted to, all aspects of CyberWorlds, informational posts about CW culture, history, etc. Language issues related to CW. Discussion of education, health, environmental issues , politics, elections, etc. Discussion of books, articles, webarticles, movies, etc., about CW or the 3D Internet in general. Discussion of minority issues, including language, within CW. Job opportunities within CW. Discussions involving PeaceKeepers and GateKeepers. Suggestions and tips for newcomers. Suggestions and tips for World Owners. Additions and alternative implementations of the CW client or server. COF Inc. posts relevant to the CW community and public meetings.

News.cyberworlds.com/cwcommunity newsgroup is for anyone who is interested in CW and who can follow Usenet newsgroup netiquette, basic rules of polite human interaction, and any further restrictions imposed by this charter. There is no test or requirement as to how much of an CW citizen a person is who wants to make a submission and participate. Any restrictions concerning the contents of a post are intended to keep to the topic of CW, and are not intended to restrict anyone's expression of opinions. Free speech exists within the context of CW as a topic as defined in this charter. If the topic is not about CW, forums other than news.cyberworlds.com/ cwcommunity newsgroup are probably more appropriate. Submissions unrelated to CW shall be rejected. Commercial advertisements unrelated to CW shall be rejected; all personal ads shall be rejected. Submissions containing ethnic slurs, or submissions intended to hurt any given race, religion, gender, or sexual orientation, shall be rejected. Personal attacks on individual posters will also be rejected. Attacks on COF Inc., its employees, contractors or partners will be rejected.

When major changes to the charter are to be considered, an announcement will be made on news.cyberworlds.com/cwcommunity newsgroup inviting interested people to respond and thus participate via email. The role of the moderators is to ensure the conditions of the charter are met by any submission to news.cyberworlds.com/cwcommunity newsgroup. The moderators recognize that they should be as unbiased and objective as is humanly possible. Submissions are evaluated as to whether or not (1) they are on topic, (2) they meet netiquette, (3) they are appropriate for the group membership as a group (rather than something that belongs in e-mail to an individual(s), and (4) meet any other submission standards as defined in the charter. The deletions of the rejected submissions to news.cyberworlds.com/ moderated newsgroup by the moderators should be in a timely manner. The total number of moderators shall be a minimum of 2 and a maximum of 5. Should a moderator reject a submission, s/he will delete the complete with no notice to the group or the submitter in a timely manner (usually within 48 hours). All of the other moderators shall be included in any notification of the deletion. Should the moderators as a group disagree with a moderator's decision about a submission, a minimum a coin toss majority is required to override it. Other details will be refined during the initial existence of news.cyberworlds.com/moderated newsgroup, recognizing that it is impossible to anticipate all of the details of moderation in advance. Submitters to news.cyberworlds.com/cwcommunity newsgroup should recognize the volunteer nature of the moderators, possible equipment problems with the server, etc., and keep such issues in mind when considering whether or not a post or deletion was made in a timely way. The moderators will also work among themselves to define the details of moderation, for example, addressing such issues as how many moderators are actively moderating at a time and how to deal with threads that appear to have strayed from the subject of CW. Additional moderators to the initial 2 may be recruited from the readership

Appendix 5

Peacekeepers guidelines on ejection

V.   Area of operation

The area of operation for the Peacekeepers is in the world CWGate, or any other world set as the default world by CWCom.

VI.   Eject

The authority to eject is an important tool to be carefully and judiciously used by a Peacekeeper, in order to achieve the ultimate goal of voluntary compliance with the code of conduct. It is important that Peacekeepers do not over use, nor abandon the privilege to eject, due to their personal preferences. It can be as damaging to not eject when required, as to eject when not warranted; which is why all Peacekeepers will go through a training session with their Team Leader to determine what situations may or may not warrant the use of this privilege. If you need assistance in this matter, do not hesitate to call for assistance from the Team Leader or the Peacekeeper personnel.

A.   The Customs Aide Bot has been placed at the Gate to serve as an assistant to the Peacekeepers in a couple of different areas, one area being that of ejection. The bot is programmed to automatically eject a person for saying any one of a list of programmed obscenities. When a person is ejected by the Customs Aide Bot, it will whisper to you who it ejected. It will also let the person who was ejected know what happened to them and why. The list of words that the bot ejects for is available to the Peacekeepers. Talk to your TL if you would like to have it.

The Customs Aide Bot will also provide the rules of conduct to whomever says 'world rules', either in the chat screen or by whispering to the Bot.

B.   A person may be ejected with or without prior warning based upon the Peacekeepers judgement of the situation. The number of prior warnings given, if any, is also a matter of discretion for either the Peacekeeper. When possible, it is preferable to warn a person before ejecting, particularly in the case of a citizen, who may be warned by telegram. Circumstances which warrant ejection without prior notice include, but are not limited to:

1   Prevent repetition of a severe offense such as racial or ethnic attacks; or gross obscenity or profanity.
2   Gain control of the chat text from continuous scrolling acts.
3   Stop an offender who just returns from prior ejection and initiates the same conduct.

C. The appropriate period of time an offender should be ejected for is also a judgement decision made by the Peacekeeper based upon the offenders conduct, the circumstances and the nature of the offense. Normally a minor, first offense warrants a 5 minute ejection after appropriate warnings. As the nature of the offense increases or when the offenses are repeated, longer periods of time are justified.

When performing duties as Peacekeepers, it is a requirement that all personnel maintain a chat log of their session. In the event it becomes necessary to eject a person, the chat text leading up to the ejection will be forwarded to the Team Leader; along with any other information available, such as length of time ejected, and prior incidents involving this person. If you do not know how to accomplish this, contact your Team Leader for assistance.

Appendix 6

Actions that can be taken by Peacekeepers

ACTION THAT CAN BE TAKEN	
EJECTING	Ejecting means the user is disabled from the current world location for periods of 5 min to up to an hour, stronger options are also available. The Peacekeepers are not required to warn you of this happening.
LOCKDOWNS	This means the CWCorp takes control of your account for a limited time. This is used when a citizen becomes disruptive or problematic.
ACCOUNT CLOSURE	If the above actions have not produced a positive outcome then Peacekeepers will recommend an account closure to Cyberworld.com
CONTACTING AN ISP	When previous action has not resolved a situation, a report can be compiled and sent to your Internet Service Provider with recommendation of account closure.

Appendix 7

Peacekeeper CORE website

PEACEKEEPER CORE (PKCore)		
PK36 Belfalest	Chief of the organisation	
PK24 armygeddon	Assitant Chief of the organisation, Archivist, Staff Manager	
PK39 Baron	Technical Advisor, Head of Special Response Team	
PK45 Thurstan	Web Master	
PK20 GolderUK	Head of Peacekeeper Academy	

The PKCore is the overseeing body of the Peacekeepers, where the governing guidelines
are debated and adapted to reflect the changes in community and software
Members of the PKCore may look into all of areas within the Peacekeepers.
The PKCore handles all requests for the lockdown of accounts.
All PKCore members can suspend a Peacekeeper at anytime.
No PKCore member can just make someone a Peacekeeper.

All members of the PKCore receive the email that is sent to the Peacekeeper@
cyberworlds.com email address. All members of the PKCore watch over the
Peacekeepers and correct them if they see anything wrong.

Because of the diverse personalities within the core group we can discuss, debate,
many issues within cyberworlds.

We always strive to change what is needed within the Peacekeeper to keep up with
cyberworlds.

Appendix 8

Peacekeeper Special Response Team web page

SPECIAL RESPONSE TEAM (SRT)			
PK39	Baron (SRT Head)		
PK14	Tomas	PK24	armygeddon
PK48	Medic1	PK65	Skyzack
PK67	Class 3	PK68	Fuzkat

This team handles the cases that are the hardest.
Harassment and Obscenity on a major level, vandalism of privately owned worlds, hacking of citizen accounts.

They will work with the world owners, review world logs and what ever other logs checked that are needed. They help world owners and users with technical and security issues.

Appendix 9

Peacekeeper Academy web page

The Peacekeeper Academy

The Peacekeeper Academy was established to extensively train and instruct those who wish to become effective moderators and support staff within cyberspace chat programs. The Academy is always receiving, reviewing and training new applicants who are put through an extensive six week structured program under the careful guidance of nine experienced teachers.

The program includes instruction in incident documentation, effective chat software use, user interaction and program simulations of vandalism and harassment.

Cyber Worlds Program Teachers

Within the Cyber Worlds 3D interactive chat program, users are identified by nicknames, the teachers nicknames can be found below, also each Peacekeeper has an assigned account number so they can be quickly identified by the users

Peacekeeper 20	GolderUK (Director of the Academy)
Peacekeeper 14	Tomas
Peacekeeper 16	Lady Pippin
Peacekeeper 22	RedSatin o
Peacekeeper 27	Bassa
Peacekeeper 44	Leadfoot
Peacekeeper 65	Skyzack
Peacekeeper 74	ALexander o

Glossary

ARPANET (Advanced Research Projects Agency Network) The precursor to the Internet. Developed in the late 1960s and early 1970s by the US Department of Defense as an experiment in wide-area-networking to connect together computers that were each running different systems so that people at one location could use computing resources from another location.

ASCII (American Standard Code for Information Interchange) This is the de facto world-wide standard for the code numbers used by computers to represent all the upper and lower-case Latin letters, numbers, punctuation, etc. There are 128 standard ASCII codes each of which can be represented by a 7 digit binary number: 0000000 through 1111111.

ASL **Internet** slang for 'Age, Sex and Location?'.

Avabuse The term used to describe derogatory verbiage (usually textual) directed at an **avatar**.

Avatar An online graphical representation of an **Internet** user. Often found within **VR** communities.

Bandwidth The amount of information that can be sent through an **Internet** connection. Usually measured in **bits-per-second**. A full page of English text is about 16,000 **bits**. A fast **modem** can move about 57,000 **bits** in one second. Full-motion full-screen video would require roughly 10,000,000 **bits-per-second**, depending on compression.

Baud In common usage the baud rate of a modem is how many bits it can send or receive per second. Technically, baud is the number of times per second that the carrier signal shifts value – for example a 1,200 **bits-per-second modem** actually runs at 300 baud, but it moves 4 **bits** per baud (4 × 300 = 1,200 **bits-per-second**).

BBS (Bulletin Board System) A computerised meeting and announcement system that allows people to carry on discussions, upload and download files, and make announcements without the people being connected to the computer at the same time. In the early 1990s there were many thousands of BBSs around the world; most are very small, running on a single IBM clone PC with 1 or 2 phone lines.

Binary Information consisting entirely of ones and zeros.

Bit   (Binary DigIT)   A single digit number in base-2, in other words, either a 1 or a 0. The smallest unit of computerized data. Bandwidth is usually measured in **bits-per-second**.

bps   (Bits-Per-Second)   A measurement of how fast data is moved from one place to another. A 56K modem can move about 57,000 **bits** per second.

BRB   **Internet** slang for 'Be Right Back'.

Browser   A **client** program (software) that is used to look at various kinds of **Internet** resources.

BTW   **Internet** slang for 'By The Way'.

Byte   A set of **bits** that represent a single character. Usually there are 8 **bits** in a byte, sometimes more, depending on how the measurement is being made.

Client   A software program that is used to contact and obtain data from a server software program on another computer, often across a great distance. Each client program is designed to work with one or more specific kinds of server programs, and each server requires a specific kind of client. A web browser is a specific kind of client.

CMC   (Computer-Mediated Communication) The processes via which interlocutors interact over computer **networks**. CMC can take both synchronous and asynchronous forms. Internet Relay Chat is considered synchronous while email is characterised as asynchronous. There are some discussions that erode this distinction, arguing that some modes of CMC straddle the divide between synchronous and asynchronous.

Cyberpunk   Cyberpunk was originally a cultural sub-genre of science fiction taking place in a not-so-distant, dystopian, over-industrialised society. The term grew out of the work of William Gibson and Bruce Sterling and has evolved into a cultural label encompassing many different kinds of human, machine, and punk attitudes. It includes clothing and lifestyle choices as well.

Cyberspace   Term originated by author William Gibson in his novel *Neuromancer*. The word cyberspace is currently used to describe the whole range of information resources available through computer **networks**.

Ethernet   A very common method of networking computers in a LAN. There is more than one type of ethernet. By 2001 the standard type was '100-BaseT' which can handle up to about 100,000,000 **bits-per-second** and can be used with almost any kind of computer

FAQ   (Frequently Asked Questions) FAQs are documents that list and answer the most common questions on a particular subject. There are hundreds of FAQs on subjects as diverse as pet grooming and cryptography. FAQs are usually written by people who have tired of answering the same question over and over

Fire Wall   A combination of hardware and software that separates a **network** into two or more parts for security purposes.

Flame   Originally, 'flame' meant to carry forth in a passionate manner in the spirit of honourable debate. More recently flame has come to refer to any kind of derogatory comment made online no matter how witless or crude.

Flame War   When an online discussion degenerates into a series of personal attacks against the debaters, rather than discussion of their positions. A heated exchange.

Flooding   The sending of large, repetitive messages via email or chat rooms, often causing disruption to the user and/or the server as a whole.

Gigabyte   1,000 or 1,024 **megabytes**, depending on the scale of measurement.

Home Page (or Homepage)   Several meanings. Originally, the web page that your **browser** is set to use when it starts up. The more common meaning refers to the main web page for a business, organisation or person, or simply the main page out of a collection of web pages.

Host   Any computer on a **network** that is a repository for services available to other computers on the **network**. It is quite common to have one host machine provide several services, such as SMTP (email) and HTTP (web).

HTML   (HyperText Markup Language) The coding language used to create **Hypertext** documents for use on the **World Wide Web**. HTML looks a lot like old-fashioned typesetting code, where you surround a block of text with codes that indicate how it should appear. The 'hyper' in **hypertext** comes from the fact that in HTML you can specify that a block of text, or an image, is linked to another file on the **Internet**. HTML files are meant to be viewed using a web **browser**. HTML is loosely based on a more comprehensive system for markup called SGML.

Hypertext   Generally, any text that contains links to other documents – words or phrases in the document that can be chosen by a reader and which cause another document to be retrieved and displayed.

IMHO   **Internet** slang for 'In My Humble Opinion'.

Internet   The vast collection of inter-connected **networks** that are connected using the TCP/**IP** protocols and that evolved from the **ARPANET** of the late 1960s and early 1970s. The **Internet** connects tens of thousands of independent **networks** into a vast global **Internet** and is probably the largest **wide area network** in the world.

Intranet   A private **network** inside a company or organisation that uses the same kinds of software that you would find on the public **Internet**, but that is only for internal use.

IP Number   (Internet Protocol Number) Sometimes called a dotted quad. A unique number consisting of four parts separated by dots, e.g. 165.113.245.2. Every machine that is on the **Internet** has a unique IP number – if a machine does not have an IP number, it is not really on the **Internet**. Many machines (especially servers) also have one or more domain names that are easier for people to remember.

IRC   (Internet Relay Chat) A large multi-user live chat facility. There are a number of major IRC servers around the world which are linked to each other. Anyone can create a channel and anything that anyone types in a given channel is seen by all others in that channel. Private channels can be created for multi-person conference calls.

ISP   (Internet Service Provider)   An organisation that provides access to the **Internet** in some form, usually for money.

LAN   (Local Area Network)   A computer **network** limited to the immediate area, usually the same building or floor of a building.

Listserv®   The most common kind of maillist, 'Listserv' is a registered trademark of L-Soft international, Inc. Listservs originated on BITNET but they are now common on the **Internet**.

Login   Noun or a verb. Noun: the account name used to gain access to a computer system. Not a secret (contrast with password). Verb: the act of connecting to a computer system by giving your credentials (usually your username and password)

LOL   **Internet** slang for 'Laugh Out Loud'.

Maillist   (or Mailing List/Discussion List) A (usually automated) system that allows people to send email to one address, whereupon their message is copied and sent to all of the other subscribers to the maillist. In this way, people who have many different kinds of email access can participate in discussions together. Often employed in online social science research, e.g. in the moderation of online focus groups.

Megabytes   A unit of computer memory or data storage capacity equal to 1,048,576 **bytes**.

Modem   (MOdulator, DEModulator) A device that connects a computer to a phone line. A telephone for a computer. A modem allows a computer to talk to other computers through the phone system.

MOO   (**MUD**, Object Oriented) One of several kinds of multi-user role-playing environments.

MUD   (Multi-User Domain) A (usually text-based) multi-user simulation environment. Some are purely for fun and flirting, others are used for serious software development, or education purposes and others for all that lies in between. A significant feature of most MUDs is the ability to 'build' within the online environment. Artefacts can be 'left behind' when users log off allowing them to permanently engrave their identities online.

Netiquette   The etiquette on the **Internet**.

Netizen   Derived from the term citizen, referring to a citizen of the **Internet**, or someone who uses networked resources. The term connotes civic responsibility and participation.

Network   Any time you connect two or more computers together so that they can share resources, you have a computer network.

Newbies   Individuals who are new to the **Internet, BBS,** or email.

Newsgroup   The name for discussion groups on **USENET**.

P2P Network (Peer-to-Peer)   Computer **networks** that are decentralised. Each computer on the **network** hosts sharable information which can be downloaded by any user. Because there is no central server it is difficult to close down P2P networks. The majority of **IP** theft occurs through these **networks**.

Posting   A single message entered into a **network** communications system.

Security Certificate   A chunk of information (often stored as a text file) that is used by the SSL protocol to establish a secure connection.

Spam (or Spamming)   An inappropriate attempt to use a mailing list, or USENET or other networked communications facility as if it were a broadcast medium (which it is not) by sending the same message to a large number of people. The term probably comes from a famous Monty Python skit which featured the word spam. The term may also have come from someone's low opinion of the food product with the same name, which is generally perceived as a generic content-free waste of resources (Spam® is a registered trademark of Hormel Corporation, for its processed meat product).

Telnet   The command and program used to login from one Internet site to another. The telnet command/program gets you to the **login** prompt of another host.

Threading   Common to many forms of online synchronous and asynchronous communication. Used to describe the overlapping of conversations in the same document or chat window. Different but simultaneous conversations within the same document or chat window are called threads.

Trojan Horse   A computer program that is either hidden inside another program or that masquerades as something it is not in order to trick potential users into running it. For example a program that appears to be a game or image file but in reality performs some other function. The term 'Trojan horse' comes from a mythical ruse of war. A Trojan horse computer program may spread itself by sending copies of itself from the host computer to other computers, but unlike a **virus** it will (usually) not infect other programs.

URL   (Uniform Resource Locator) The protocol used to identify web pages on the **Internet**.

USENET   A world-wide system of discussion groups, with comments passed among hundreds of thousands of machines. Not all USENET machines are on the **Internet**. USENET is completely decentralised, with over 10,000 discussion areas, called **newsgroup**s.

Virus   A chunk of computer programming code that makes copies of itself without any conscious human intervention. Some viruses do more than simply replicate themselves, they might display messages, install other software or files, delete software or files, etc. A virus requires the presence of some other program to replicate itself. Typically viruses spread by attaching themselves to programs and in some cases files; for example, the file formats for Microsoft word processor and spreadsheet programs allow the inclusion of programs called 'macros' which can in some cases be a breeding ground for viruses.

VR (Virtual Reality) The term used to describe the partial sensory immersion of an individual into a non-physical three-dimensional graphical space. To date VR environments on the **Internet** allow for three-dimensional visual immersion. Some more experimental VR environments also include audio as part of the sensory experience.

WAN (Wide Area Network) Any **Internet** or **network** that covers an area larger than a single building or campus.

Worm A worm is a **virus** that does not infect other programs. It makes copies of itself, and infects additional computers (typically by making use of **network** connections) but does not attach itself to additional programs; however a worm might alter, install, or destroy files and programs.

WWW (World Wide Web) World wide web (or simply web for short) is a term frequently used (incorrectly) when referring to the **Internet**. WWW has two major meanings. First, loosely used, the whole constellation of resources that can be accessed using Gopher, FTP, HTTP, telnet, USENET, WAIS and some other tools. Second, the universe of **hypertext** servers (HTTP servers), more commonly called 'web servers', which are the servers that serve web pages to web **browsers**.

Notes

1 Introduction

1 For a synopsis of the methodology see Appendix 2. A more thorough discussion of the 'components' of the virtual ethnography can be found in Stewart and Williams (2005) and Williams (2006).

2 For a detailed discussion of the use of online focus groups see Stewart and Williams (2005). A brief synopsis of the use of online focus groups within Cyberworlds is provided in Appendix 2.

3 MOOs (object oriented MUDs) are another type of one-to-many text-only online social space.

4 Deviance and anti-social/normative activity are taken to be banned or controlled behaviour which are likely to attract punishment or disapproval on the part of a social audience (Downes and Rock 2003).

2 The Internet, crime and society

1 It is acknowledged that in recent times the 'digital divide' has been subject to erosion as a result of government e-inclusive initiatives (such as those within the UK, UKonline, and the EU, eEurope).

2 The criticism of the *virtuality* of community is still valid, and is recognised by replacing the term virtual with online.

3 The Council of Europe published the Preliminary draft of the First Additional Protocol to the Convention on Cybercrime on the criminalisation of acts of a racist or xenophobic nature committed through computer systems on 19 February, 2002.

4 The use of the term harm in this context is not to be confused with tortuous behaviour. There is no intention to convey harmful online acts as less serious than some terrestrial crimes whose resolution can only take place via civil action. Using a harm/crime distinction as a heuristic device allows for an appreciation of the complexities and contemporary nature of some online deviant behaviours that may, in time, progress to crimes via maturation in jurisprudence.

5 It is acknowledged that a small volume of terrestrial criminal activity is not dependent upon perpetrator-victim/target temporal-spatial coalescence, e.g. certain white collar crimes.

6 However, the OCJs Survey also indicated that those from council estates and other low-income areas were more likely to admit to these crimes compared to those from affluent family, suburban and rural areas. This contrary evidence may be a result of the nature of the self-report methodology utilised. However, it is worth noting that the so called 'digital divide' is subject to erosion, due in part to governments' (both national and European level) e-inclusive initiatives.

7 Under the Telecommunications Act of 1984 (UK), a person who sends, by means of a public telecommunication system, a message or other matter that is grossly offensive or of an indecent, obscene or menacing character can be imprisoned for up to a maximum term of six months.

8 Calculations of financial loss and the actual harms suffered by corporations are difficult to perform accurately. In the case of financial organisations, for example, reports of losses at the time of reporting may be an underestimation due to the unforeseen impact security breaches may have on customer confidence.

9 Several worldwide surveys, such as those produced by the Information Security Forum and Chief Information Officer Magazine, report equally varied findings.

10 Of course, the financial gain from automated systems may outweigh the potential losses from cyber-criminal activity.

11 Such a dramatic decrease is more likely to be a result of victims shifting their reporting from online voluntary organisations to 'terrestrial' police that have instituted measures to deal with cybercrime than an actual decrease in the prevalence of cyber violence.

3 Control in cyberspace

1 The voluntary policing organisation set up to regulate the behaviour of citizens and tourists within Cyberworlds. Peacekeepers embark on training where they learn about the deviant acts that plague their community and the available sanctions at their disposal (see Appendices 6–9).

4 Establishing online community

1 A synopsis of the methodology used to gather both online observational and focus group data is provided in Appendix 2. As text can function as a part of identity online the content of responses from the focus group has been preserved in its original form. As a result several spelling and grammatical errors appear in the data extracts that were not corrected. Pseudonyms were used to protect participants' identities.

2 It is recognised that recently geographical proximity has been less of a concern for the constitution of offline community, and that sociologists and the like are less preoccupied with physicality instead recognising communities of interest and understanding.

3 Methodological details of how visual data were digitally recorded within Cyberworlds is provided in Appendix 2.

4 Coordinates used to locate avatars or spaces within Cyberworlds.

5 Magic shop.

6 Circle of Fire, former name of corporate entity of Cyberworlds.

7 Ground Zero, social space into which all avatars must first enter when visiting Cyberworlds.

5 Online deviance

1 Ejections are a form of immediate punishment dispensed by a trained Peacekeeper. Peacekeepers act as prosecutor, judge and jury in the majority of minor cases (such as the continuous use of profane language) and ejections occur rapidly based on officer discretion. More serious incidents are escalated to the appropriate authorities (including cases of harassment) such as the world owner/administrator, the corporate entity of Cyberworlds (which has the power to cancel a subscriber's account), the ISP or local terrestrial police.

2 It is acknowledged that such percentage comparisons are fundamentally flawed due to the vast differences between on and offline environments. In particular, the characteristics of the online environment under study restrict certain deviant acts often found offline, while allowing others that are so dependent upon technology that their terrestrial occurrence is precluded. Comparisons are then drawn as mere illustrations and are not intended to be taken as analytical supposition.

3 A crosstabulation was first run on category of offence by status of offender which showed a significant difference in the proportions of citizens and tourists taking part in all deviant activity ($\chi2$ (8, N=640)=198.12, p=.000). Note that these calculations were within the deviant subgroup and not the overall population of Cyberworlds.

4 Crosstabulations were then run individually on each offence by status of offender: 41.2 per cent of citizens and 20.6 per cent of tourists were ejected for harassment ($\chi2$ (1, N=640)=29.42, p=.000); 1.0 per cent of citizens and 1.6 per cent of tourists were ejected for sexual harassment ($\chi2$ (1, N=640)=0.36, p=n.s.); 25.1 per cent of citizens and 64.9 per cent of tourists were ejected for profanity ($\chi2$ (1, N=640)=86.78, p=.000); 0.5 per cent of citizens and 0.9 per cent of tourists were ejected for impersonating a Peacekeeper ($\chi2$ (1, N=640)=0.29, p=n.s.); 1.0 per cent of citizens and 0.7 per cent of tourists were ejected for racial harassment ($\chi2$ (1, N=640)=0.19, p=n.s.); 2.5 per cent of citizens and 9.8 per cent of tourists were ejected for flooding ($\chi2$ (1, N=640)=10.36, p=.001); 19 per cent of citizens and 0 per cent of tourists were ejected for vandalism ($\chi2$ (1, N=640)=92.04, p=.000); 9.0 per cent of citizens and 0.2 per cent of tourists were ejected for obscenity ($\chi2$ (1, N=640)=37.02, p=.000); 0 per cent of citizens and 1.4 per cent of tourists were ejected for unknown offences ($\chi2$ (1, N=640)=86.78, p=n.s.).

5 At the time of writing Alabama, Alaska, Arizona, California, Connecticut, Hawaii, Illinois, New Hampshire, New York, Oklahoma and Wyoming had specifically included laws against cyber stalking in their state legislation. At the federal level the Violence Against Women Act (2000) made cyber stalking a part of the interstate stalking statute.

6 A detailed analysis of the application of Hirschi's bond (attachment, commitment, involvement and belief) to the online environment is provided later in this chapter.

7 This is the rational, calculative element of Hirschi's bond. Citizens and tourists make conscious decisions to become involved in certain legitimate activities.

8 See Appendix 2 for a synopsis of the online focus group utilised in this study.

8 Community, deviance and regualtion beyond Cyberworlds

1 Existing 'terrestrial' laws such as the Public Order Act 1986, the Telecommunications Act 1984, the Computer Misuse Act 1990 and the Sexual Offences Act 2003 can and have been employed to prosecute 'cyber criminals'.

Bibliography

Ahmed, E., Harris, N., Braithwaite, J. and Braithwaite, V. (2001) *Shame Management Through Reintegration*, Cambridge: Cambridge University Press.

Akdeniz, Y. (1997) 'Governance of pornography and child pornography on the global internet: a multi-layered approach', in L. Edwards and C. Waelde (eds) *Law and the Internet: Regulating Cyberspace*, London: Hart Publishing. Available online: http://www2.warwick.ac.uk/fac/soc/law/elj/jilt/1997_1/akdeniz1/.

Akdeniz, Y., Walker, C. and Wall, D. (2000) *The Internet, Law and Society*, London: Longman.

Allen, J., Forest, S., Levi, M., Roy, H., Sutton, M. and Wilson, D. (2005) *Fraud and Technology Crimes: Findings from the 2002/03 British Crime Survey and 2003 Offending, Crime and Justice Survey*, Home Office Online Report 34/05.

Althusser, L. (1971) 'Ideology and ideological state apparatuses', in B. Bruster (ed.) *Lenin and Philosophy*, London: Monthly Review Press.

Anderson, B. (1983) *Imagined Communities: Reflections on the Origin and Spread of Nationalism*, London: Verso.

APACS (2005) 'UK Card Fraud losses reach £504.8m', press release www.apacs.org.uk.

Argyle, M. and Dean, J. (1965) 'Eye contact, distance and affiliation', *Sociometry*, 28, 289–304.

Atkinson, P. (1990) *The Ethnographic Imagination: Textual Constructions of Reality*, London: Routledge.

Austin, J.L. (1975) *How To Do Things With Words*, Cambridge, MA: Harvard University Press.

Bakhtin, M. (1965) *Rabelais and his World*, Cambridge: MIT Press.

Baldwin, J. and Bottoms, A.E. (1976) *The Urban Criminal: A Study in Sheffield*, London: Tavistock.

Barker, M. and Bridgeman, C. (1994) *Preventing Vandalism: What Works*, London: HMSO.

Barlow, J.P. (1996) *A Cyberspace Independence Declaration*, available online http://www.eff.org/ ~barlow (Accessed 12/07/98).

Baron, L. and Straus, M.A. (1989) *Four Theories of Rape in American Society: A State-Level Analysis*, New Haven, CT: Yale University Press.

Baudrillard, J. (1975) *The Mirror of Production*, St Louis, MO: Telos Press.

Baudrillard, J. (1998) *Selected Writings*, Cambridge: Polity Press.

Baym, N. (1995a) 'The emergence of community in computer-mediated communication', in S. Jones (ed.) *CyberSociety*, Newbury Park, CA: Sage.

Baym, N. (1995b) 'The performance of humor in computer-mediated communication', *Journal of Computer-Mediated Communication*, 1: 2, available online http://www. ascusc.org/jcmc/vol1/issue2/baym.html (Accessed 03/04/98).

Baym, N. (1998) 'The emergence of online community', in S. Jones (ed.) *Cybersociety 2.0*, Newbury Park, CA: Sage.

Beck, U. (1992) *Risk Society: Towards a New Modernity*, London: Sage.

Becker, H. (1963) *Outsiders: Studies in the Sociology of Deviance*, London: Free Press of Glencoe.

Becker, P.J., Byers, B. and Jipson, A. (2000) 'The contentious American debate: the First Amendment and internet-based hate speech', *International Review of Law, Computers and Technology*, 14, 1: 33–41.

Bell, D. (1976) *The Cultural Contradictions of Capitalism*, New York: Basic Books

Beniger, J.R. (1987) 'Personalization of mass media and the growth of pseudo-community', *Communication Research*, 14, 3: 54–62.

Boas, F. (1911) *The Mind of Primitive Man*, New York: Macmillan.

Bonnici, J.P.M. and Cannataci, J.A. (2003) 'Access to information: controlling access to information as a means of internet governance', *International Review of Law, Computers and Technology*, 17, 1: 51.

Boyle, J. (1997) 'Foucault in cyberspace: surveillance, sovereignty and hard-wired censors', *University of Cincinnati Law Review*, 66: 177–205, available online http://www.law.duke.edu/boylesite/foucault.htm#N_1_ (Accessed 15/04/02).

Braithwaite, J. (1989) *Crime, Shame and Reintegration*, Cambridge: Cambridge University Press.

Bruyn, S. (1966) *The Human Perspective in Sociology: The Methodology of Participant Observation*, Englewood Cliffs, NJ: Prentice-Hall.

Burkhalter, B. (1999) 'Reading race online: discovering racial identities in Usenet discussions', in M. Smith and P. Kollock (eds) *Communities in Cyberspace*, New York: Routledge.

Butler, J. (1997) *Excitable Speech: A Politics of the Performative*, London: Routledge.

Capeller, W. (2001) 'Not such a neat net: some comments on virtual criminality', *Social and Legal Studies*, 10: 229–49.

Castells, M. (1996) *The Rise of the Network Society, The Information Age: Economy, Society and Culture*, Vol. I, Oxford: Blackwell.

Castells, M. (1997) *The Power of Identity, The Information Age: Economy, Society and Culture*, Vol. II, Oxford: Blackwell.

Castells, M. (1998) *The End of the Millennium, The Information Age: Economy, Society and Culture*, Vol. III, Oxford: Blackwell.

CIA (2005) *The World Fact Book*, available online http://www.cia.gov/cia/publications/factbook/

Clark, L.S. (1998) 'Dating on the net: teens and the rise of "pure" relationships', in S. Jones (ed.) *Cybersociety 2.0*, London: Sage.

Clarke, R.V.G. (1983) 'Situational crime prevention: its theoretical basis and practical scope', in M. Tonry and N. Morris (eds) *Crime and Justice: An Annual Review of Research*, Vol. 4, Chicago, IL: University of Chicago Press.

Clarke, R.V.G. (1995) 'Situational crime prevention', in M. Tonry and D. Farrington (eds) *Building a Safer Society: Strategic Approaches to Crime Prevention*, Vol. 19, Chicago, IL: University of Chicago Press.

Clarke, R.V.G. (1997) *Situational Crime Prevention: Successful Case Studies*, 2nd edn, Guilderland, NY: Harrow and Heston.

Clarke, R.V. and Felson, M. (1993) *Routine Activity and Rational Choice: Advances in Criminology Theory*, Vol. 5, New Brunswick, NJ: Transaction Books.

Clifford, J. and Marcus, G.E. (1986) *Writing Culture: The Poetics and Politics of Ethnography*, Berkeley, CA: University of California Press.

Clinard, M.B. and Wade, A.L. (1958) 'Toward the delineation of vandalism as a sub-type in juvenile delinquency'. *The Journal of Criminal Law, Criminology and Police Science*, 48: 152–65.

Cloward, R. and Ohlin, L. (1960) *Delinquency and Opportunity: A Theory of Delinquent Gangs*, Glencoe, IL: Free Press.

Cohen, A. (1955) *Delinquent Boys: The Culture of the Gang*, Glencoe, IL: Free Press.

Cohen, S. (1973) 'Property destruction: motives and meanings', in C. Ward (ed.) *Vandalism*, London: Architectural Press.

Compaine, B.M. (2001) *The Digital Divide: Facing a Crisis or Creating a Myth*, Cambridge, MA and London: MIT Press.

Computer Industry Almanac (2005) *Internet Users by Country*, Arlington Heights, IL: Computer Industry Almanac Inc.

Correll, S. (1995) 'The ethnography of an electronic bar: the lesbian café', *The Journal of Contemporary Ethnography*, 24, 3: 485–96.

Council of Europe (2000) 'Proposal for the extension of Europol's mandate to the fight against cybercrime' *Note from Presidency to Article 36 Committee*, available online http://www.xs4all.nl/~respub/europol/cyberpol.html (Accessed 03/07/03).

Danet, B. (1998) 'Text as mask: gender, play, and performance on the Internet', in S. Jones (ed.) *CyberSociety 2.0*, Newbury Park, CA: Sage.

Danet, B. (2001) *Cyberplay: Communicating Online*, New York: Berg Publishing.

Davis, C.N. (2000) 'Personal jurisdiction in online expression cases: rejecting minimum contacts in favour of affirmative acts', *International Review of Law, Computers and Technology*, 14, 1: 43–54.

Delgado, R. (1993) 'Words that wound: a tort action for racial insults', in M.J. Matsuda, C.R. Lawrence, R. Delgado and K.W. Crenshaw (eds) *Words That Wound: Critical Race Theory, Assaultive Speech, and the First Amendment*, Boulder, CO: Westview Press.

Denning, D. (1995) 'Crime and Crypto on the Information Superhighway', *Journal of Criminal Justice Education*, 6, 2: 323–36.

Denzin, N.K. (1999) 'Cybertalk and the method of instances', in S. Jones (ed.) *Doing Internet Research*, London: Sage.

Dibbell, J. (1993) 'A rape in cyberspace; or, how an evil clown, a Haitian trickster spirit, two wizards, and a cast of dozens turned a database into a society', *The Village Voice*, available online, http://www.levity.com/julian/bungle.html (accessed 01/08/00).

Dietrich, D. (1997) '(Re)-fashioning the techno-erotic woman: gender and textuality in the cybercultural matrix', in S. Jones (ed.) *Virtual Culture: Identity and Communication in Cybersociety*, London: Sage.

Downes, D. and Rock, P. (2003) *Understanding Deviance*, Oxford: Clarendon Press.

Durkheim, E. (1951) *Suicide*, New York: Free Press.

Ellison, L. and Akdeniz, Y. (1998) 'Cyber-stalking: the regulation of harassment on the internet', *Criminal Law Review, Special Edition: Crime, Criminal Justice and the Internet*, pp. 29–48.

European Commission (1997) *Communication: Action Plan on Promoting Safe Use of the Internet*, available online http://www2.echo.lu/legal/en/internet/actplan.html (accessed 01/08/00).

European Commission (1998) *Green Paper on the Protection of Minors and Human Dignity in Audiovisual and Information Services*, Brussels: Council of Europe.

European Committee on Crime Problems (2001) *Convention on Cybercrime*, Brussels: Council of Europe.

Ezponda, J.E. (1998) '21 theses on the third environment, telepolis and daily life', Paper presented at XIV Congreso de Estudios Vascos, Spain.

Felson, M. (1994) *Crime and Everyday Life*, Thousand Oaks, CA: Pine Forge Press.

Fernback, J. (1997) 'The individual within the collective: virtual ideology and realisation of collective principles', in S. Jones (ed.) *Virtual Culture*, London: Sage.

Fielding, N.G. (1993) 'Ethnography', in N. Gilbert (ed.) *Researching Social Life*, London: Sage.

Fielding, N.G. and Lee, M.R. (1995) 'Confronting CAQDAS: choice and contingency', in R.G. Burgess (ed.) *Studies in Qualitative Methodology: Computing and Qualitative Research*, Vol. 5, London: JAI Press.

Fielding, N.G. and Lee, M.R. (1998) *Computer Analysis and Qualitative Research*, London: Sage.

Fine, G.A. (1983) *Shared Fantasy: Role-Playing Games as Social Worlds*, Chicago, IL: University of Chicago Press.

Foresight (2000) *Turning the Corner. Report of the Office of Science and Technology Crime Prevention Panel*, Department of Trade and Industry Report. London: HMSO.

Foucault, M. (1986) *Discipline and Punish: The Birth of the Prison*, Harmondsworth: Penguin.

Garland, D. (2001) *The Culture of Control: Crime and Social Order in Contemporary Society*, Chicago: University of Chicago Press.

Geertz, C. (1973) *The Interpretation of Cultures*, New York: Basic Books.

Geis, G. (2000) 'On the absence of self-control as the basis for a general theory of crime: a critique', *Theoretical Criminology*, 4, 1: 35–53.

Gibson, W. (1994) *Neuromancer*, London: HarperCollins.

Giddens, A. (1990) *The Consequences of Modernity*, Oxford: Polity Press.

Giddens, A. (1994) 'Risk, trust, reflexivity', in U. Beck, A. Giddens and S. Lash (eds) *Reflexive Modernization*, Cambridge: Polity Press.

Gill, M. (1994) *Crime at Work: Studies in Security and Crime Prevention*, Leicester: Perpetuity Press.

Glaser, B. and Strauss, A. (1967) *The Discovery of Grounded Theory*, Chicago, IL: Aldine.

Goffman, E. (1955) 'On face-work: an analysis of ritual elements in social interaction', *Psychiatry* 18: 213–31.

Goffman, E. (1971) *The Presentation of Self in Everyday Life*, Harmondsworth: Penguin.

Gordon, L.A., Loeb, M.P., Lucyshyn, W. and Richardson, R. (2005) *CSI/FBI Computer Crime and Security Survey*, Computer Security Institute, available online.

Gottfredson, M. and Hirschi, T. (1990) *A General Theory of Crime*, Stanford, CA: Stanford University Press.

Grabosky, P. and Smith, R. (1998) *Crime in the Digital Age*, Sydney: The Federation Press.

Grabosky, P. and Smith, R. (2001) 'Digital crime in the twenty-first century', *Journal of Information Ethics*, 10: 8–26.

Grace, S. (1996) *Testing Obscenity: An International Comparison of Laws and Controls Relating to Obscene Material*, Home Office Research Study 157.

Greenawalt, K. (1989) *Speech Crime and The Uses of Language*, New York: Oxford University Press.

Greenleaf, G. (1998) 'An endnote on regulating cyberspace: architecture vs law?', *University of New South Wales Law Journal*, 21: 593–622.

Gupta, A. and Ferguson, J. (1997) 'Discipline and practice: "the field" as site, method, and location in anthropology', in J. Ferguson and A. Gupta (eds), *Anthropological Locations: Boundaries and Grounds of a Field Science*, Berkeley, CA: University of California Press.

Haddon, A.C. (1911) *The Wanderings of Peoples*, Cambridge: Cambridge University Press.

Hammersley, M. and Atkinson, P. (1995) *Ethnography: Principles in Practice*, 2nd edn, London: Routledge.

Harmon, D. and Boeringer, S.B. (1997) 'A content analysis of internet-accessible written pornographic depictions', *Electronic Journal of Sociology*, available online http://www.sociology.org/ (accessed 18/09/98).

Hartling, L.M. and Luchetta, T. (1999) 'Humiliation: assessing the impact of derision, degradation, and debasement', *The Journal of Primary Prevention*, 19, 4: 259–78.

Healy, D. (1997) 'Cyberspace and place: the internet as middle landscape on the electronic frontier', in D. Porter (ed.), *Internet Culture*, New York: Routledge.

Herring, S. (1999) 'International coherence in CMC', *Journal of Computer-Mediated Communication*, 4: 4, available online http://www.ascusc.org/jcmc/vol4/issue4/herring.html (accessed 23/05/01).

Hillery, G.A. (1955) 'Definitions of community: areas of agreement', *Rural Sociology*, 20, 2: 118.

Hindelang, M.J. (1976) 'With a little help from their friends: group participation in reported delinquent behaviour', *British Journal of Criminology*, 16: 109–25.

Hine, C. (2000) *Virtual Ethnography*, London: Sage.

Hirschi, T. (1969) *Causes of Delinquency*, Los Angeles, CA: University of California Press.

Hirst, P. and Thompson, G. (1995) 'Globalisation and the future of the nation state', *Economy and Society*, 24: 408–22.

Hobbes, T. (1957) *Leviathan*, Oxford: Basil Blackwell.

Holland, K. (1995) 'Bank fraud, the old fashioned way', *Business Week*, 4 September: 88.

Hosein, G., Tsavios, P. and Whitley, E. (2003) 'Regulating architecture and architectures of regulation: contributions from information systems', *International Review of Law, Computers and Technology*, 17, 1: 85.

Information Security Breaches Survey (ISBS) (2004) London: Department of Trade and Industry

Jameson, F. (1991) *Postmodernism, or, The Cultural Logic of Late Capitalism*, London: Verso.

Jewkes, Y. (2003) *Dot.cons: Crime, Deviance and Identity on the Internet*, Uffculme: Willan Publishing.

Johnson, D.R. and Post, D. (1996) 'Law and borders: the rise of law in cyberspace', *Stanford Law Review*, 48: 1367–80.

Joinson, A.N. (1998) 'Causes and effects of disinhibition on the internet', in J. Gackenbach (ed.) *The Psychology of the Internet*, New York: Academic Press.

Joinson, A.N. (2003) *Understanding the Psychology of Internet Behaviour*, London: Palgrave Macmillan.

Jones, S. (1995) *Cybersociety: Computer Mediated Communication and Community*, Newbury Park, CA: Sage.

Jones, S. (1997) *Virtual Culture: Identity and Communication in Cybersociety*, London: Sage.

Jones, S. (1998) *Cybersociety 2.0: Revisiting Computer Mediated Communication and Community*, Newbury Park, CA: Sage.

Jones, S. (1999) *Doing Internet Research: Critical Issues and Methods for Examining the Net*, London: Sage.

Kaspersen, H. (1998) 'Fraud in relation to EFT and telebanking/teleshopping systems and applicability of criminal law', in Y. Poullet and G. Vandenberghe (eds), *Telebanking, Teleshopping and the Law*, Deventer: Kluwer Law and Taxation Publishers.

Katz, J. (1988) *Seductions of Crime*, New York: Basic Books.

Kiesler, S. and Sproull, L. (1992) 'Group decision making and communication technology', *Organizational Behaviour and Human Decision Processes*, 52: 563–78.

Kiesler, S., Siegel, J. and McGuire, T.W. (1984) 'Social psychological aspects of computer-mediated communication', *American Psychologist*, 39, 10: 356–70.

Kitchin, R. (1998) *Cyberspace: The World in the Wires*, London: John Wiley and Sons.

Klein, D.C. (1991) 'The humiliation dynamic: an overview', *Journal of Primary Prevention*, 12, 2: 93–121.

Kolko, B. and Reid, E. (1998) 'Dissolution and fragmentation: problems in on-line communities', in S.G. Jones (ed.) *Cybersociety 2.0: Revisiting Computer-Mediated Communication and Community*, Thousand Oaks, CA: Sage.

Kramarae, C. (1998) 'Feminist fictions of future technology', in S. Jones (ed.) *Cybersociety 2.0*, Newbury Park, CA: Sage.

Laclau, E. (1996) 'Why do empty signifiers matter to politics?', in E. Laclau (ed.) *Emancipation(s)*, London: Verso.

Lajoie, M. (1996) 'Psychoanalysis and cyberspace', in R. Shields (ed.) *Cultures of Internet: Virtual Spaces, Real Histories, Living Bodies*, London: Sage.

Lash, S. (2001) 'Technological forms of life', *Theory, Culture and Society*, 18, 1: 105–20.

Latour, B. (1999) *Pandora's Hope: Essays on the Reality of Science Studies*, Cambridge: Harvard University Press.

Latour, B. (2000) 'When things strike back: a possible contribution of science studies to the social sciences', *British Journal of Sociology*, 51, 1: 231–55.

Lawrence, C.R. (1993) 'If he hollers let him go: regulating racist speech on campus', in M.J. Matsuda, C.R. Lawrence, R. Delgado and K.W. Crenshaw (eds) *Words*

That Wound: Critical Race Theory, Assaultive Speech, and the First Amendment, Boulder, CO: Westview Press.

Lea, M. and Spears, R. (1991) 'Computer-mediated communication, de-individuation and group decision-making', *International Journal of Man-Machine Studies,* 34, 2: 283–301.

Lea, M. and Spears, R. (1992) 'Paralanguage and social perception in computer-mediated communication', *Journal of Organizational Computing,* 2: 569–80.

Lessig, L. (1999) *Code: And Other Laws of Cyberspace,* New York: Basic Books.

Levi, M. (2001) '"Between the risk and the reality falls the shadow": evidence and urban legends in computer fraud', in D.S. Wall (ed.) *Crime and the Internet,* London: Routledge.

Levy, S. (1984) *Hackers: Heroes of the Computer Revolution,* New York: Bantam Doubleday Dell.

Lockard, J. (1997) 'Progressive politics, electronic individualism and the myth of virtual community', in D. Porter (ed.) *Internet Culture,* London: Routledge.

Lombard, M. and Ditton, T. (1997) 'At the heart of it all: the concept of presence', *Journal of Computer-Mediated Communication,* 3: 2 available online http://www. ascusc.org/jcmc/vol3/issue2/lombard.html (accessed 23/03/00).

Lyng, S. (1990) 'Edgework: a social psychological analysis of voluntary risk taking', *American Journal of Sociology,* 95, 4: 876–921.

Machlup, F. (1962) *The Production and Distribution of Knowledge in the United States,* Princeton, NJ: Princeton University Press.

MacKinnon, R.C. (1995) 'Searching for the Leviathan in Usenet', in S. Jones (ed.) *Cybersociety: Computer Mediated Communication and Community,* Thousand Oaks, CA: Sage.

MacKinnon, R.C. (1997a) 'Punishing the persona: correctional strategies for the virtual offender', in S. Jones (ed.) *Virtual Cultures: Identity and Communication in Cybersociety,* London: Sage.

MacKinnon, R.C. (1997b) 'Virtual rape', *Journal of Computer-Mediated Communication,* 2: 4, available online http://www.ascusc.org/jcmc/vol2/issue4/ mackinnon.html (accessed 16/08/2000).

Maguire, M. (2002) 'Crime statistics: the "data explosion" and its implications', in M. Maguire, R. Morgan and R. Reiner (eds) *The Oxford Handbook of Criminology,* Oxford: Oxford University Press.

Malinowski, B. (1926) *Crime and Custom in Savage Society,* London: Routledge.

Maltz, T. (1996) 'Customary law and power in internet communities', *Journal of Computer-Mediated Communication,* 2: 1, available online http://shum.cc.huji. ac.il/jcmc/vol2/issue1/custom.html (accessed 20/11/98).

Mann, D. and Sutton, M. (1998) 'Netcrime: more change in the organisation of thieving', *British Journal of Criminology,* 38, 2: 201–29.

Mann, D. and Tuffin, R. (2000) 'Conflict on the net: a study of racism in internet newsgroups', paper presented at the British Society of Criminology Conference, Leicester University.

Mann, D., Sutton, M. and Tuffin, R. (2003) 'The evolution of hate: social dynamics in white racist newsgroups', *Internet Journal of Criminology,* available online www.flashmousepublishing.com (accessed 12/04/03).

Marcus, G. and Fischer, M. (1986) *Anthropology as Cultural Critique: an Experimental Moment in the Human Sciences,* Chicago, IL: University of Chicago Press.

Marcus, G.E. (1998) *Ethnography Through Thick and Thin*, Princeton, NJ: Princeton University Press.

Marenin, O. and Reisig, M. (1995) 'A general theory of crime and patterns of crime in Nigeria: an exploration of methodological assumptions', *Journal of Criminal Justice*, 23, 6: 501–18.

Markham, A. (1998) *Life Online: Researching Real Experience in Virtual Space*, California: Sage.

Matheson, K. and Zanna, M.P. (1988) 'Self-awareness in computer-mediated communication', *Computers in Human Behaviour*, 4: 263–85.

Matsuda, M.J., Lawrence, C.R., Delgado, R. and Crenshaw, K.W. (1993) *Words That Wound: Critical Race Theory, Assaultive Speech, and the First Amendment*, Boulder, CO: Westview Press.

Matza, D. (1964) *Becoming Deviant*, Englewood Cliffs, NJ: Prentice Hall.

McConnell International (2000) *Cybercrime ... and Punishment: Archaic Laws Threaten Global Information*, Washington, DC: McConnell International.

McLaughlin, J. (2000) 'The name still remains the same', *WebNet Journal*, Jan–Mar 2, 1: 356–65.

Mehta, M.D. and Plaza D.E. (1994) 'A content analysis of pornographic images on the internet', Paper presented at the Symposium for Free Speech and Privacy in the Information Age, Waterloo, Canada.

Meloy, J.R. (1998) 'The psychology of stalking', in J.R. Meloy (ed.) *The Psychology of Stalking: Clinical and Forensic Perspectives*, London: Academic Press.

Merton, R.K. (1938) 'Social structure and anomie', *American Sociological Review*, 3: 672–82.

Merton, R.K. and Kendall, P.L. (1946) 'The focused interview', *American Journal of Sociology*, 51: 541–57.

Miller, D. and Slater, D. (2000) *The Internet: An Ethnographic Approach*, Oxford: Berg.

Mnookin, J. (1996) 'Virtual(ly) law: the emergence of law in LambdaMOO', *Journal of Computer-Mediated Communication*, 2: 1, available online http://www.ascusc.org/jcmc/vol2/issue1/lambda.html (accessed 15/02/98).

Morely, D. and Robins, K. (1995) *Spaces of Identity: Global Media, Electronic Landscapes and Cultural Boundaries*, London: Routledge.

Morgan, D.L. (1997) *Focus Groups as Qualitative Research*, London: Sage.

Morris, P. (1994) *Bakhtin Reader*, London: Edward Arnold.

Murray, P. (1997) 'Using virtual focus groups in qualitative health research', *Qualitative Health Research*, 7, 4: 187–201.

Neumann, P. (1995) *Computer Related Risks*, Reading, MA: Addison-Wesley.

Newman, G. and Clarke, R.V. (2003) *Superhighway Robbery: Preventing E-Commerce Crime*, Cullompton: Willan Publishing.

Nguyen, D.T. and Alexander, J. (1996) 'The coming of cyberspacetime and the end of polity', in R. Shields (ed.) *Cultures of Internet: Virtual Spaces, Real Histories, Living Bodies*, London: Sage.

Nicholas, S., Povey, D., Walker, A. and Kershaw, C. (2005) *Crime in England and Wales*, London: Home Office.

NUA (2003) Internet Survey, available online, http://www.nua.com/surveys/how_many_online/index.html (accessed 22/07/03).

O'Connell, R. (2000) 'Through the looking glass: a perspective of child sex iconography in cyberspace', paper presented at British Society of Criminology Conference, Leicester University.

Oldenburg, R. (1999) *The Great Good Place*, New York: Marlowe and Company.

Paccagnella, L. (1997) 'Strategies for ethnographic research on virtual communities', *Journal of Computer-Mediated Communication*, 3: 1, available online, http://www.ascusc.org/jcmc/vol3/issue1/paccagnella.html (accessed 12/01/98).

Pease, K. (1997) 'Crime prevention', in M. Maguire, R. Morgan and R. Reiner (eds) *The Oxford Handbook of Criminology*, Oxford: Oxford University Press.

Pease, K. (2001) 'Crime futures and foresight: challenging criminal behaviour in the information age', in D.S. Wall (ed.) *Crime and the Internet*, London: Oxford University Press.

Peck, M.S. (1987) *The Different Drum: Community Making and Peace*, New York, NY: Simon and Schuster.

Petherick, W. (2000) *Cyber-Stalking: Obsessional Pursuit and the Digital Criminal*, available online, http://crimelibrary.com/criminology/cyberstalking (accessed 02/05/01).

Piore, M. and Sabel, C. (1984) *The Second Industrial Divide*, New York: Basic Books.

Poplin, D.E. (1979) *Communities: A Survey of Theories and Methods of Research*, New York: Macmillan Publishing.

Porat, M.U. (1977) *The Information Economy: Definition and Measurement*, The Office of Telecommunications Special Publications, Washington, DC: Government Printing Office.

Poster, M. (1990) *The Mode of Information: Poststructuralism and Social Context*, London: Blackwell.

Poster, M. (1998) 'Virtual ethnicity: tribal identity in an age of global communications', in S. Jones (ed.) *Cybersociety 2.0*, Newbury Park, CA: Sage.

Prandy, S.L., Norris, D., Lester, J. and Hoch, D.B. (2001) 'Expanding the guidelines for electronic communication with patients: application to a specific tool', *Journal of the American Medical Informatics Association*, 8, 4: 129–45.

Presdee, M. (2000) *Cultural Criminology and the Carnival of Crime*, London: Routledge.

Reicher, S.D., Spears, R. and Postmes, T. (1995) 'A social identity model of deindividuation phenomena', *European Review of Social Psychology*, 6: 458–79.

Reid, E. (1995) 'Virtual worlds: culture and imagination', in S. Jones (ed.), *Cyber Society: Computer Mediated Communication and Community*, Thousand Oaks, CA: Sage.

Reid, E. (1999) 'Hierarchy and power: social control in cyberspace', in P. Kollock and A. Smith (eds) *Communities in Cyberspace*, London: Routledge.

Reinharz, S. (1983) 'Experiential analysis: a contribution to feminist research', in G. Bowles and R.D. Klein (eds) *Theories of Women's Studies*, London: Routledge and Kegan Paul.

Reiss, A. (1951) 'Delinquency as the failure of personal and social controls', *American Sociological Review*, 16: 213–39.

Reno, Rt. Hon. J. (1997), *Keynote Address to the Meeting of the G8 Senior Experts Group on Transnational Organised Crime*, Chantilly, VA, available online http://www.usdoj.gov/criminal/cybercrime/agfranc.htm (accessed 20/03/02).

Reno, Rt. Hon. J. (1999) *Report on Cyberstalking: A New Challenge for Law Enforcement and Industry*, A Report from the Attorney General to the Vice President, August 1999, available online http://www.usdoj.gov/criminal/cyber-crime/cyberstalking/html (Accessed 20/03/02).

Rezabek, R. (2000) 'Online focus groups: electronic discussions for research', *Qualitative Social Research Forum*, 1: 1, available online http://www.qualitative-research.net/fqs-texte/1-00/1-00rezabek-e.htm (accessed: 15/06/01).

Rheingold, H. (1993) *The Virtual Community: Homesteading on the Electronic Frontier*, New York: HarperCollins.

Rhodes, R.A.W. (1994) 'The hollowing out of the state: the changing nature of the public services in Britain', *Policing Quarterly*, 65: 138–51.

Richardson, R. (2000) *CSI/FBI Computer Crime and Security Survey*, California: Computer Security Institute.

Richardson, R. (2003) *CSI/FBI Computer Crime and Security Survey*, California: Computer Security Institute.

Rimm, M. (1995) 'Marketing pornography on the information superhighway: a survey of 917,410 images, descriptions, short stories, and animations downloaded 8.5 million times by consumers in over 2,000 cities in forty countries, provinces and territories', *The Georgetown Law Journal*, 83: 1849–934.

Robson, K. (1998) '"Meat" in the machine: the centrality of the body in Internet interactions', in J. Richardson and A. Shaw (eds) *The Body in Qualitative Research*, London: Ashgate.

Robson, K. and Robson, M. (1999) 'Your place or mine? Ethics, the researcher and the internet', in J. Armitage and J. Roberts (eds) *Exploring Cybersociety: Social, Political, Economic and Cultural Issues*, Vol. 2, Newcastle: University of Northumbria.

Roehl, B. (1996) 'Shared worlds', *VR News*, 5, 8: 14–19.

Roehl, B. (1996) 'Shared worlds', *VR News*, 6, 9: 10–15.

Ross, E.S. (1995) 'E-mail stalking: is adequate legal protection available?' *John Marshall Journal of Computer and Information Law*, 13: 405–32.

Schafer, J.A. (2002) 'Spinning the web of hate: web-based hate propagation by extremist organisations', *Journal of Criminal Justice and Popular Culture*, 9, 2: 69–88.

Schwartz, R. and Orleans, S. (1967) 'On legal sanctions', *University of Chicago Law Review*, 34: 274–300.

Selwyn, N. and Robson, K. (1998) 'Using e-mail as a research tool', *Social Research Update*, Issue 21, available online http://www.soc.surrey.ac.uk/sru/SRU21.html (accessed 02/04/99).

Sennett, R. (1998) *The Corrosion of Character: The Personal Consequences of Work in the New Capitalism*, New York: W.W. Norton.

Sharf, B. (1999) 'Beyond netiquette: the ethics of doing naturalistic discourse research on the internet', in S. Jones (ed.) *Doing Internet Research: Critical Issues and Methods for Examining the Net*, Thousand Oaks, CA: Sage.

Shaw, D.F. (1997) 'Gay men and computer mediated communication: a case study of the Phish.Net fan community', in S. Jones (ed.) *Virtual Culture: Identity and Communication in Cybersociety*, London: Sage.

Short, J.F. and Strodtbeck, F. (1965) *Group Processes and Gang Delinquency*, Chicago, IL: University of Chicago Press.

Shroeder, R. (1997) 'Networked worlds: social aspects of multi-user virtual reality technology', *Sociological Research Online*, 2: 4, available online http://www. socresonline.org.uk/2/4/5.html (accessed 05/08/00).

Siegel, J., Dubrovsky, V., Kiesler, S. and McGuire, T.W. (1986) 'Group processes in computer-mediated communication', *Organizational Behaviour and Human Decision Processes*, 37: 242–60.

Silver, M., Conte, R., Miceli, M. and Poggi, I. (1986) 'Humiliation: feeling, social control and the construction of identity', *Journal for the Theory of Social Behaviour*, 16, 3: 269–83.

Spears, R. and Lea, M. (1992) 'Social influence and the influence of the "social" in computer-mediated communication', in M. Lea (ed.) *Contexts of Computer-Mediated Communication*, Hemel Hempstead: Harvester.

Spears, R., Lea, M. and Lee, S. (1990) 'De-individuation and group polarization in computer mediated communication', *British Journal of Social Psychology*, 29, 2: 121–34.

Sproull, L. and Kiesler, S. (1991) *Connections: New Ways of Working in the Networked Organization*, Cambridge, MA: MIT Press.

Stephenson, N. (2000) *Snow Crash*, New York: Spectra.

Sternberg, J. (1998) 'It's all in the timing: synchronous versus asynchronous computer-mediated communication', paper presented at 3rd Annual Conference of the New Jersey Communication Association, Montclair, New Jersey, available online http://homepages.nyu.edu/~js15/p-time.htm (accessed 16/05/99).

Stewart, F., Eckermann, E. and Zhou, K. (1998) 'Using the internet in qualitative public health research: a comparison of Chinese and Australian young women's perceptions of tobacco use', *Internet Journal of Health Promotion*, 12, available online http://www.monash.edu.au/heath/IJHP/1998/12 (accessed 12/08/99).

Stewart, K. and Williams, M. (2005) 'Researching online populations: the use of online focus groups for social research', *Qualitative Research*, 5, 4: 395–416.

Stinchcombe, A.L (1964) *Rebellion in a High School*, Chicago, IL: Quadrangle Books.

Sussmann, M.A. (1999) 'The critical challenges from international high-tech and computer-related crime at the millennium', *Duke Journal of Comparative and International Law*, 9: 451.

Sykes, G.M. and Matza, D. (1957) 'Techniques of neutralization: a theory of delinquency', *American Sociological Review*, 22: 664–70.

Taylor, P. (1999) *Hackers: Crime in the Digital Sublime*, London: Routledge.

Taylor, P. (2001) 'Hacktivism: in search of lost ethics?', in D.S. Wall (ed.) *Crime and the Internet*, London: Routledge.

Tester, K. (1994) *The Flâneur*, London: Routledge.

Tönnies, F. (1979) *Gemeinschaft und Gesellschaft. Grundbegriffe der reinen Soziologie*, Reprint of the edition of 1935, Darmstadt: Wissenschaftliche Buchgesellschaft.

Turkle, S. (1995) *Life on Screen: Identity in the Age of the Internet*, London: Weidenfeld and Nicolson.

Turner, V. (1967) *The Forest of Symbols: Aspects of Ndembu Ritual*, Ithaca, NY: Cornell University Press.

UN Commission on Crime and Criminal Justice (1995) *United Nations Manual on the Prevention and Control of Computer-Related Crime*, New York: United Nations.

Van Maanen, J. (1988) *Tales of the Field: On Writing Ethnography*, Chicago, IL: Chicago University Press.

Van Maanen, J. (1995) 'An end to innocence: the ethnography of ethnography', in J. Van Maanen (ed.) *Representation in Ethnography*, Thousand Oaks, CA: Sage.

Virilio, P. (1997) *Open Sky*, London: Verso.

Virtual Rape Consequences (1994) available online http://vesta.physics.ucla.edu/~smolin/lambda/laws_and_history/failed/antirape.html (accessed 14/11/98).

Walker, C. and Akdeniz, Y. (1998) 'The governance of the internet in Europe with special reference to illegal and harmful content', *The Criminal Law Review, Special Edition on Crime, Criminal Justice and the Internet*: 5–18.

Wall, D.S. (1998) 'Policing and the regulation of cyberspace', *The Criminal Law Review, Special Edition on Crime, Criminal Justice and the Internet*: 79–91.

Wall, D.S. (1999) 'Cybercrimes: new wine, no bottles?', in P. Davies, P. Francis, and V. Jupp (eds) *Invisible Crimes: Their Victims and their Regulation*, London: Macmillan.

Wall, D.S. (2001) 'Maintaining order and law on the internet', in D. Wall (ed.) *Crime and the Internet*, London: Routledge.

Webster, F. (1995) *Theories of the Information Society*, London: Routledge.

Wellman, B. and Gulia, M. (1999) 'Net surfers don't ride alone: virtual communities as communities', in B. Wellman (ed.) *Networks in the Global Village*, Boulder, CO: Westview Press.

Whine, M. (2000) 'Far right extremists on the net', in D. Thomas and B. Loader (eds) *Cybercrime: Law Enforcement, Security and Surveillance in the Information Age*, London: Routledge.

Wiener, M. and Mehrabian, A. (1968) *Language Within Language: Immediacy, a Channel in Verbal Communication*, New York: Appleton-Century-Crofts.

Williams, M. (2000) 'Virtually criminal: discourse, deviance and anxiety within virtual communities', *International Review of Law, Computers and Technology*, 14, 1: 95–104.

Williams, M. (2001) 'The language of cybercrime', in D.S.Wall (ed.) *Crime and the Internet*, London: Routledge.

Williams, M. (2004) 'Understanding King Punisher and his order: vandalism in a virtual reality community – motives, meanings and possible solutions' *Internet Journal of Criminology*, available online http://www.internetjournalofcriminology.com/Williams%20-%20Understanding%20King%20Punisher%20and%20his%20Order.pdf.

Williams, M. (2006) 'Avatar watching: participant observation in graphical online environments', *Qualitative Research*, 6, 4.

Williams, M. and Robson, K. (2003) 'Re-engineering focus group methodology for the online environment', in S. Sarina Chen and J. Hall (eds) *Online Social Research: Methods, Issues and Ethics*, New York: Peter Lang.

Witmer, D.F. Colman R.W. and Katzman S.L. (1999) 'From paper-and-pencil to screen-and-keyboard', in S. Jones (ed.) *Doing Internet Research*, London: Sage.

Wittel, A. (2000) 'Ethnography on the move: from field to net to internet', *Qualitative Social Research Forum*, 1, 1, available online http://www.qualitative-research.net/fqs-texte/1–00/1–00wittel-e.htm (accessed 05/06/01).

Wittel, A. (2001) 'Towards a network sociality', *Theory, Culture and Society*, 18, 6: 542–62.

Wittes, B. (1995) 'Witnessing the birth of a legal system', *The Connecticut Law Tribune*, Supplement, Special Section: Technology: 8A.

Woolgar, S. (2002) *Virtual Society? – Technology, Cyberbole, Reality*, Oxford: Oxford University Press.

Young, L. F. (1995) 'United States computer crime laws, criminals and deterrence', *International Yearbook of Laws, Computers and Technology*, 9, 6: 1–16.

Zender, L. (2002) 'Victims', in M. Maguire, R. Morgan and R. Reiner (eds) *The Oxford Handbook of Criminology*, Oxford: Oxford University Press.

Zimring, F.E. and Hawkins, G.J. (1973) *Deterrence: The Legal Threat in Crime Control*, Chicago, IL: University of Chicago Press.

Press articles

CNN.com 06/08/00 available online.
www.cnn.com/2000/US/06/08/barrel.bodies.02/ (accessed 20/08/00).
Reuters 16/06/03 available online.
UEL: http://www.reuters.co.uk/newsArticle.jhtml?type=searchNewsandstoryID=29 3676 (accessed 23/16/03).

Cases

AandM Records, Inc. v. Napster, Inc., 114 F. Supp. 2d 896 (N.D. Cal. 2000).

California Software, v. Reliability Research, Inc., 631 F. Supp. 1356 (C.D. Cal. 1986).

Chaplinsky v. New Hampshire, No. 225, 315 U.S. 568, 1942.

Cubby v. Compuserve, Inc., 776 F. Supp. 135, 138 (S.D.N.Y. 1991).

Stratton Oakmont, Inc. v. Prodigy Services Co., No. 94–31063, (N.Y. 1995).

Index

Note: UK and US acts and regulations are followed by either (UK) or (US) to indicate country of origin. A page number followed by *Fig.* indicates an illustration or table.

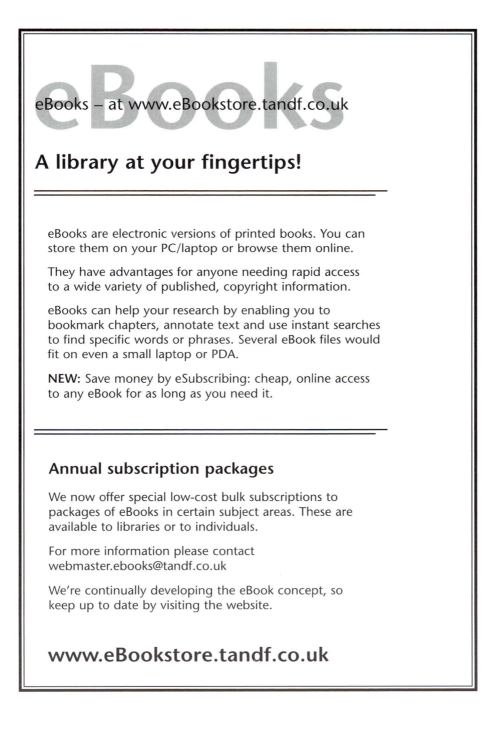